SNAKES AND LADDERS

SNAKES AND LADDERS

FERGUS FINLAY

New Island Books/Dublin

SNAKES AND LADDERS
First published 1998 by
New Island Books
2 Brookside
Dundrum Road
Dublin 14
Ireland

Reprinted September 1998

British Library Cataloguing in Publication Data
A catalogue record for this book is available from the British Library

ISBN 1 874597 99 5

Cover design: Slick Fish Design, Dublin
Cover photograph: Derek Speirs/Report
Typesetting: New Island Books
Printed in the UK by Biddles Limited

Contents

Introduction   ix

1   Say Yes Dick   1

2   The Learning Curve   9

3   Carrying the Scars   36

4   Fighting Back   51

5   Leader of the Opposition   62

6   Beating the Big Guys   80

7   The Year of the Golden Circle   96

8   Top of the World   108

9   Meeting Albert   129

10   Building a Partnership   147

11   Partnership at Work   164

12   Peace Work   180

13   Partnership Tested   205

14   Triumphs and Disasters   217

15   Partnership Shattered   242

16   A New Marriage   266

17   Divorce and Breakdown   295

18   Back to Square One   306

19   Looking Back   325

Fergus Finlay worked for three governments from 1982 to 1997, as adviser to Dick Spring. He is the author of two previous bestsellers: *A President with a Purpose*, about Mary Robinson's election, and a political thriller, *A Cruel Trade*. He lives in Dublin with his wife and four daughters.

For Vicky,
who delayed completion of this book in a good cause,
and in the process proved that she can do whatever
she sets her mind to.

Introduction

I set out to write an objective, third-hand account of all the things I had observed over fifteen years in active politics. After a few failed attempts, I realised I couldn't do it, and therefore this isn't it.

It gradually got personal. At first I resisted, and then finally realised that the only thing I could write, honestly, was a personal account. So this isn't "what I saw". It's "what I saw, and how it affected me".

I hope, though, that it's an honest and not too self-serving account. It's certainly as honest as I could make it.

I wanted to write about the last fifteen years, not just because they were mine, but because they were among the most eventful and turbulent in our political history. An awful lot has changed, in every walk of Irish life, in that time. I wanted to try to describe how it felt to be part of all that, because I have found it intensely exciting.

And I suppose I wanted to set the record straight too. I left politics convinced that Labour had been treated unfairly, that our role in the implementation of change had been under-valued. That feeling has diminished over time—and my own feeling that politics, by and large, gets the media it deserves, has reasserted itself.

But media and history are two different things. In all my years in politics, I never expected the media to be objective, because the media is human too. I did expect it to be fair, and often it was. But sometimes it wasn't, and I have a general sense to this day that the media in Ireland is always prepared to admire the work that Labour does in opposition, but seldom prepared to recognise the real things it has done in government.

I believe that the period when Labour was in government from 1993 to 1997 was one of the most productive periods of government that Ireland has ever seen.

The objectives we brought to that time, the structural changes we made, and the systems we established, all contributed to the profound and long-lasting changes that were wrought. A fair examination of the record does, I think, demonstrate an extraordinary commitment to change for the better.

But it goes deeper than that too. When I started to work in politics, Ireland was in deep economic crisis, caused largely by the irresponsible politics that followed the 1977 election. The country was riven by debate about family planning, marital breakdown, abortion—and it was often bitter, filthy debate.

"Participation" in every sense of the word was a concept that had never been mentioned. The conduct of politics was unconstrained by any rules or regulation, and the relationship between politics and business was entirely secret, and often unhealthy. Issues of social policy—housing, education, welfare and health, the rights and needs of people with disabilities—all of these were areas of neglect.

Above all that, Northern Ireland was a conflagration. The unwritten policy of successive Irish governments was one of containment—whatever happens, don't let it spill over down here.

All of that, and a lot more, has changed. Ireland today, with all the things that still need to be done, is unrecognisable from the Ireland of 1983. And we contributed our fair share—and maybe a bit more—to that change.

We didn't do it alone, and we didn't do it without making mistakes. But many of the changes—for the better—that Ireland has seen in that time would not have happened without an effective and committed Labour Party—effective and influential in opposition as well as in government.

I wanted to say all that at the outset, because this book doesn't so much report on the changes as on how they happened and how it felt to be there. I discovered something as I was writing the book—character matters more to me than events do. Character shapes events and the reaction to events. This book is much more about character than about events, but maybe it will help to explain why things happened the way they did. And as I say, I hope it explains honestly.

In the last fifteen years, I've had my heroes and my villains. I've tried to paint them both equally fairly. Among my heroes are all the people I worked with. I hope that nobody among my colleagues feels that the role they played has been undervalued. One of the best and most important features of the work I've done in politics has been to be part of a team—and it was a great team, that most of the time was able to withstand incredible pressures. In the end, nothing any of us did could have been done without the rest of us.

Because this is, after all, a personal account, there will be a lot left out. I have a great memory for how things felt, but I often couldn't tell you to save my life whether they happened a year ago or six years ago.

William Scally (as kindly as he could) told me recently that whatever great strengths I might have, keeping records isn't one of them. I've never kept a diary, and I've always operated on the principle that, in the public service, keeping files is by definition an act of wasteful duplication. The key thing in the public service is not to keep the file—but always to know where it is!

So getting the sequence of events right was the most difficult part of the book as a result. I hope I have, and if I have I'm indebted to a few people who don't even know of my debt.

For instance, Stephen Collins' great book *Spring and the Labour Story* helped me to place a lot of events in their proper time and context. I had forgotten, until I read it again recently, what good sources Stephen had!

And it's not a secret that I've had something of a public feud going with the *Irish Times* for a while now. It may not cause champagne corks to pop in the editor's office, but I hereby declare it over. I couldn't have written this book without the help of the *Irish Times* library, and especially the annual summary of events they produce. And the advice and support of Dick Walsh meant more to me than he knows.

John Foley, Greg Sparks, Sally Clarke, Anne Byrne and Finbarr O'Malley also helped me to remember dates and places. William Scally put in long hours to help me be as accurate as possible. Pat Magner got me into all this in the first place, and has been an invaluable source of anecdotes.

But they did much more than help with the writing. Their friendship and encouragement has sustained me for years, and particularly in the last few months as this work has been done.

Hugh Mohan has also been hugely helpful, and generous with his red wine at the same time.

I specially want to thank Frances O'Rourke and Joe Joyce for working with me throughout. Their patience has been extraordinary, and their skills have been invaluable. Any errors, omissions, or lapses in this book are entirely down to me, and not to them.

I was lucky, for fifteen years, to work for a man whom I will always be able to regard as a friend. He is essentially a private man, despite his public profile, and he probably won't welcome another book in which he features prominently. But he gave me a chance that few people get to do a job that really matters, and for that I will always be grateful to Dick Spring.

Finally, this book is dedicated to my daughter Vicky. She and her sisters, Mandy, Emma, and Sarah, are four of the five most important people in my life. They put up with a lot while this book was being written, and they never (well, hardly ever!) complained. Their mother, Frieda, is the one who makes everything I do worthwhile.

1

Say Yes Dick

Dick Spring negotiated his first government in the month of December 1982. It was the toughest, and loneliest, negotiation he ever conducted.

There were several reasons. Dick had only been party leader for a couple of months, and a TD for a year and a half. He had spent a good deal of that time in hospital, following a horrific car crash, and had come to the leadership of the party in the aftermath of Michael O'Leary's resignation and defection to Fine Gael. The party he led into the 1982 election was demoralised, terribly split, and above all, a virtual stranger to its leader.

But they had survived the election. Every commentator had predicted Labour's decimation. How could it be otherwise? Labour had played the fool for the previous two years. In the year of GUBU, while Charlie Haughey wrecked the economy and played havoc with public life, while the Attorney General had been forced to resign because of the arrest of a deranged murderer in his apartment, Labour had acted out one of its interminable internal battles about ideological purity.

It had culminated in the dramatic moment when O'Leary had walked away, and the party had turned to a taciturn, reserved, Kerryman for leadership. It was a decision made more in hope than in confidence. He was young, inexperienced, and largely unknown.

And suddenly he was fighting an election at the head of his demoralised troops, and in the face of unanimous predictions of total calamity.

But it didn't work out that way—at least, not quite. The party's vote, which had been in continuous decline, rose ever so slightly, and the party won an extra seat. Fine Gael's vote, on the other hand, went up enough to give them seven more seats.

The two parties came out of the election with enough seats for an overall majority of three in the Dáil.

That first election result under Dick Spring was secured largely because, although people didn't know him, they saw enough to realise that there was a toughness and a solidity that had been missing. Here was a politician who was serious, who managed to exert enough authority within his fractious party to allow a disciplined and united campaign to emerge. It was a reasonable start.

Now he had to deliver, by negotiating a coalition deal that he could sell. For other political parties, the question of coalition was a tactical one. For Labour, it was an issue of soul. These negotiations were bound to be difficult.

And they were made all the more so because Fine Gael sought to take every advantage possible of his inexperience. A politician with no background or training in economic policy was expected to negotiate with Garret FitzGerald and Alan Dukes about how the currency could be stabilised, and about how spiralling public expenditure could be managed—and he was expected to do it in the seclusion of a convent in the Donnybrook area of Dublin.

Ostensibly, the purpose of the arcane setting was to keep the negotiations away from the prying eyes of the media, but if it helped to ensure that the inexperienced Labour leader was isolated from whatever back-up and support he could count on, so much the better.

Fine Gael introduced Peter Sutherland to the negotiations on their side—perhaps for his legal and constitutional expertise, but perhaps also because he was a much more senior figure at the bar than Dick, and this would automatically put Dick at a disadvantage.

It was obvious that they were playing him for a patsy. If there was any doubt in Dick's mind, it was confirmed when Garret FitzGerald told him that he was taking three days off from the negotiations, to attend a European Christian Democrat conference in Paris.

That's when Fine Gael saw the other side of Dick Spring— the side you don't mess with. It was unconscionable that a party leader, in the middle of negotiations on the formation of a government, knowing that a hard bargain had to be struck, would choose to absent himself entirely, leaving the whole affair to underlings. And Spring told him so.

In fact, he arranged for FitzGerald to get a clear and precise message that if the putative Taoiseach wasn't prepared to cancel his plans for a weekend in Paris, he could regard the negotiations as being over.

After some bluster, the plans were cancelled, and things went much better after that. In addition, and little by little, help and advice began to come on board. One recruit was William Scally, who had worked as an adviser to the Fine Gael/Labour government in the 1970s, and whose wisdom and judgement were invaluable. David Grafton, who had worked for Michael O'Leary and remained loyal after O'Leary's defection, did a lot of work for the Labour negotiators too, as did Eithne FitzGerald.

Barry Desmond and Frank Cluskey were key players—Dick quickly learned to introduce Frank to especially difficult meetings, because he had an uncanny ability to unnerve Garret FitzGerald.

But Dick's principal source of advice was two of his oldest friends, John Rogers and Joe Revington. They made themselves available to him around the clock, and even if they were as inexperienced as he was in government formation—and economic policy—they were a constant source of strength and confidence.

Pat Magner didn't know Dick well before the election. He had gone to Dublin from Cork to meet Dick a week earlier, with one clean shirt, and had been immediately struck by the fact that Dick was negotiating almost alone. He had joined Dick's team without hesitation, and spent the rest of the week acting as a kind of chief of staff for the Labour negotiations.

Unlike Dick and his immediate circle, Pat had an intimate knowledge of the party and its resources. If a paper needed to be written, or a set of talking points prepared, Pat knew who to ask, and how to get it done.

That's how I got involved.

Pat was then, as he still is, a charismatic individual, with the ability to sweep people along in his enthusiasms. Within a year of my moving to Cork, he had become a firm friend, and had persuaded me not only to join the Labour Party, but to go to work for Toddy O'Sullivan as a voluntary PRO. During the 1981 and '82 election campaigns, we had worked together until the small hours, night after night, to try to ensure Toddy's election.

And it had worked. I've always believed that the lion's share of the credit for the fact that Toddy O'Sullivan had won back a seat in Cork that seemed lost to Labour forever belonged to Toddy himself, as a man who radiated decency and integrity, and who had made an outstanding success of his term as Lord Mayor. But in the course of those elections, Pat and I formed a bond that has stood the test of time.

And among other things, it meant that he knew I was prepared to work through the night if necessary. So I wasn't too surprised to get a phone call from Pat at half-five on a Thursday, just as I was preparing to go home for the evening. I didn't realise the call was to change the course of my life.

After more than ten years as a trade union official, during which my family had grown up without me, I was settling into the relatively quiet life of a Personnel Manager. I had gone to work for an American multinational in Cork, a good company but with the unlikely name of Ridgid Tool. I counted it already among my achievements that I had persuaded them to change the name of the company, at least for the purpose of incoming phone calls, to Ridge Tool! It was a sedentary and quiet life, and I was sort of enjoying it.

When Pat rang, he explained that he couldn't say much on the phone—they had been advised that they should all operate on the assumption that their phones were being tapped.

"But we need a speech," he said. "The negotiations are more or less over, and Dick has to address a special delegate conference on Sunday. It's absolutely vital that we get it right—the conference is where all the critical decisions will be made. We're all too shagged to start writing it now, and I said I was sure you'd be willing to help."

"Sure," I said, "what does he want to say?"

"I can't tell you that," Pat replied. And he went on to tell me that the details of the negotiations were being kept top-secret until Sunday morning, and that he wasn't at liberty to say what Dick would be recommending.

"How am I supposed to write a speech for a conference like that if I don't know if he's recommending participation in government or not?"

"I don't know," said Pat, "but I told them you could handle it all right."

"Can you tell me anything at all, Pat?" I asked—I suspect there was beginning to be an edge in my voice.

"Only two things," Pat said. "One, he's a very up-front guy—I've discovered that much. And two, I promised him he'd have it by eleven o'clock tomorrow morning!"

And he was gone before the stream of expletives had an opportunity to form.

I'd never met Dick Spring. I'd spoken to him only once, and that had been an impertinence. I had read in the *Examiner* that he was spending the day at home, in the first week of the election campaign, to try to figure out how to respond to pro-life pressure. Garret FitzGerald and Charlie Haughey had already agreed to the insertion of a pro-life amendment in the Constitution, and the pro-life movement was now demanding that all party leaders should make the same commitment before polling day.

I was horrified at the thought that any leader of my party might agree to capitulate to such pressure, and I had plucked up enough courage to ring Dick Spring's house to tell him so.

He was quiet-spoken, and courteous. When I explained my mission, he told me I had nothing to worry about. He wasn't about to agree to anything as complex as a constitutional change without the most careful study, and he would be saying so publicly.

And that was it. I had now agreed to write a speech for a man to whom I had spoken, several weeks earlier, for a minute and a half, about negotiations in which I had no involvement, the purpose of which I didn't know.

We had just taken possession, in Ridge Tool, of the very latest in office technology—a golf-ball typewriter with a correcting ribbon. As I loaded it into the boot of my car to bring it home, I realised I was in for a long evening.

My mother has an expression that she uses when she's writing and inspiration isn't coming—"the icy challenge of the empty page". By half-eleven that night, I was ready to admit that the challenge had beaten me.

When Frieda came in to tell me she was going to bed, I told her that I couldn't write this speech. It was an impossible task, trying to put words you didn't know into the mouth of a man you didn't know.

"At least," Frieda said, "you know the audience he'll be delivering it to."

It was true. I had believed in the Labour Party all my life, and even though I had never joined the party until my trade union days were over, I was totally committed to its place in Irish life. I knew precisely the sort of anxiety that even the most pro-leadership delegate would feel at the special delegate conference.

Even if I didn't know what Spring was going to say to reassure them, I knew what he should say. He should talk about what the party meant to him—his roots and his history—and he should undertake that the unity and the seriousness of the party were his most important priorities, whatever the next couple of years might bring.

And so I wrote the speech I wanted to hear. I worked at it all through the night, giving the correcting ribbon plenty of exercise. At six o'clock the next morning, I had a quick shower, drove into Cork city, and took the train to Dublin.

I had never been in Leinster House before, and Joe Revington met me at the Kildare Street gate. Even fifteen years later, when I've come to regard myself like a piece of somewhat battered furniture in the House, I can still remember the feeling I had as we walked through the winding corridors to the 1932 annexe, where the Labour Party offices were (and still are).

I have no recollection of being introduced to Dick. All I can remember is sitting in front of him as he read the speech, like a schoolboy in front of the headmaster. Every now and then he would pick up a pen and scribble something in the margin, or underline a word or phrase. I sat there feeling like a complete fool, certain that I had missed the point of the whole exercise.

Eventually he finished, and looked up at me with a grin.

"This is perfect," he said, "just what I was hoping for. I'm going to have to make a few changes here and there, but it's pretty well what I wanted."

And that was it. I was ushered out of the office, and Dick handed the speech to Sally Clarke, his personal assistant, for re-typing. She looked anything but pleased at the prospect. (I was to discover later that she had had virtually no sleep for three nights. In those days the business of re-drafting took a terrible toll on the person who had to type each draft afresh.) And then I was on the next train back to Cork, reflecting on my one and only brush with politics and power.

I never saw that speech again. I was supposed to be a delegate at the special conference, but the birth of our last daughter Sarah was imminent, and I didn't go. (She was actually born two days later, on the day the government was formed, and Pat Magner got through to the labour ward to tell me that Dick was to be Tánaiste. They wouldn't call me to the phone until he told the nurse he was my father!)

The conference was held in private session, and the speech wasn't circulated to the media. My only satisfaction on the day was listening to Seán Duignan reporting from Limerick that many delegates had told him that it was Spring's speech that helped them to support him.

I heard nothing further until Christmas. And then Pat rang again, to tell me that Dick would like to meet me in Dublin.

I met the new Tánaiste and Minister for the Environment in a pub, Kennedys in Lincoln Place. John Rogers was with him. It took us a while to find a quiet corner, because there were still an awful lot of well-wishers around.

"I want you to come and work for me," Dick said. "We don't know each other, but you write as if you know me. And I need some help, especially to mark Peter Prendergast, who's going to be government press secretary. But before you agree, there's a few things you ought to know. And I need to know, if I tell you them and it doesn't work out, can I trust you?"

"You can trust me absolutely," I said. And I meant it. Here was the Deputy Prime Minister, a man with a reputation already for closeness, prepared to open up secrets to a relative stranger. They had clearly decided already that I was trustworthy, and I wasn't going to let that down.

"First," Dick said, "I took this job in the Department of the Environment because I believed it was going to give me a chance to do big things—build houses, cut the waiting lists. Well, it isn't. We put a contingency fund of £100 million in the programme for government, but when we opened the books we discovered there isn't a spare penny. In fact, it's worse than that. I'm looking at the possibility of introducing local authority charges—bringing back the rates—because if I don't do it, I'm going to have to lay off 4,000 workers. Second, we're in for a very rough budget—there's simply no choice. The books have been cooked for the last twelve months, and if we don't take tough action the economy will go into a tail-spin. Third, and I can't tell you the details, there's very heavy stuff going down on the security front."

He looked at me, and smiled.

"In short," he said, "I'm offering a very bumpy ride. I have no idea whether this government will last a fortnight. What do you say?"

I turned to John Rogers.

"What is one supposed to say to all that?" I asked him.

"Say what the rest of us have said," he replied. "Just say 'yes Dick'."

2

The Learning Curve

In some ways, the next four years are a blur. I remember it as one crisis after another, days that started at seven in the morning and frequently didn't end until three or four the following morning—often with the only meal of the day, in Jury's coffee dock. But I remember it as exciting, and tense—so much so that I can remember one of our colleagues being physically sick in the Tánaiste's toilet in the middle of a late night meeting.

I remember another occasion too, when the Tánaiste returned to his office late at night, in the middle of one very intense crisis. After some fumbling with the lights and combination locks, we were able to gain access, only to be confronted with the sight of a naked behind, engaged in intense activity. Two civil servants from the Department in question were taking a somewhat unwarranted advantage of the deep pile of the Tánaiste's carpet. Both subsequently accepted transfer suggestions as gracefully as possible in the circumstances.

Moments of light relief were rare, however. Most of the time, the pressure was intense, and it came from all sides. The first thing it meant—unexpectedly—was that those of us who didn't live in Dublin essentially said goodbye to home. For the first year and a half, I commuted to Dublin every Monday morning—and sometimes didn't get home again until Sunday afternoon. The strain on Frieda was intolerable, and usually, I was too exhausted to notice. Eventually the strain became too much for both of us, and we moved to Dublin. By then I was committed—I had made my bed in politics, and I was going to have to make the most of it.

When I started, at the end of January in 1983, most of the others had settled in, and no-one had time to break in a new boy. My appointment was to the grand title of Deputy Head of the Government Information Service and Deputy Government Press Secretary. It was a longer title than most, but if I expected the title to start making things happen, I was in for a rude awakening.

I reported to Seán O'Riordan, who was then Personnel Officer in the Taoiseach's Department, and my first contact with Government Buildings. He was extremely courteous, and told me that they had prepared an office for me. And then he led me up several flights of stairs, to a small bare room at the very top of the building. There was nothing in it except a desk, a chair, and a telephone. This was where I was going to run my empire of news management—as far away as possible from even a hint of action. It occurred to me that perhaps it was intended that I should think great thoughts, and write them out with a quill pen.

When he left me alone, I investigated—mainly by opening the two desk drawers and rummaging inside. To my astonishment, I found that one of them was full of a very attractive blank letterhead, with the address "Abbeville" and a little crest on it. Whoever had occupied this office before me had handled the previous Taoiseach, Charlie Haughey's, personal correspondence! I carried a box of that letterhead around with me for a couple of years, with the occasional thought that I might send out a couple of hundred invitations to a cocktail party in Charlie's house some Christmas. Alas, I have to admit I never quite summoned up the nerve to do it.

Throughout that four-year period, I had two jobs—my day job, and the other one, which seemed to take about twelve hours a day. My day job was marking Peter Prendergast, and the other one was working with the Labour Ministers—writing speeches, researching, reacting, occasionally (very occasionally) initiating. Dick had two advisers, William Scally for economics and Joe Revington for constituency matters. Sally Clarke worked the round of the clock as his PA and expert on party matters. Together, we began to make a team.

The man I was supposed to mark, Peter Prendergast, was, and remains, a phenomenon. He had worked as Garret FitzGerald's General Secretary in the 1977-81 period. While

Garret was supplying an injection of charisma to a party that was in sore need of it, Peter was applying high-level marketing and organisational skills to the job of revolutionising Fine Gael.

He was respected and feared, admired and hated, throughout the Fine Gael party. When I met him, as a raw novice in the arts of politics, he was already something of a legend.

And it wasn't hard to see why. Peter didn't just possess marketing ability—he had internalised his techniques to such an extent that he was always selling. And what he sold was Garret. As far as he was concerned, Fine Gael, and the FitzGerald/Spring Government, was Garret's. The Cabinet had decided that Peter would be briefed about government decisions after each meeting by John Boland, who was Minister for the Public Service. Peter never acted on a single one of those briefings without consulting Garret first.

Laid back and gregarious, always charming, he had an intensity about him that I have seldom encountered. Even when he was obviously setting out a particularly partisan point of view, he did it with such conviction and passion that his sincerity was never questioned.

Over the four years that I worked with him, I learned to like him enormously. But I never learned to fully trust him. His agenda wasn't mine, and our relationship was almost entirely partisan. Ultimately, I think it was destructive.

The Labour Party was in government at a time of severe economic retrenchment, without the resources or experience to handle the difficulties it faced. We fought every day to protect our constituency from the effects of the worst cutbacks—and part of the fight involved trying to get a message out about what we were doing. Frequently, that involved me trying to beat Peter to the newspapers—getting my message out before he got his.

He had the advantage of a daily five o'clock briefing with the political correspondents, and he knew them all very well. I was "up from the country", and it took me weeks even to find my way around Leinster House. The basic argument between us was a simple one. I was determined to resist the absorption of Labour policies and personalities into an overall government perspective—he wanted to project a government that was utterly cohesive.

"Utterly cohesive" meant that Labour Ministers were to be seen as acquiescing on a daily basis in policies that were anathema to the majority of their supporters. And they were negotiating all the time from a position of weakness, undermined from within and from outside.

It was never possible, during that period, for Dick Spring and any of his Ministers to be able to rely on an appeal to the wider public interest. They were under siege from the day the government was formed. Those of us who were paid to advise them were viewed with the deepest suspicion by elements in the party, and indeed by some of the Ministers.

From the very beginning, there was an air of crisis. Very early on in the government's life, Gemma Hussey, Minister for Education, was forced to cut back on free school transport. Dick Spring was forced to announce the introduction of local service charges, and spent months trying to get the necessary legislation through the Dáil. Michael Noonan, in Justice, announced that he had uncovered the fact that members of Charles Haughey's government had not only tapped journalists' phones, but were also bugging each other's conversations. Alan Dukes announced the size of the current budget deficit he would be proposing in his first budget as Minister for Finance. It would have meant massive cuts in public expenditure on essential services.

That, about four weeks into the life of the government (and before I had started work) caused the first inter-party crisis. Dick Spring, who was in hospital having pins removed from his back, let it be known publicly that the Minister for Finance would bring in whatever cuts the government agreed, and not whatever he decided himself. Garret FitzGerald agreed with Dick, and Alan Dukes was overruled.

Some have argued ever since that the decision to overrule Alan Dukes laid the seed for the ultimate economic failure of that government. My view has always been different. It is possible for governments to take, and to survive, unpopular decisions. But they have to do it together, in solidarity with one another, and with sufficient time and space to prepare the ground for the decision. Dick Spring was right to object to Alan Dukes' pre-emptive strike—because if he hadn't done so he would never have had the authority in his own ranks to keep that government alive.

As it was, Michael Bell, our Deputy from Louth, and Fintan Kennedy, a senior SIPTU official whom Dick had nominated for the Senate, both resigned the party whip over the social welfare implications of that budget. It could have been worse—Frank Prendergast from Limerick also announced his intention to vote against the social welfare provisions. He was dissuaded from doing so only after a very intense piece of lobbying by William Scally and myself.

ERRATUM

This page contains references to Mick O'Connell, the former Kerry Footballer and County Councillor. The author and publisher acknowledge that the article allegedly written by Mr O'Connell was not in fact written and that the statements attributed to him are entirely without foundation. Both the author and the publisher deeply regret the hurt and damage caused to Mr O'Connell and his family by these unfounded allegations and unreservedly apologise for them.

Dick was horrified, and determined to stop it. Lawyers were called, and advised that such a piece would be clearly libellous. But the editor of the *Kerryman*, Seamus McConville, refused to budge. He was determined to publish the piece unchanged.

Eventually, the managing director of the Independent Group, Bartle Pitcher, was contacted, and told that we were prepared to seek an injunction to halt the publication of the newspaper. After a good deal of argument, it was agreed that publication of the paper would be sufficiently delayed to allow an article of equal size to O'Connell's to be submitted by Dick Spring as a right of reply.

It meant that we had no more than a couple of hours to prepare a considered response—because Dick was not prepared to back down from his basic position against a referendum in the face of the charge of being an abortionist. In the end, both articles appeared together on the front page of the newspaper, after an exhausting night spent researching with one hand and writing with the other.

Relations between the Spring family and the *Kerryman* had never been good, but that incident soured them completely. I was to observe many times over the following years that if Dick ever needed a break from a newspaper, the one place he needn't bother looking was his own home town.

(The *Kerryman* had its revenge some years later, on the eve of Dick's most successful party conference. The conference in question was being held in Tralee, and was a bonanza for the town outside the normal tourist season. The thousand delegates who arrived to visit Dick's home town were greeted by the headline "Spring beats up journalist" in Dick's local newspaper.

The incident referred to an altercation between Dick and a somewhat tired and emotional journalist in a Dáil corridor. The altercation had ended with Dick taking off the journalist's glasses and slapping his face. It was an unseemly enough episode, which had merited a mention in most newspapers, but only Dick's home town paper had used it as their lead story.)

In those early years, every situation that arose was serious. It was quite usual to spend a night dealing with something like the *Kerryman* abortion story—working until two or three in the morning to try to get it right—and then discover the following morning that something fresh and different, and just as demanding, had blown up.

I learned very early on that the primary skill a great politician needs, more often than not, is a talent for crisis management. The time and space to develop visions and dreams, to work out how to change society for the better, is almost never given to a politician in government. If he or she doesn't arrive in government with a highly focussed agenda of change on day one, change won't happen on their watch. Even when they do, the daily grind of government can wear them down.

Dick Spring had never had the time to develop a platform of change. And his first experience of government was one where he was entirely on the defensive, where every day generated a fresh crisis. If in the end of the day his major achievement in that government was that he survived it, and learned a lot about government from it, that was no small achievement.

As time went by, I moved my office downstairs, until eventually I was occupying the room that had up to then served as an ante-room to Peter Prendergast's office. Although I've always been certain that Peter resented the intrusion, and undoubtedly thought I was spying on him, he was always too polite to say so.

It meant that we both had rooms on the same corridor as the cabinet room, and could be quickly reached and briefed about any significant development. It also meant, however, waiting for interminable cabinet meetings to be over.

And they were staggeringly interminable. It was not unusual for government meetings to begin at eleven in the morning, and still be going on twelve hours later. I can still remember meeting Ministers tottering out from those meetings, pale with exhaustion, and totally unable to remember what they had discussed in the first five hours of the day.

For a long time I assumed that the length of the meetings derived from the intractable nature of the problems they were dealing with. In reality, it was Garret FitzGerald's chairmanship that wore his government out.

Garret FitzGerald was the outstanding figure in my early days in politics. I was in awe of him at the start, and in some ways I remain so to this day. I've never come across a man with such energy and passion, and I will always believe that it was a great tragedy that, for example, Garret FitzGerald and Martin Mansergh never had a chance to work together. The nature of adversarial politics makes that sort of relationship impossible— but it would have made history.

In the early years that I worked for Garret FitzGerald's government, I used to believe that there was no way of avoiding long cabinet meetings. Now, I know that one of Garret FitzGerald's biggest failures was an inability to focus on the politics of government. He would immerse himself in so much detail, and involve himself in so many Ministries other than his own, that he was unable to steer his colleagues towards any sense of a bigger picture.

His previous government had fallen on the issue of VAT on children's shoes—and during the course of the subsequent election it was discovered that Bord Gáis profits had been understated by an amount that made the tax hike unnecessary.

Garret FitzGerald refused to allow preparatory work on the 1986 divorce referendum to begin until he had completed his consultations with the Catholic Bishops—and his government found itself unable to answer basic questions during the referendum campaign.

These were political misjudgements, the mistakes of a man who became befuddled by detail. Garret FitzGerald was a man of extraordinary vision, and a master of fine points—it was always somewhere in between, in that area where political judgement comes into play, that he lost his way.

He loved government—its overall potential for change, but even more its potential for getting involved in every detail. It was John Boland, I believe, who circulated the story that at one cabinet meeting, Garret had said about some proposition put forward by his Ministers, "it sounds very good in practice, but will it work in theory?"

It was certainly the case that Ministers of both parties heaved huge sighs of relief on any occasion that Garret was away, and his Tánaiste was chairing the Cabinet meeting. The agenda would be concluded, leaving Garret to wonder afterwards had enough work been done on analysing the issues.

The agenda for cabinet meetings became so cluttered that Ministers began to have serious difficulty in raising an item of urgent importance. An agenda heading was introduced to deal with this, known as "12 o'clock items". The intention was that the prescribed agenda would be set aside at noon, to enable Ministers to raise anything that they needed to bring to the government's attention urgently, and which could be dealt with quickly. Within a month or so of this device being introduced, things had deteriorated to such an extent that it was often three in the afternoon before they got around to the 12 o'clock items, and the first one raised might take them up to six o'clock!

It was heavy going. One night the meeting ran so late that the secretariat was sent out to buy fish and chips for the Government. When they arrived, Garret thought it unseemly for the Taoiseach to be eating from a plastic bag, and poured his chips into a crystal bowl in the centre of the table—without realising that Alan Dukes had been using it as an ashtray for the previous six hours or so. Solidarity prevailed, however, and each member of the government gave up a few chips for the Taoiseach.

Many of the tensions in that government arose as a result of personality and ideological conflicts. Some involved Dick Spring, some Frank Cluskey, and almost all of them involved John Bruton.

I had worked for Dick for several weeks before I met Frank Cluskey for the first time. He made it clear, right from the beginning, that he neither liked me nor trusted me.

I never found out why, but as a result, I was never able to form any kind of working relationship with him. And yet he was someone I had admired for a long time. His roots and his socialism went back a long way, and his convictions were totally straightforward. But he could be fearsome, and it was clear that he was uncomfortable with the position he found himself in, defending tough and unpopular decisions, and playing second fiddle to a party leader with only a fraction of his experience. He always seemed to me to be spoiling for a fight.

There was plenty of opportunity. One weekend Garret went on radio and gave one of those interviews that only he could give, where he forgot he was Taoiseach and outlined an economic analysis for the nation—including the fact that the government urgently needed to cut a half-billion pounds from the Budget.

It sounded like another pre-emptive strike, and once again Dick was forced to take crisis action. He tried to contact Garret the following morning to tell him that Labour Ministers wouldn't be attending that day's cabinet meeting until he had met his Labour Ministerial colleagues, and until the issue of how government budgetary decisions were made had been discussed between Taoiseach and Tánaiste.

Car phones didn't exist then, and Garret was in his car. I was the one who was deputed to tell him the bad news when he arrived at Government Buildings for the cabinet meeting. I found him already aghast at what he had said, and at the newspaper coverage of his remarks. He explained that he hadn't realised that so many journalists were numerate, and had managed to translate half a billion into five hundred million!

Unfortunately, Frank didn't get the message either, that instead of being at the cabinet meeting he should be meeting his party leader in protest. When he was called out of the cabinet room and told what was going on, he went back in to collect his papers and took the opportunity to let a few choice expressions fall about the duplicity of Fine Gael Ministers.

The row over the budgetary cuts was patched up before the day was out, but someone (I always suspected Frank himself, but had no way of knowing) told Michael Mills of the *Irish Press* that Frank Cluskey had given his Fine Gael colleagues a tongue-lashing over their attitude to negotiating the budget. It made the lead story in the following day's *Press*, and it had two effects.

First, it made it look as if it was Frank, and not his Party leader, who had defended party interests. And second, Garret took great umbrage at the public impression that he had been forced to back down, and put Dick completely on the defensive for weeks over the leak of a cabinet row.

It has to be said, though, that Frank Cluskey did some extraordinary things as a Minister. I knew of his reforming reputation in the 1970s, but I formed the view of him that he no longer had the stamina or interest to deal with any really big issue. I was wrong, and the collapse of the PMPA proved it.

The PMPA was the largest insurer of motor business in Ireland. It was controlled by Joe Moore, a rough businessman and a close personal friend of Charlie Haughey. If the news broke that the PMPA was in deep financial trouble, it would be enough to cause a major crisis.

Except that the news didn't break until Frank had developed a response to the situation. He saw to that. Frank and his brilliant Department Secretary, Joe Holloway, carried the secret of the PMPA crisis for several weeks while they came up with legal and financial solutions. It was the only time I was let close to Frank, because he needed someone who could handle media queries when the story broke.

And in the short period of time that I was involved, I watched Frank display a total mastery of the crisis. In order to avoid chaos in motor insurance, they had to prevent the liquidation of the company. One obvious route was nationalisation, but that might have involved paying a large sum of money to the people who had caused the crisis in the first place. So Frank devised the concept of administration—a halfway house between receivership and liquidation which allowed the courts to effectively place the company under new management. Legislation was drawn up in secret, and only published on the day that it went into the Dáil to be passed into law.

The dimensions of the potential crisis were huge. So was the complexity of the solution. But it worked, and Frank Cluskey virtually single-handedly averted what could otherwise have been a major disaster. It's not often remembered now, but I certainly learned never again to underestimate the man or his ability.

Barry Desmond also demonstrated an uncanny knack for generating crisis in those years, but for different reasons.

Barry was a reformer, who always believed in telling people unpalatable truths—the more unpalatable the better. The day he was appointed Minister for Health and Social Welfare, he got the job he was born for.

Within months he developed a total and intimate knowledge of every social welfare scheme, every hospital, every aspect of the health service. He would astound delegations who came to see him about their local hospitals by being able to refer to hospital staff by their first names—and usually by referring to their level of competence or skill!

Barry was totally committed to change and modernisation of the health service, and totally frustrated by the lack of resources to do the things he wanted to do. For four years he defended the budgets for the service, never giving an inch to those who wanted to make savings. As a result, spending on health, as a proportion of GNP, was never reduced under his auspices.

But he would never tell anyone about the battles he fought, and instead of being seen as a saviour of the service, he came to be regarded as a hard Minister, who only wanted to make savings.

He was a public relations nightmare. For example, I always remember Barry briefing me about the fact that he was going to announce the closure of nine psychiatric hospitals the following day.

"They have to go," he said. "They're kips—Dickensian, totally unsuitable today. We're going to replace them with really decent facilities."

I pleaded with him not to bite off so many hospitals in one go, to think again about how the closures would be presented, to be certain that people would understand that this was in the interest of progress and not just of financial savings.

He promised to consider everything I said, and rang me back later to tell me that I had made a big impression, and that he was going to moderate his announcement. I was really pleased with myself—until the following day, when I heard Barry in the Dáil. Instead of closing nine hospitals, he closed eight—and the heavens opened over his head.

Barry wasn't just determined, he was also stubborn. He fought many a battle with Alan Dukes, including one about cigarette smoking. Each year, in the run-up to the budget, Barry would propose an increase in the cost of cigarettes, accompanied by a proposal that the revenue which accrued would be earmarked for the health service. Each year, Alan Dukes ignored him, and imposed just enough tax on cigarettes to ensure that there would be no effect that would lead to a decline in sales.

Eventually Barry decided to take a stand, and sent a whopping memorandum to government proposing a huge increase in the cost of a packet of twenty cigarettes. It was accompanied by a wealth of statistics outlining mortality rates, the impact on young people, and so on.

Alan replied with a memorandum rejecting Barry's proposal. His essential argument was that so large an increase would have a drastic effect on demand, and actually make less revenue available for such areas as health care.

Barry pounced on this. It didn't matter, he declared in his next memo, because if cigarette smoking went into decline, a lot less hospital beds would be needed for the heart and cancer patients that smoking caused.

But he lost the argument. Alan's final memo patiently explained that the beds no longer required for heart attack sufferers would be quickly filled up by all the people who were now living longer and beginning to suffer the ailments associated with old age!

Barry did have one victory when it came to tobacco—and it led to a fascinating discovery. He banned Skoal Bandits, and learned about Irish power and morality in the process.

He called me to his office one day, and told me about this pernicious new product that was about to be launched on the Irish market. Skoal Bandits were a form of chewing tobacco, sold in sachets. They were popular in Scandinavia, and there was evidence linking them to mouth cancer.

Barry was determined to stop them catching on in Ireland, and had asked his officials to investigate whether he had the power to ban their importation.

It appeared he had—the officials had unearthed a section of the 1949 Health Act which had never been used before, but which allowed the Minister to ban the importation of any product or "thing" that he deemed injurious to the nation's health.

This was the section that he used to save Ireland from the scourge of Skoal Bandits. But Barry being Barry, he had also asked the civil servants to investigate why, if this power had never been used before, it had been put into the Act in the first place.

His civil servants had dug out the file, and told him that the section had been inserted into the Act at the insistence of the then Archbishop of Dublin, Dr John Charles McQuaid. According to the correspondence, the Archbishop was gravely concerned about the damage that another product then newly on the market, the tampon, could do to the well-being and morality of young Irish women, and wanted Ministers for Health to have the power to remove such temptation from them!

But most of the rows in that government involved John Bruton. I remember him from that period as a man who was buzzing with ideas, and immensely headstrong. He could never allow an argument to end until he had won it. He caused more trouble in that government—with his own as well as with Labour Ministers—than any other member.

In my early days with the government, I believe I did John Bruton a huge favour—although he was anything but grateful. It was a day when Peter Prendergast was away, and I was in charge of the Government Information Service for the day. A speech was sent over from John Bruton's office for immediate release.

In it, the Minister announced a brave new idea. He wanted to launch a programme of liberalisation of protective legislation, to make it easier to hire and fire employees. The outcome of such a programme, he said, would be the creation of thousands of jobs in such areas as domestic service. I insisted on holding over the speech until Peter returned—I never found out how Peter had persuaded John not to release it, but I doubt if it was easy.

One of the ironies of that government was that Garret was afraid of John Bruton. He would never take him on in argument, and always relied on others to do so. John had responsibility, among other things, for the troubled Irish Steel company. In the mid-80s, when it was going through a major cash crisis, John decided it had to be closed down. Dick was implacably opposed to the closure, and Garret FitzGerald left it between them to decide.

It led to a blazing row in Dick's office. I sat outside, waiting to be briefed on the outcome, and I can still remember the muffled sound of shouting inside. Eventually, though, they fought each other to a draw. Irish Steel secured a cash injection, in return for some rationalisation. Although the company was saved, and although some of the union officials involved knew the efforts that Dick had made, it was the Labour Party that was attacked for the fact that the company had to trim some jobs.

The biggest row between Dick and John concerned the National Development Corporation. The NDC was a Labour priority, to some extent a totem pole, which was designed as a holding company for state enterprise and for establishing and investing in indigenous industry. Because of John's ministerial brief, it was his responsibility to develop it. Unfortunately, he was opposed to the concept as it had been set out in the programme for government.

In the run-up to one of our party conferences, we were under intense pressure to be seen to be delivering on the NDC. Eventually, on the eve of our conference, after a long struggle with John's office, we agreed a number of paragraphs to insert into Dick's keynote speech, which would copper-fasten the principle of state investment in small and medium Irish industry.

Despite being opposed to the whole thing, John found it galling that Dick would be announcing the outcome of the negotiations, so he put out a statement as our conference began, claiming credit for the establishment of the NDC. I was surrounded by reporters as the conference got under way, and asked to comment on John Bruton's statement. Unwisely, I accused him of pettiness, and suggested that it was hypocritical to oppose something and then claim credit for it when it happened. Naturally, the row overshadowed whatever positive publicity we were hoping for from the announcement of the NDC, and I subsequently had to apologise for my remarks.

In those days, while we worked closely with Dick Spring and the other Ministers, there was a clear difference between them and us. We were briefed, usually though not always, by Dick, on a strict "need to know" basis. What happened in the cabinet room was seldom shared outside it—even though we would often complain that it was just as important to know the dynamic behind a decision as it was to know the decision itself.

I tended to be told about things that were likely to get into the papers, William Scally was consulted frequently about economic matters, and Joe Revington and Sally Clarke were briefed about things that would have implications within the party or in the constituency. There were times when we all wondered whether Dick realised that everything spilled over into everything else.

The consequence was that we all briefed each other. We would meet every day, usually in the morning, and we always learned more about what was going on in government from each other than we did from any of the Ministers.

Very early on in the life of that government, William Scally told me about the developing situation in the Dublin Gas company. And the first time he mentioned it, he warned me that it was going to produce a crisis that would rock the government. I didn't take it seriously at the time—it was just another company in trouble, how could it be any worse than Irish Steel or the many other companies that were in dire straits in those years? Several times in the following couple of years, he tried to get Ministers from both parties to take seriously the potential policy crisis that would have to follow from whatever choice was made in relation to Dublin Gas. When the crisis blew up, William had warned them—but they didn't listen until it was too late.

To my untutored way of thinking, Dublin Gas was a vital utility in deep financial crisis. It was a privately-owned company, whose proprietors were totally unwilling to hand it over to the state sector. There were three alternatives for dealing with it—allow it to close (which would have had unthinkable consequences for gas-dependent companies and thousands of families), nationalise it, or bail it out. Every option was going to cost money—lots of it.

But what none of us knew was how deeply Frank Cluskey felt about the situation. We didn't know because he didn't tell us. William predicted that Frank would oppose any bail-out that didn't involve state ownership, and he was right. But we were not in a strong negotiating position. It would perhaps have been strengthened if the government had known the true depth of Frank's feelings, but he never mentioned the word resignation until the decision had gone against us, and especially him.

Even then, it wasn't really a surprise. Frank had been a loner all his political life, and he was uncomfortable in that government from the start. His closest friend in the cabinet was not any of his Labour colleagues, but John Boland, a Fine Gael Minister. They would frequently drink together until very late hours, and they tended to back each other up in argument.

In the end of the day, the decision to give large amounts of money to Dublin Gas, while leaving it in private ownership, was forced through the cabinet by John Bruton, and it was that fact, I think, that finally precipitated Frank's resignation. They couldn't stand each other, and came to see every argument as a battle of wills. Frank left rather than continue the fight.

Dick never, to my knowledge, considered leaving that government because of Frank's resignation. He decided instead that John Bruton's sails would have to be trimmed, and set about having the energy portfolio removed from him in the ensuing re-shuffle. He also, almost, persuaded Mervyn Taylor to take Frank's place at the cabinet table.

Late one night, in the middle of that crisis, I walked into Dick's Leinster House office unannounced. Dick wasn't there, but Mervyn was—and he was being briefed by the Cabinet Secretary, Dermot Nally, on the procedures for divesting himself of business and professional responsibilities in order to take up cabinet office.

I learned later that Mervyn had had a sleepless night, torn between becoming the first Jewish member of an Irish cabinet (an aim in which he was to succeed six years later) and the responsibilities of his busy solicitor's practice. He was, I think, troubled too by the thought that he would be seen as abandoning the left of the party if he were to join the government. In the end, he changed his mind, and declined the offer to serve.

In some ways, the reshuffle forced by Frank's departure made the government stronger and more cohesive. The party pressure on Dick, which derived from events and also from the continuing strong strain of anti-coalition sentiment within the party, often had the paradoxical effect of forcing Labour Ministers to find their greatest solidarity in the Cabinet room. While Dick was frequently resentful—and rightly so—of the fact that Fine Gael frequently displayed little sensitivity to the difficult position he was in, he never lost his determination to make the government work.

It wasn't always easy. After Dick became Minister for Energy, he quickly discovered that one of the key items in his portfolio was the thorny subject of oil terms. That is to say, there had been a debate for some years about the terms that should be applied to any commercial discovery of oil off the Irish coast. The degree to which the state would benefit from such a discovery would depend on the right mix of taxation and royalties being applied.

The dilemma of course was simple. If the state looked for too much, nobody would see any commercial value in exploration and exploitation. And Irish oil interests were led by Tony O'Reilly, the proprietor of most of the printed word in Ireland, and a long-time advocate of a policy that would have allowed the first people who brought oil ashore to keep most, if not all, of the profits for themselves. His company, Atlantic Resources, would have been the major beneficiary of any such a policy approach.

From the moment Dick became Minister, he discovered that coping with pressure to make concessions on this issue was a daily fact of life. A Fine Gael backbench committee was established to push for policy concessions, and it withered on the vine when we discovered that most of its members owned shares in Atlantic Resources.

On one occasion, William Scally took an urgent phone call from Garret FitzGerald in the Department. Garret, it transpired, was going to have dinner with Tony O'Reilly that evening. He was in a difficult position—one of the topics of conversation at dinner could be the oil terms, and Garret wanted a full briefing there and then. When he was told that work was ongoing in the

Department, but that there was little progress to report, he expressed very considerable frustration—but he didn't press the point.

Tony O'Reilly never got the concessions he was looking for from that government—although the oil terms were changed, the terms applied would still have produced a yield for the exchequer that was considerably in excess of what the *Independent* newspaper experts reported as fair or reasonable.

It may have been that issue that soured Independent Newspapers on that government. Or it may have been Barry Desmond. As Minister for Health, Barry introduced a comprehensive limitation on cigarette advertising. It coincided with the introduction of full colour printing capacity by Independent Newspapers—the sort of capacity that depended on cigarette advertising to pay for itself. Independent Newspapers made strong representations to Barry, seeking the postponement of the ban on the grounds that it would make a huge hole in their revenue-raising capacity. He refused to budge.

It may have been just paranoia on our part, but then a spate of stories that were highly critical of Barry began to appear in Independent publications.

The Nursing Council, for instance, prepared a report on nurse training, recommending that there should be a rationalisation of nurse training schools. When it was sent to Barry—and before he had read it or commented on it—the lead story in the *Herald* was "Desmond to axe nurse training".

The *Sunday World*, another O'Reilly publication, coined an awkward, ugly acronym "Garbardick"—Garret, Barry, and Dick—to sum up its disgust at how awful a government it was. And there were many other examples, all going to show that either we were paranoid or it was very unwise to ignore certain commercial interests.

Sometimes we gave them ammunition, of course. There was, for instance, the August bank holiday weekend when, in the absence of Alan Dukes (who was on holidays), the cabinet decided that Ireland's credit rating was in imminent danger of being undermined, and that immediate drastic action would have to be taken. At the end of a long day, they agreed to eliminate food subsidies, to save about £40 million.

Sadly, Garret wasn't in a position to make the announcement himself, because he left to go on holidays immediately after the meeting. The cabinet decided instead to instruct the Government Information Service to release the decision through civil service channels, apparently hoping that the fact that it was a holiday weekend would mean that no-one would notice.

I was on a day off, and I noticed, because it was the first item on the news, as was the failure of the government to make any effort to explain the background to the decision. I drove into Government Buildings, and persuaded Dick, somewhat against his will, that if the Taoiseach and the Finance Minister weren't available, he would have to take the flak as the most senior member of the Government.

He did it, accompanied by John Boland, in the interests of decent government. For several years afterwards, as a result, he was occasionally criticised as the man who personally abolished food subsidies—a fact of which he would occasionally remind me when I was urging more invaluable advice on him.

A month after that, Dick felt it was necessary to put down several markers in government. As part of the interminable expenditure reviews that resulted from the economic crisis we were in, it was being proposed that social welfare payments—including pensions—should be "de-indexed". In other words, payments that had been tied to the rate of inflation would increase at a slower rate in future.

Dick knew that measures like this were simply unsustainable in political terms, and decided to make a public speech in which he set down his opposition to them. He chose to do it at a meeting of the two Cork city constituencies.

The Cork Labour Party had other ideas. They never listened to a word he had to say—so that a major policy speech fell on completely deaf ears. Instead, speaker after speaker at the meeting lashed Dick for his involvement in the food subsidies, and they tried to move a motion of no confidence in him. Had it not been for some adroit procedural manoeuvring by Pat Magner which prevented a vote being taken, Dick would have been hugely damaged by it.

It was usual, when Dick travelled in the country, to arrange for a series of deputations to see him at the end of the meeting. Because this meeting went on so long, it was well after midnight when the last deputation was brought in to see the Tánaiste. They were a group of artificial inseminators from west Cork, and they were deeply upset by the incipient practice among farmers of what they called D.I.Y.A.I. This practice, they explained to a bemused and exhausted Tánaiste, was destroying their livelihoods. It wasn't until they had left that a local councillor explained that what they were complaining about was do-it-yourself insemination. I don't think the explanation left Dick much the wiser.

That meeting in Cork was a sort of microcosm for the dilemma we had. Major policy statements and arguments were lost on the party, which was obsessed by its own internal faction-fighting at the time. And while you were struggling to get a message across, life—often the most mundane life possible—still had to go on.

Despite all the tension, Dick and Garret were determined that they were not going to be brought down by internal wrangling. Indeed it was one of the features of that government that its two principals, who had very little in common with each other at any level, worked so well together most of the time. Even when they disagreed, they stood by each other.

The one major thing that soured their relationship for a while was the succession to Peter Sutherland. Peter was the Attorney General, and when a vacancy arose for a European Commissioner, he staked a claim for the job. Dick argued for Justin Keating, but in the end arrived at an understanding with Garret that if Peter got the Commissionership, Labour would fill the vacant office of Attorney General—an office which the party had never held in the history of the state.

I had urged Dick to hold out for the office, and to seek to have John Rogers appointed. I regarded John as more than capable of doing the job—but more importantly, I believed he would be a source of strength and confidence to Dick in the Cabinet Room. We only had four members of government out of fifteen, each of them with busy portfolios, and we were never in a position to negotiate policy from strength. Even though John wouldn't be an extra vote, he would be an extra, and a key, presence.

Garret balked, and did everything he could to try to prevent John's appointment. Outsiders sneered, and mocked that Dick was prepared to lose policy arguments in government but would go to the wall for a pal. They missed the point entirely— the main reason we lost policy arguments was because Dick didn't have enough people to support him in the cabinet room.

Eventually, Garret gave in, but there was a sour taste about the way in which he had handled it. He acknowledged fully in later years that John performed brilliantly in the job, and was a totally reliable and non-partisan legal adviser to the government.

I worked closely with John on the great project he wanted to accomplish during his term—bringing some kind of an end to the Stardust Tragedy. Forty eight young people had been killed in a disastrous fire in the Stardust ballroom some years previously, and their families had been tied up in the courts over compensation issues for years. Although they had a strong case, the issue of who was liable had bedevilled them, and no families, and none of the survivors, had been compensated for their terrible loss or injuries.

John was determined from the moment he got the job to cut through the legal quagmire involved. He was strongly advised not to touch it, because any concession on the issue of liability would establish legal precedents that would be used against the State in future. So he single-handedly, virtually, designed a new model of compensation tribunal, that was able to address the suffering of families without addressing the issue of liability at all, and without depriving the families of their right to proceed with litigation if that was their wish. Not one family, to my knowledge, went on with litigation, and the result was that many families were enabled to live with a pain that could never be cured.

One of the great pressures on that government throughout all those years was Northern Ireland. Garret FitzGerald was determined to make his mark in that area, and spent months trying to engage Mrs Thatcher in serious negotiations. To his eternal credit, I believe, he refused to abandon the search for progress after the infamous "out, out, out" statement with which she dismissed the entire contents of the New Ireland Forum Report.

That report, after months of negotiation, had recommended three different possible ways in which nationalism would be prepared to move forward towards an accommodation with unionism. Some of the options in the report were essentially restatements of traditional nationalist sentiment—they were there, in the government's view, as a form of cover for the introduction of the principle of consent, whereby the status of Northern Ireland would remain unchanged unless the consent of a majority of the people of Northern Ireland was secured for change. But Mrs Thatcher's rejection of the entire report had plunged Garret into despair.

His own political resilience came to the rescue, but he was helped immeasurably by the support of others in his cabinet, especially Dick and Peter Barry, the Foreign Minister, who threw themselves wholeheartedly into the search for an agreement. Both men in that period made a number of secret trips back and forth to England, as gradually the Anglo-Irish Agreement began to take shape.

All except one of the major political developments in relation to Northern Ireland can be traced back to that Agreement. The single exception, of course, was the position of Sinn Féin.

The Anglo-Irish Agreement was designed specifically to strengthen constitutional nationalism in its struggle against violent nationalism—it was an integral part of a strategy which assumed that the more progress moderates could make, the more likely it was that violence would wither, and "armed struggle" would be marginalised.

Because that strategy, although entirely logical, was based on a misapprehension about the strength of the republican movement and its hold over the community, the Agreement failed in its central objective. But within ten years all strands of Irish nationalism had embraced the principle of consent to a greater or lesser degree, and the development of a peace process was facilitated by a dialogue in which that became the central principle.

The day the Anglo-Irish Agreement was signed, in Hillsborough Castle, was the high point of Garret's government. It was also the day I met Mrs Thatcher (alas, the only day).

The arrangement was that the two government delegations would line up side by side outside the ballroom of the Castle, and march in to meet the world's media. Mrs Thatcher took personal charge, lining everyone up according to rank. Suddenly she paused.

"Where's Geoffrey?" she snapped. "Where's Geoffrey?"

Geoffrey Howe, the British Foreign Secretary, was nowhere to be seen. And neither was Peter Barry.

Within a minute, Geoffrey appeared in a doorway down the corridor, and came scurrying up to take his place in the line, Peter Barry in his wake.

"Sorry about that, Margaret," he said, "it was all Peter's fault."

Mrs Thatcher sniffed, and set about straightening the Foreign Secretary's jacket. Then, noticing a speck of dandruff on Peter Barry's lapel, she reached to flick it off. The Foreign Minister from Cork, a direct political descendant from Michael Collins, recoiled in horror, and Mrs Thatcher had the good sense to let him flick his own lapel.

The Anglo-Irish Agreement was bitterly opposed by Charlie Haughey. I've always believed that if, in the face of that opposition, Garret had sought a new mandate to seek to build on the Agreement, and had made it the centre-piece of an election, he might well have got it. As it was, the popularity of the government soared for a few weeks in the immediate aftermath of Garret's historic achievement, before the economic realities of the time reminded people that they had better kick the government around.

They got their next opportunity to do so in the divorce referendum of 1986. A series of opinion polls convinced the government that the time was right to take on the issue of divorce, despite the drubbing that the coalition partners had got in the abortion referendum a few years before. That had been a nightmarish campaign, with enormous quantities of hate mail being received by anyone who had the temerity to take a stand against the pro-life movement. This time we felt the opposition would be more reasonable.

It was not to be. Garret delayed the holding of the referendum for months, while he consulted the various churches, apparently in the belief that he could persuade them (especially, of course, the Catholic church) that the time was right to introduce a modest measure of reform. To make matters worse, his procrastination also delayed the preparation of the necessary background papers, to equip the government to deal with every issue that might arise in the course of the campaign. When he eventually gave the go ahead for a Referendum Bill, we were woefully unprepared.

And deeply unpopular. The opponents of divorce were able to rely on a mixture of fear about property and land, and a message that this was a government that couldn't be trusted. I came to believe in the course of that campaign that a great many women, who had been prepared to vote for divorce before it started, began to see divorce as a reward for philandering husbands.

We ran a ham-fisted campaign. I always remember getting a phone call from Geraldine Kennedy, the political correspondent of the *Irish Times* (I think she was with the *Sunday Tribune* then) when it was all over. She asked me if I knew whether any of the principals in the campaign had read the book by William Binchy, *The Case against Divorce*. Binchy had been the mastermind of the anti-divorce campaign, and his book had set out, in simple, readable form, all the arguments they were going to use against any change in the law. As far as I could discover, nobody on our side had read it!

Despite all that government tried to do, it ended in failure and disagreement. In its last few months, Garret tried to reshuffle the cabinet, to give it a brighter and fresher look, and to take people out of portfolios where they had attracted more than their share of unpopularity. Taoisigh don't normally consult those who are about to be re-shuffled, because they end up fight a lot of rear-guard actions, and because once one Minister is told, rumours begin to spread like wildfire. He did however consult Dick.

One of the Ministers in the frame was Barry Desmond, who had endured a lot of abuse in Health, despite fighting very successfully to protect the health budget. Garret and Dick agreed that Barry should be moved—but Barry was totally opposed. He saw it essentially as a vote of no confidence in him, and decided that he would stay where he was.

At one point in the course of that bizarre night, Barry was literally barricaded in his own office, to prevent anyone getting in to try to persuade him to be reasonable. At another stage in the evening, he spent some time in Alan Dukes' room (Dukes was also being moved) trying to persuade Alan to make a stand with him, while Alan tried to persuade Barry to give in. It was like a Gilbert and Sullivan version of *Mutiny on the Bounty*. Eventually, after the entire Government had stayed up all night, Barry accepted the loss of half of his portfolio, but carried on as one of the most controversial , and one of the best, Ministers for Health that Ireland has ever seen.

In that reshuffle, John Bruton, to everyone's surprise, had secured the Finance portfolio. In the budget preparations for 1987 a set of draconian spending cuts were proposed, many of which would have had a disastrous impact on poorer families. It was obvious that there was no way we could accept them. It was equally obvious, despite several months of negotiation, that we were not going to change Fine Gael's mind.

We took a conscious decision however, that two important pieces of legislation, on Europe and extradition, would be passed before we went our separate ways. The end was due to come on January 10th, 1987. On that day, the Government would finally decide budget proposals. We knew we would resign then, to allow the budget to be published in the afternoon.

However, on the day, there was four inches of snow on the ground. One of the Fine Gael proposals was for a 10p increase in the cost of a gallon of central heating oil. Dick remarked that even by Fine Gael standards of fiscal rectitude, increasing the tax on central heating while pipes were frozen all over the country was likely to be political suicide. The decisions were postponed for a week.

So the government finally came to an end on January 20th. We stood on the steps of Government Buildings, and Dick read a short statement to the assembled media, explaining that Labour had resigned rather than support a Budget that we believed to be unjust.

Four weeks later, we watched on television, all of us gathered together in the party head office, as the party seemed to disappear down the drain. For a long time that night, as the results of the 1987 election were being counted, it looked as if Labour could return no more than six deputies. Gradually, as the night wore on, some optimism returned, as five more candidates began to look like they had a chance of winning through. But would they have a leader? The way the drama was unfolding in Kerry North, the constituency of Dick Spring, it looked like they wouldn't.

As I watched on television that night—watched the party leader whom I had come to know and admire clinging for dear life to his seat—one thought went through my mind. We'd learned a lot in four years—a lot about how to manage events; a lot about how to govern effectively; a lot about how to implement change. If Dick wasn't going to survive, how were we ever going to put it into practice?

3

Carrying the Scars

We had hired billboards for that election, great forty-eight sheet posters strategically placed around the country. One of them was in Gardiner Place, just across the road from our head office. As dusk fell on the evening of the count, we watched from the window as the giant poster of Dick Spring was covered over with large sheets of purple paper, in readiness for a new subject the following day. Purple, like a canonical shroud, seemed all too appropriate.

While we watched on television, on one of the most depressing nights I can remember, the drama surrounding Dick's count unfolded in Tralee, two hundred miles away. In the days before mobile phones, it was impossible to keep in close touch, and we had to rely on RTE for whatever updates we got. Fortunately, perhaps, it was one of the most dramatic counts in history, and RTE kept us fully informed.

John Foley was covering the count for the *Irish Independent*, and he told the story for years afterwards. By the time it was over, it was six in the morning, freezing cold, and already bright. A full moon in a clear February sky illuminated Denny Street, the fine street that dominates the centre of the town.

John still had work to do, even at that hour. He had just witnessed, at close quarters, one of the most dramatic counts in Irish political history, and now had to file copy for that day's *Evening Herald* before he could get to bed.

A Tánaiste had held on to his seat by just four votes out of more than 33,000 cast. And it had happened after an agonising re-count, while the whole country stayed glued to their televisions. Dick had gone into the election as one of the few safe Labour TDs in the country, and had emerged personally and politically scarred.

We all found it hard to believe. The most senior politician ever to have emerged from Kerry, the first party leader with a Kerry background, and a Minister who had delivered more than any other in the history of the county. How could the electorate have treated him this way? He had been personally responsible, for instance, for increasing the total number of houses in the constituency by 10% in just four years—a housing stock that had taken several centuries to accumulate.

And now, it seemed, the people of his constituency were hell-bent on humiliating him.

Sinn Féin had picked up nearly 1,200 votes in the election, and if Dick hadn't received nearly 300 of their transfers, he'd have been out—after four years of spectacular delivery for his own people.

To make matters worse, his "running mate", Jimmy Deenihan of Fine Gael, had polled more than 10,000 votes. In an election which saw Fine Gael's national share of the vote dropping by 12%, their vote in Kerry North had gone up by almost the same amount. Local people around Dick had warned him, four years earlier, that when Garret FitzGerald had appointed Deenihan as a Senator, in Dick's own backyard, he should have seen it as a hostile act.

And the local Fine Gael campaign in 1987 had been run entirely on the basis that "Dick is as safe as a house, you can afford to give Jimmy the number one this time". It paid off, and left Dick dependent on the surplus of the Fine Gael man who had nursed the constituency while Dick was away running the country—another galling wound.

The drama of the count, the figures, and the background all had to be crammed into the short piece that John was writing for the *Herald*. It was nearly seven-thirty, on that bitterly cold February morning, before he climbed into his bed in the Mount Brandon Hotel. But before he could close his eyes, the phone began ringing insistently beside his bed.

Dick was in the hotel lobby, looking for him. The Tánaiste who had barely survived had decided to play golf, and John was required to make up the foursome.

A couple of hours later, wearing a borrowed Lansdowne rugby club sweater and golf shoes that were two sizes two big for him, John set off around the Tralee golf course with the three Spring brothers, Arthur, Dick, and Donal. Another little bit of history was made that morning—it was the first time that the three of them had ever played together.

John can't remember now who won—all he can remember is that they didn't talk about politics.

They stopped after twelve holes, because none of them had had any sleep to speak of. Donal in particular had had the busiest night, because it was he who, as his brother's legal representative, had fought over every single vote in the recount that had gone on through the night. John still has a recollection of seeing Donal sitting at the bar in the golf club, ordering a pint. By the time it arrived, he was fast asleep, his head on the counter.

That game of golf was an act of bravado—and also of family solidarity. It was intended to clear heads, to translate bitterness into some kind of "us against the world" determination. It might have worked, but it didn't. The following six months were the real low point of Dick's career.

He retreated into himself, unable to come to terms with the rebuff that the people of North Kerry had handed him. It didn't matter that his reaction was illogical—it was never intended as a rebuff, but was a combination of complacency and the very vigorous, undermining campaign run by his opponents. ("Dick is dead safe" was also the motto of Fianna Fáil's Denis Foley, who argued that a switch away from Dick was the best way for the people of Tralee to elect two Tralee Deputies.)

Dick saw it as more than personal. The Spring family had served the people of Kerry for decades, and Dick's father had fought many a bitter battle. But nothing like this had ever happened—people had never misled them before, promising support and than ignoring them when it counted.

And on top of the feeling of rejection was physical and mental exhaustion. For the last six months of the FitzGerald government, Dick had been under immense strain.

Every day there had been arguments and pressures. Everyone involved knew the government was going nowhere, and Dick had been torn between the need to get out of that government with dignity, and his own sense of loyalty and duty.

He believed it was a government that had tried hard, against the odds, and had never done anything to be ashamed of. But he knew it couldn't possibly contest an election as a government—that would have torn his own party apart. The party had set up a Commission on Electoral Strategy to try to resolve the age-old row about coalition, and its report had strongly recommended that Labour should stay out of government until it had 25 seats. That certainly didn't look likely in the short term, but Dick had committed himself to accepting the report. Trying to get the balance right kept him awake night after night, as we argued the pros and cons in his office in Clare Street.

You can't take a sabbatical from leadership, but Dick tried. From February to September, he was listless and apathetic. He spent as little time as possible in Dublin, going through the motions on the daily Order of Business and otherwise doing nothing except constituency work. The moment the Dáil rose for the summer, he and Kristi left for the States for a six-week holiday. Almost as soon as they had gone, we had to fight off a rumour that he had been offered a partnership in a law firm in Arizona, and wouldn't be coming back. (Like all the best rumours, it was absolutely false, but built around the tiniest grain of truth. Dick's eldest son Aaron had contracted a form of juvenile arthritis, which was painful and worrying. Part of the rumour was that Dick and Kristi had been advised that the dry heat of Arizona was the best possible place to treat their son.)

He left behind terrible problems. We had spent more than £200,000 on the election—money we didn't have. Because constituencies had been so dispirited in the run-up to the election, we had organised leaflets and posters centrally, and had supplied them to candidates. It had made a difference, and encouraged people to go out and fight for seats instead of spending weeks trying to gather basic material together.

It was the first time that we had ever taken a central role in equipping constituencies, and it worked. But it had left demoralising debts behind—there were days when Ray Kavanagh, the party's general secretary, had to beg for time from the Revenue Commissioners, because we were so far behind in PAYE and PRSI payments.

Just because Dick was standing still, the rest of the world wasn't. The election had thrown up an odd result. At 6.4%, our share of the vote was the lowest we had had in 54 years. Four of our TDs had lost their seats, one (Joe Bermingham) had left the party just before the election and had retired, and Eileen Desmond had decided not to contest. Numerically, it should have been a disaster. But three new TDs had been elected—Brendan Howlin, Michael D Higgins (who was regaining his seat), and Emmet Stagg. There were now twelve Labour Deputies—down only two on the number that had gone into the election.

One sweet result was that of Frank Cluskey, who knocked his old enemy Dr John O'Connell out of the Dáil. Frank and I had had a row during the election, when he had failed to turn up for an important radio interview about economic policy, and had sent his friend Flor O'Mahony in his place.

I was furious—not because Flor wasn't a good representative for the party (he probably knew more about the subject than Frank did) but because I was convinced we needed Frank's higher national profile. He also failed to turn up when Dick made one his rare forays to Dublin and visited the Guinness brewery. It seemed like a deliberate snub.

I didn't know it at the time, but Frank was already suffering from the throat cancer that killed him shortly afterwards, and it was affecting his voice badly. I assumed, especially when I spoke to him on the phone, that he had failed to turn up because he was drinking.

It took me several months to discover the truth, but I apologised to him for the injustice when I found out. We shook hands, and I think he forgave me. It was the last time I saw him.

But the election had made a further significant difference. The balance in the party had shifted, and the new force in the party didn't take long to make his intentions clear. Immediately he was declared elected, Emmet Stagg drove to RTE, and waited impatiently to take his place on the analysis panel. There was no room for him, because Barry Desmond was already there as the party's representative. During an ad break, Emmet approached Barry and made it clear to him that he wanted to go on the panel. Rather than make a scene, Barry concurred, and Emmet immediately took the opportunity to launch a scathing attack on the leadership, calling for a radical new direction for the party.

We all saw it, and promptly decided that it was a case of Emmet being a poor winner. We were wrong. Emmet was absolutely determined to take over control of the Labour Party, just as he had taken control of the Kildare constituency. And for most of the next two years, the battle against Emmet was to occupy most of our time and effort.

It wasn't as if we hadn't been warned. Kildare had been a Labour seat, held by William Norton, since 1932. We had lost it when Norton died, and it had taken Joe Bermingham years to get it back. But Joe had held the seat against all comers for fourteen years, until Emmet had moved in on him.

Joe was one of the great characters of the Labour Party. Born in 1919, he was well into middle age when he became a Dáil deputy. A life-long bachelor, with a crusty reputation but a genuine sense of humour, Joe had always been a party loyalist. He backed the leader of the day unswervingly, and could always be relied on to stand up and be counted in any crisis.

He also had a huge appetite. In my early days with the party, it was my job to brief the media after each parliamentary party meeting. Because I didn't attend the meetings, I relied on a briefing from Joe about what happened, and his instructions were to wait for him in the members' restaurant in the Dáil, so that he could get straight to his lunch after the meeting, without being delayed by the demands of the media.

I can still remember the day, in or about 1986, when the parliamentary party spent the morning wrestling with Barry Desmond's Contraceptive Bill. There was more than usual media interest in the outcome of the debate, and I fretted in the restaurant while I waited for Joe. As soon as he arrived, he ordered roast beef—"and two extra slices of the well-done beef, with lashings of gravy".

"You're hungry, Joe," I observed.

"Those hoors have spent the whole morning talking about contraception," he announced, "and I've had to listen to every bloody one of them talking about creams and jellies until I'm blue in the face. I'm starving after it!"

In 1985, a spate of ugly personal rumours began to circulate about Joe. A young man who worked as his assistant was approached one night and told that if he stood in the local elections, one of the local newspapers would carry stories about a sexual relationship between him and Joe.

Joe was horrified, and demanded an investigation into the source of the rumours. The administrative council of the party set up a small committee to try to find out what was going on, and very quickly, circumstantial evidence began to accumulate which suggested that the rumours (which were completely untrue) had emanated from people around Emmet Stagg.

Emmet himself denied absolutely that he had had anything to do with the matter, except that he admitted hearing the rumours, and claimed to have done no more than alert Joe to their existence.

There was no proof of Emmet's involvement and besides, there was the dilemma that further action on the matter would have opened up the whole affair to the media. Inevitably, the rumours about Joe would find their way into the newspapers. So the investigation fizzled out.

Joe Bermingham, however, was convinced that Emmet was behind a plot to do him in, and when Emmet subsequently succeeded in getting a nomination to contest the next general election, he resigned from the party in protest. Almost the last thing he said to Dick before he resigned was that he (Dick) would be Emmet's next target.

There is a strange irony in the fact that some years later, it was identical rumours, which this time turned out to have more than a grain of truth in them, which did terrible damage to Emmet's own career.

Some time after the hounding of Joe Bermingham, I was also the subject of a rumour campaign, when I applied for the post of general secretary of the party. I did myself no favours in seeking the job, by doing a lousy interview. But it was also widely, and falsely, rumoured that I couldn't be considered because I had told the interview board that I wouldn't travel because I had a mentally handicapped daughter, and because my father had passed union pickets in a bitter Aer Lingus strike (my father worked in Aer Lingus management, and like all his colleagues had carried on working during the strike).

Wherever these and other rumour campaigns had come from, they were entirely symptomatic of the bitter and divided atmosphere in the party in the run-up to the 1987 election and in its immediate aftermath. It was bound to boil over.

What we didn't know was that it wasn't just Emmet who had an agenda. Relations between the party leadership, especially Dick and Barry, and senior figures in the trade union movement, had plummeted throughout the time we were in government. We believed that the trade unions regarded us as little more than a dog that would bark whenever they kicked us, and we resented the way in which they felt entirely free to attack any measure.

John Carroll, in particular, would routinely put out a statement every time the Book of Estimates was published, attacking the government for its Thatcherite policies—and this after Dick and Barry had fought for weeks to protect essential social spending. Eventually Dick snapped at this kind of treatment, and issued a sarcastic statement in response to one of John Carroll's, suggesting that it was time he learned to read. It didn't go down well.

There were other tensions. During the lifetime of the government, the closure of Clondalkin Paper Mills led to demands for its nationalisation, and a bitter dispute which involved two of the workers going on hunger strike. Fianna Fáil put down a Private Members Motion in the Dáil condemning the government's handling of the situation.

On the night the vote was to be taken on the motion, a delegation of senior trade union people came to see the Labour

Ministers. For an hour they harangued the Ministers about how critical it was for the future of the Labour Party that we should not be caught on the wrong side of this vote. Eventually, they put their cards on the table. It was Billy Attley who spelled out the demand.

"We're here to make sure that you vote against the government tonight," he said. "If you don't, the party's finished."

It was a delicate moment, requiring tact and diplomacy. Instead, Barry spoke.

"As usual, Bill, you're missing the point," he said. "We won't be voting against the government. We are the government!"

Incidents like these ensured that by the time the government came to an end, senior people in both wings of the Labour movement were barely on speaking terms with one another. When Emmet Stagg began campaigning for a change in direction in the party, and for more "democracy" in how the leader of the party should be elected, he quickly found allies in the trade union movement.

This was Emmet's masterstroke. He proposed a motion for the party conference, which was due to be held in Cork, that in future the leader of the party should be elected by party conference. Up to that point, the leader had always been chosen by the TDs in the parliamentary party. Changing the rules would mean that the trade union block vote would have a decisive influence on who would lead the Labour Party in the Dáil in future. The fact that it would be hard to imagine a less democratic method of imposing a parliamentary leader didn't matter much. The whole purpose of the motion, and the inspiration behind its drafting, was to fatally undermine Dick Spring, and place him in the same position that Michael O'Leary had been in a few years earlier.

We went into that conference like lambs to the slaughter. A political party, if it has any sense, treats its annual conference as a glorious opportunity to communicate—with itself and with the wider public. It's the only chance a party leader gets to address the electorate as a whole, without the filter of the media, and as a result he puts a lot of effort into his televised speech. Dick wanted to use this speech to speak to the party and to the public—to begin the job of binding wounds in the party, and to show a united and confident front to the public.

It has to be done in 56 minutes—no more and no less. As long as RTE allots a broadcast hour to the speech, you have to use it as well as possible. Cutting the speech short means that the public is watching proceedings in which it is even less interested—allowing it to go on for thirty seconds longer than it should means the public sees you being cut off in mid-sentence. Timing, preparation, and rehearsal become every bit as important as content.

That's why the leader needs a bit of space. It's a nerve-wracking business, trying to perform on live television, and it can go horribly wrong. Shortly before Dick's first term as Tánaiste came to an end, he was invited to present the *People of the Year* awards on RTE. The only thing he had to do was make a short speech, and at the end announce the name of the overall winner, the person of the year. None of the other awards was a surprise, and the award winners knew in advance of their selection. But one among them was to be surprised, right at the end of the evening.

Dick read his speech, and turned to the last page of the script for the name of the overall winner. It wasn't there. Somehow, the last page had come adrift from the stapled script. He stared at the camera for eight seconds (I timed it on videotape), obviously wracking his brains to try to recall which of the eight winners was the overall one. Eventually it came to him, but I was able to calculate that it takes precisely eight seconds for a bead of sweat to trickle from Dick Spring's forehead to the top of his moustache!

The lesson Dick learned from that experience was to leave nothing to chance. And his conference speech in Cork in 1987 was a good deal more important, so he threw himself into its preparation for a couple of weeks before the conference. He didn't know that it was only going to be a sideshow. The real business was going to be the battle between right and left.

The conference agenda was arranged so that debate and voting on the leadership motions would take place on the Saturday night, after Dick's speech. We thought that would be an advantage. It would give us time to take a reasonable measure of the mood of the delegates throughout Saturday; they would be in a more receptive mood anyway after Dick's speech; and there would be time to organise, if organisation was necessary. Dick had taken the precaution of ensuring that his own branch, the Rock Street branch in Tralee, had put down a compromise amendment on the leadership election issue, calling for the establishment of a commission to examine new ways of electing a party leader for the future.

It was John Rogers who spotted first that the mood was entirely wrong. He came to me at lunchtime on the Saturday, saying that he had spoken to some of the ITGWU delegates, and he was convinced they would be voting for Emmet's motion. It was clear too that there was intensive campaigning going on in the hall.

Emmet himself was campaigning for the position of party vice-chair, and Mervyn Taylor was running hard for the post of party chairman against Ruairi Quinn. They had both come well prepared, with rosettes and leaflets. Our side had nothing.

John and I decided we had better do something. We approached Niall Greene, who, despite being a successful businessman, was respected on all sides of the party as a person of long experience and commitment, and asked him if he would suss out Billy Attley, to see what his position was. He was back in an hour, to tell us that the entire trade union vote was going to go against us. In his view, there was nothing to be done, except take the medicine.

"Are you suggesting," John asked him, "that he ought to resign?"

"He's a big boy," Greene replied curtly. "He can make up his own mind."

Around five o'clock, I went to Dick's hotel room, for one final rehearsal of the speech. I found him in a dark mood, ready to give up. He had got the message again and again throughout the day that his friends were deserting him in droves.

Constituencies that he could expect to rely on, like Wicklow and Carlow–Kilkenny, had sent far fewer delegates than they were entitled to. Most of the Dublin constituencies, by contrast, were there in strength. And Emmet's Kildare constituency had more delegates than had travelled from Kerry.

To make matters worse, Barry Desmond and Bill Attley had attacked each other during their speeches in the afternoon. Whatever chance there was of Attley drawing back from a confrontation with the leadership, it was well and truly gone.

"Why should I bother?" Dick was saying. "We've fought on our backs for the last four years to try to protect the party's interests, and nobody gives a damn. They've just come here looking for blood, and I don't see any reason I should go on fighting."

For the rest of the hour, we argued the toss, ignoring the speech that had to be delivered at eight o'clock. In fact, at one stage Dick more or less decided that he was going to scrap the speech entirely, and tell the delegates on live TV that they could pick a new leader there and then. Even after we left his hotel room and went down to the empty auditorium in the City Hall to check the lights and sound (Conference had broken for a tea break), I still wasn't sure what he was going to do.

Pat Murray, the artistic director of the Cork Opera House, had designed the stage set, and was waiting for us in the hall. Pat is a perceptive and sensitive man—qualities he hides behind a very large, very bluff, and very camp exterior. He's not a member of the party, and pretends not to understand politics, but he would have had his ear to the ground all day. He took one look at Dick's face, and came bustling over to us.

"Yerrah, fuck 'em boy!" he said. "They don't know a good thing when they have one!"

For the first time in several days, I saw Dick grin. He put his hand on Pat's arm.

"Then we'd better show them what a good thing looks like," he said.

Throughout his televised speech, I had to forget the drama that still waited to unfold. I sat behind the stage, beside the autocue operator, keeping a close watch on the clock. It was my job to let Dick know if he was going too fast or too slow, and to cut the material down if he had fallen behind time. A scrap of paper, with "speed up" or "slow down" written on it, held in front of the autocue camera, was visible to him but to no-one else.

I sometimes think it's almost as hard a job to get right as actually delivering the speech. The first time I did it, in the Mansion House in Dublin, I had to cut twenty minutes of material out of the speech as he spoke. The autocue operator and I were working in a tiny cramped space at the back of the stage. I had the autocue roll (which looks for all the world like a toilet roll), spread out all over the floor, frantically marking passages for her to scroll through quickly. All Dick could see, on the monitor in front of him, was great gobs of text flashing by every time there was a round of applause. He had to stand there and look unconcerned, hoping against hope that the text would stop flashing by when the applause stopped. We just barely got away with it, and I ended the speech in a state of collapse, with a temperature of 102°.

It was easier in Cork, because the applause was seldom more than polite. There was no need to remove any of the material in the speech. Dick was hesitant, reading the speech as if he wanted to be somewhere else, seldom capturing any of the spirit of it. And there was a palpable sense throughout the hall that the delegates were waiting for the main business, the business of choosing how the next leader would be elected— and humiliating and destroying the present one in the process. We were powerless to do anything about it.

Later, when the leadership debate started, I stood at the back of the hall with John Rogers, watching. Speaker after speaker, especially the trade union ones, took pleasure in their veiled attacks on Dick's leadership, reciting all the perceived failures of the previous four years. Throughout it all, Dick sat in the centre of the platform, his head cupped in his hand, his jacket thrown over the back of his chair.

And then Michael D. Higgins, who was chairing the conference, called on Dick to move his Rock Street amendment. Dick reached for his jacket, then obviously decided to leave it where it was.

His face set and grim, he marched to the speaker's podium. There were a few audible sniggers, and one or two cat-calls. My heart sank.

"Jesus!" I muttered to John. "He's going to tell them to shove it!"

"Dick Spring, Rock Street Branch," he began, and he was speaking very quietly. "There are delegates from Wicklow here tonight, and from Carlow, and from Kerry—and they've had a hand in the election of every party leader we've ever had."

He paused, and all around the hall you could see people starting to straighten up.

"Will I tell you how they did it?" he went on, his voice beginning to rise. "They went out, in hail, rain and snow, and despite all the odds they elected Labour TDs. That's how they did it—not by ramming through motions in a party conference—but by appealing to the people in their constituencies."

He went on, gripping the podium as he spoke, leaning forward into the microphone, his eyes sweeping the hall. It was entirely ad-lib, entirely his personal reaction to the debate. And it was making the delegates uncomfortable. From my vantage point, I could see them shifting in their seats.

"I am the leader of this party," he said. "I'm properly elected to do that job. If you don't want me to do it, you can pass a motion of no confidence any time. But let me say this. I don't regard the job as my personal property. I don't regard it as conferring any personal privileges. Except one—the courtesy of being consulted. That's all I'm asking for—the right to be consulted in how the leader should be elected. The right to ensure that the decision we make takes account of all the aspects—and that it's a decision that will serve the long-term interests of the party."

Nobody present had ever seen this side of Dick Spring. Some who had served with him in cabinet had seen him angry before, but never like this. His eyes were blazing, and there was no doubt that he was throwing down a challenge to his critics.

He spoke for no more than three or four minutes, and when he was finished, there was silence in the hall. Gradually, applause began, tentative at first, then swelling. While it was his own people who were applauding—throughout sections of the hall, his critics were sitting on their hands—there was suddenly a sense that maybe, just maybe, we weren't beaten after all.

And then the vote was called. A sea of hands went up in support of the Rock Street Amendment. From where John and I stood at the back of the hall, it looked like a bigger sea of hands against. But when the roll-call vote was demanded, we had won—by 38 votes out of more than a thousand.

We lost a lot at that conference—the left won the chair and vice-chair, and almost won control of the Administrative Council—but for the moment, that didn't matter. We got a leader back.

When it was over, later that night, a few of us sat down for a drink. I expected to find Dick relieved, even happy. But he wasn't. He was angry—angry at himself for allowing things to get so close, angry at the tactics that had been employed against him.

"Never again," he said. "Next time, we take the fight to them. And they won't know what hit them."

4

Fighting Back

Apart from the day Deirdre O'Brien saved Barry Desmond's life, a lot of the rest of the next eighteen months was uneventful—at least on the surface. Underneath the surface, there was a war going on.

Deirdre was Barry's secretary. In the cramped conditions of Leinster House, she and Barry shared the same office. And sharing an office with Barry also meant living with the hundreds of files and reams of paper he kept. Barry was an inveterate hoarder, and he had accumulated several tons of paper during his term as Minister for Health. (On one occasion, when they were doing some housekeeping in the Cabinet Secretary's Office, it was discovered that they had a number of gaps in the files relating to cabinet agendas for the years 1983—1987. Barry was able to supply copies of all the missing agendas from his collection.)

He wasn't just a hoarder—if he had to dispose of anything, he always insisted on shredding it first. And he always did the shredding himself. I think he found it therapeutic to sit in front of the shredder, feeding paper (even blank paper) into it.

At least he did until the day he caught his tie in the shredder. Deirdre was working at her own desk when she heard Barry give a strangled yelp. She looked up to see him purple in the face, crouched low over the shredder.

If she hadn't leaped up from her desk and unplugged the machine, we might have had to cope with one of the most bizarre accidents ever to befall a TD!

In those years, Barry was one of the most important people around Dick. With his energy, he could run a one-man opposition, and Dick left an awful lot of the Dáil work to him. He concentrated instead on organising. Charlie Haughey was running the country, with Ray MacSharry implementing a series of savage cuts in social spending. We were ignoring the country, and trying to sort out the party.

Dick's instructions were specific. We were going to take on the left at every opportunity. We would fight to modernise the image and look of the party; we would ensure that by the time the next conference came around we had a clear majority; and we were going to get rid of the Militant Tendency, which was a corrosive element in the party, especially in Dublin. If necessary, we were going to do it inch by inch.

Every Wednesday night for the next eighteen months, a small group of us met in Dick's Leinster House office. Ray Kavanagh, general secretary, and his deputy Marion Boushell (who had an uncannily detailed knowledge of the party organisation) would brief us on where we were strong and where we were weak. Each week we would focus on a different constituency, and go through it virtually on a name-by-name basis. We were determined that by the time we got to the next conference, nothing would be left to chance.

The work we did was so thorough that when all the delegates' names were in for the next conference, Marion predicted the outcome of each vote. I don't think she got any of her predictions wrong by more than a vote or two.

The group that came together in that period was one of the two groups that built the party. They were focussed on one thing and one thing only—organising to ensure that a modern, efficient machine would face the electorate. Sally Clarke, Pat Magner, Anne Byrne, Pat Upton, James Wrynn, and Brendan Howlin worked with Ray and Marion day in and day out to ensure that we got to know and understand what made each and every potential delegate to our next conference tick.

At the same time, William Scally gathered a small group of people around him—Greg Sparks, John Rogers, Brendan Lynch, and Tim Burke—to start analysing and assessing ideas mainly on the direction of economic policy.

After a year's intensive work and discussion, they came up with the outline of a new economic policy for the party. It stuck firm to traditional values of redistribution, but it was written in language that was new, coherent, and positive. With the agreement of the group, Dick decided to publish it as a leadership contribution to debate, rather than seek party support for the document.

The overlap between these two groups, throughout that period, was John Rogers. His contribution was inestimable. To those who don't know him, John is a reserved, almost moody figure. In fact, he can be impetuous, and his enthusiasm for ideas and action kept us going often when all we wanted to do was curl up and sleep.

Every day, in that period, I thought of the old Winston Churchill aphorism, when he stopped a young MP in his tracks, because the MP was complaining about the enemies in the Labour Party. Churchill, pointing to the opposition benches, told the MP never to forget that the people over there were the opposition. "If you're looking for the enemy, young man," said Churchill, "always look behind you."

We knew who the enemy was, and he was organising too. Emmet had won almost a majority on the Administrative Council of the party, and we had to devise a rather peculiar method of choosing the TDs who would join the AC if he was to be deprived of total control. We came up with a rather elaborate and untested form of PR, and Emmet announced that he would challenge it legally. He even got counsel's opinion in the matter—from Mary Robinson SC! It was good advice too—I believe Emmet would have won in court if he had taken us on, but ultimately he decided not to.

He discovered at another stage that we were going through his constituency records with a fine-tooth comb. We were correlating branch records to addresses, and checking at random to see if the people listed were actually members of the party.

The oddity about Emmet's constituency was that it was cash rich. The most left-wing constituency in the country owned and operated commercial property! It was a property bought by the Nortons in Naas, and bequeathed in trust to the local party. It brought in a tidy income, which Emmet used to ensure that his membership was always paid up. The buses used to transport delegates to conference were paid for out of the same fund.

And Emmet wasn't squeamish about fund-raising either. The proprietor of the new K Club in Straffan, Co. Kildare, Michael Smurfit, was among those who received a begging letter from his local Labour TD.

When Emmet discovered that we were digging around in his constituency, he decided to do the same in Kerry North. But he didn't have the same access to party files as the party leader had. So he decided to take it. He turned up at our party headquarters in Gardiner Street, and simply announced that he was helping himself. While Ray Kavanagh argued the toss with Emmet, Angie Mulroy, who was in charge of membership records in head office, rang Leinster House. The first I knew of it was when I heard Dick bellowing down the corridor, "C'mon! We're needed in head office now."

Twenty minutes later, I was literally holding them apart. I had no doubt in my mind which of them would win a fist fight, but it was equally clear that both of them would have been very damaged politically, had any physical injuries been inflicted.

One of the keys to Emmet's organising ability in those days was a strange American called Michael Taft. I worked very long hours then, and would often be the last person to leave the Labour Party offices in Leinster House—the last, that is, except for Taft. He worked full-time for Emmet, as a speechwriter, researcher, and organiser. He wasn't on the Houses of the Oireachtas payroll, and seemed to have no visible means of support, yet he was supporting a family in one of the more fashionable parts of Dublin. He had been very active in the first Divorce Action Campaign, and seemed to be associated with a number of left-wing causes. We tried every means possible to investigate the mystery behind him but we were never able to solve it.

Little by little, our confidence began to grow that we could make this thing work. Barry Desmond and Brendan Howlin, ably supported by Ruairi Quinn and Mervyn Taylor, were performing brilliantly on the floor of the Dáil. Brendan in particular proved himself to be a superb party whip and strategist. Haughey's minority government lost six votes in the Dáil in that period, and Brendan organised five of those defeats.

Week after week, the hostilities between the two sides of the party raged—although most of the time, it was under the surface. The *Irish Times* in those days ran an occasional series of history items in its educational supplements, where they would take historic events and report them as if they were current news. The page that they devoted to the insurrection led by Robert Emmet was dominated by the headline "Emmet hanged in Thomas Street". Late one night I enlarged the headline on the photocopier, and hung it as a notice over Emmet's desk!

But we knew that this was a war to the death. Dick could not sustain another conference like the Cork one. At the same time, the most frustrating aspect of the struggle was that we knew the party's image was in desperate need of modernising, if we were ever to begin to haul back from the results of the 1987 election. The energy being devoted to an internal struggle was enough to revolutionise our electoral chances.

And what made it even worse was that this was never a struggle about values. It was, pure and simple, a struggle for power within the party. Naturally, Emmet made every effort to paint himself on the left of the party, and to brand everyone who supported Dick as careerist and right-wing. He made one speech at that time which compared the party under Dick's leadership to the "political wing of the Vincent de Paul society". The only reaction he got was a strong letter of protest from the Vincent de Paul society!

For those who wanted to look at the issues objectively, the proof about the nature of the struggle was contained in the document that Dick published in 1988, an economic policy document called "Labour's Alternative". It was strongly redistributive, and relied heavily on new models of property and wealth taxation.

When Dick offered it to the party's economic policy committee as a contribution to debate, the committee, which was dominated by trade union members and people who supported Emmet, insisted that the property taxation elements be significantly watered down. Essentially, while Emmet's rhetoric was always louder and more radical than Dick's, his instincts were populist.

The battle was fought out in every possible forum. We sent people under cover to every meeting of Emmet's organisation, Labour Left, and received detailed reports of everything said. Niamh Bhreathnach agreed to take Emmet on for the position of vice-chair at the next conference. At meeting after meeting of the Administrative Council, the gauntlet was thrown down.

Despite the fact that nearly everyone who worked for Dick was a heavy smoker, he succeeded in getting a ban on smoking at AC meetings adopted by the Council. Emmet was the heaviest smoker of all, and even though the ban irritated Pat Magner, it drove Emmet berserk.

We forced through a vote to hold the next conference in Dick's home town of Tralee, because that would make it more expensive and difficult for Emmet to get his delegates there. At one of the party's Christmas parties, Dick got himself involved in some pushing and shoving in response to a smart remark by Dave Moynan, Emmet's constituency assistant. All the time the message was the same—there'd be no backing off.

More seriously, we began to compile a dossier of members of the Militant Tendency, the pernicious Trotskyist organisation which had succeeded in infiltrating a number of the party's constituencies. Dick was determined to get rid of them, because their influence was totally negative and destructive. Although there was ample evidence that they existed as a "party within the party", with a well-funded organisation and a head office of their own, we could only get rid of them by dealing with their members on an individual basis.

Because the rules of the party are designed to ensure fair play for members, we had to proceed very carefully and slowly. Each "Milly" had to be identified by name, and given an opportunity to choose between their own organisation or the party. Then, in the case of any Milly who was expelled by the party, they had to be given a right of appeal to the next conference.

At successive meetings of the AC, Millies were put up for the chop. Most of the time, they would be picketing outside the meeting, and members had to walk through a gauntlet of placards and boos. Once or twice the media made a meal of it, but it became boring after a while, and the image of a cold and heartless Dick Spring expelling young and idealistic members of the party never caught on in the way that Militant hoped it would.

As we got closer to the next conference, it became clear that the stakes were already pretty high. Most of my colleagues thought I had lost my head entirely when I suggested that we had to try to use the conference to appeal to a wider audience than just ourselves. To do it, I wanted to completely change the format of the leader's speech. I wanted the TV audience to be surprised—they would be used to a standard shot of a politician walking on stage to a prescribed standing ovation, followed by a ritualistic speech. I wanted them to see something different, perhaps sufficiently different for people to wonder what was going on, and not reach automatically for the remote control.

The difficulty was what to do. RTE rules about party conferences were very rigid and inflexible in those days. Their job was to point a camera at the stage for fifty-six minutes, and broadcast whatever happened there. The idea that it would be possible to use any of the high-tech facilities that go into modern TV programming was immediately knocked on the head.

Instead, we decided to begin and end the speech with music, and to intersperse it with poetry. Emmet Bergin, the actor, agreed to read the poetry, and Dick suggested a Tralee singer, Sharon Reidy, to sing the two songs we chose.

This time, we approached the conference as if it were a military campaign. Donal Spring, for instance, volunteered for the job of shadowing Michael Taft wherever he went in Tralee, and was so effective that at one point Taft objected to being stood over even at a urinal!

Niamh beat Emmet in the election for vice-chair, and we won all the votes on the expulsion of Militants. The margin was a good deal more comfortable than Cork, even though there were still some—Michael D Higgins, for instance—who made it clear that they were not in favour. One of Emmet's lieutenants, Frank Buckley, predicted in his speech that the vote on the

Militant Tendency would cause a bloodbath in the party. The majority of the delegates knew that Emmet and his people would not have objected to a bloodbath at all if they could choose the blood to be spilled.

The speech was a nerve-wracking affair—getting timing right with three people working together was enough to age both me and the RTE floor manager by ten years. But it received a rapturous reception in the end—and it enabled Dick to deal with his internal problems and at the same time to send a message out to the watching audience that Labour was determined to put up the strongest opposition to the policies being enacted by Charlie's minority government.

For two years, the government had made a target of health, social welfare, education and housing expenditure. There was a consensus that something had to be done about the national debt, which had undoubtedly spiralled while we were in government. But we were strenuously opposed to the manner in which it was being done. The poor were being expected to subsidise the poorer, in a mean series of policy cutbacks.

Alan Dukes and Fine Gael had, in our view, opted out of opposition altogether. Dukes had declared, in a speech which came to be known as the "Tallaght strategy", that he would not oppose just for the sake of it. As long as the government took a responsible attitude to the national finances, he said, they could count on Fine Gael support.

The more high-minded commentators saw this as an act of patriotism. I saw it as just stupid—playing into Charlie's hands. There was undoubtedly a patriotic motive behind the strategy, but there was also a strong impulse to give Fine Gael the space to regroup after the 1987 election—to buy time before they had to face the people again. Charlie knew full well that Fine Gael was making its offer from a position of weakness—all the more so because there was no conditionality to it, no sense of demanding social as well as economic responsibility.

For two years, Charlie laughed at Fine Gael, and adopted whatever policies suited himself. If Labour hadn't been trying to harry him at every opportunity, there would have been no opposition at all.

Gradually, as we began to get our act together in dealing with the hard left in the party, Dick's appetite for the fight grew. We added another item to the agenda on our Wednesday night meetings—how to harry and harass the government.

This presented something of a dilemma for us too—one that we discussed a lot. The government was in a fragile position, working in a minority situation. Every time they were defeated in the Dáil, it made that position more difficult—and a general election more likely. We knew that an election wouldn't suit us any better than Fine Gael, because we had an enormous amount of work to do before we could face the electorate with any confidence. We were also under threat at that time from the Workers Party, who had been making steady inroads into our vote in Dublin.

The relatively new Progressive Democrat party, under Des O'Malley, was also making a huge impact. Because they had won more seats than us in the 1987 election, they were the second opposition party. It gave O'Malley the advantage that on every set-piece occasion in the Dáil, he would be called on to speak before Dick. And with his long experience, he was a very effective performer—especially on issues of fiscal responsibility.

The ideal scenario, from our point of view, would be to test our recovery in the European elections, due in the summer of 1989. Barry was going to run for us in Dublin, and all the signs were that he would top the poll. All we needed, we felt, was a clear run—a European win would provide a huge morale-booster for the party.

In the end, though, Dick decided that the job of opposition was to oppose—especially when there were so many issues of huge social concern. So I spent a good deal of my time, working principally with Barry and Brendan, perfecting a mastery of the rules of the House. We used the Standing Orders in ways that they hadn't been used for years, to try to catch the government on the hop as often as possible. Every time we had an opportunity to have a motion of our own debated, we tried to devise one that would provide maximum embarrassment for the government, and for any member of the opposition that declined to support it.

When the government decided to close down Barrington's Hospital in Limerick, for instance, we trapped the Progressive Democrats into supporting an opposition motion. O'Malley couldn't vote for the closure of the oldest hospital in his constituency—but by voting against the government on the issue, he damaged forever his reputation for total consistency when it came to the need to cut public spending.

When Brendan Howlin put down a motion calling on the government to provide financial aid and support for haemophiliacs who had contracted the AIDS virus through blood transfusions, we were also confident of united opposition support. In fact, we were fairly sure that the government itself wouldn't oppose the motion, and that they would find the relatively small sum of money involved. The people most directly affected by the motion were in a terrible position— many of them had been deprived of life insurance, or had been let go from their jobs. They were people who were facing the double agony of a greatly decreased life expectancy, combined with a hugely reduced capacity to provide for their loved ones. And it was a state agency that had put them in that position. They had an unanswerable case.

To our amazement, Charlie decided to take a stand on the issue. As the debate began, rumours went around Leinster House like wildfire that Charlie, who was on a trade mission to Japan, had sent a message home that he would dissolve the Dáil if he were beaten on the issue. We would all be into a general election eighteen months before we were ready.

Some of our people began to panic. At one stage, while Brendan was speaking in the Dáil, one of his colleagues was literally tugging at his jacket, urging him not to push the issue to a vote. During his closing speech in the debate, the entire Fianna Fáil cabinet took their seats in the House, something that had never happened before in private members time. In his usual seat was Charlie himself, just back from Japan and looking decidedly grumpy.

When the vote was called, there was a hush in the chamber as the government was declared beaten. Charlie bowed to the Ceann Comhairle, and muttered something along the lines of "I must now go and do what I have to do". He glided from the chamber, taking his crestfallen cabinet with him.

And then he seemed to change his mind. For several weeks, he dithered about whether to dissolve the Dáil. The European elections were scheduled to be held in a few weeks, and the certainty grew in all our minds that the general election would be held the same day.

We weren't ready, but at least by then, with the Tralee conference behind us, we were in control.

5

Leader of the Opposition

The first time I saw Proinsias De Rossa's poster, I knew that Barry was in trouble. It was positioned at the bottom of the stairs in Westland Row DART station, and it hit me like a blow to the stomach. A fresh-faced De Rossa, his coat slung over his shoulder, accompanied by the slogan, "A Breath of Fresh Air", looked every inch a natural leader. He was contesting the European elections in 1989, as well as the Dáil election, and was determined to mount a strong campaign against our candidate in Dublin, Barry Desmond. His poster and slogan, conceived by Eoghan Harris, was a masterpiece.

We had gone to great trouble with Barry's poster. We had taken a photographer and a stepladder to the roof of Liberty Hall. I held the ladder with the photographer perched on top, while Barry clung to the railings of the balcony and tried to look magisterial—and as if the city spread out far below belonged to him. Despite the biting wind and cold, I had insisted on Barry posing in his shirtsleeves.

The result was a ghastly picture of Barry, looking as miserable as he undoubtedly was, produced too late for us to do anything about it except hang it all over Dublin. While Proinsias De Rossa strode along Dollymount Strand like a young god, Barry glowered down at the people of Dublin from every lamppost in the city.

Simple is best in election campaigns. I should have learned that back in 1985, when I had organised an elaborate stunt to launch our local elections campaign. We needed a lift back then, and I thought what better way to provide it than to invite the media to watch an aeroplane swoop down, pick up a large banner with a giant LABOUR on it, and soar off into the sky over Dublin.

I chose the wettest day of the year for the launch. When we got to the aerodrome where our plane was waiting, the banner lay out in the grass, absolutely sodden and several times its normal weight. We had to carry it into a hanger to dry, and Dick passed the time by posing for photographs, peering out through some of the letters with his colleagues. The photograph that appeared the next day showed Dick and Bernie Malone peering out through the letters BO!

Worse was to come. The banner was eventually spread out on the ground, to be picked up by the aeroplane's tail hook. Once, twice, three times the plane swooped in, and each time it missed the banner. The cameras whirred, and the smiles on the politicians' faces grew more fixed and desperate. At the fourth attempt, the plane finally engaged the once again sodden banner, and lifted off into the air, with "LABOUR" hanging straight down beneath it, instead of fluttering behind it.

We all heard the plane cough and splutter as it tried to rise. Suddenly, the pilot released the banner—he had to, otherwise its weight would have forced the plane into a stall. Our once proud banner drifted slowly to earth, and ended up on waste ground near one of the Ballymun Towers.

For years after that, every time I thought I had a bright idea for a publicity stunt, one of my colleagues—and as often as not my party leader—would remind me about our day in Weston Aerodrome. Not that I need reminding—I still have a video of the footage that *Today Tonight* lovingly took of the whole episode, and used as the centrepiece of their coverage of us during those elections. I fancy that when I arrive in hell, the devil will have that video to show me.

Anyway, in the elections of 1989, four years later, we were determined to keep it simple. As far as the Euro campaign went, we had good candidates, and Barry was our banker in Dublin. In the middle of the campaign, the Dublin city carnival occupied O'Connell Street for a weekend. I sent a gang of students out to prowl the carnival, armed with cheaply produced leaflets extolling Barry's virtues. The feedback from the eleven year-olds on the chairoplanes was apparently quite encouraging.

De Rossa, meanwhile, hired a white open-topped double-decker bus, which was festooned with balloons and crowded all day with kids and their parents, all along for a free ride up and down O'Connell Street.

Late on Sunday afternoon, when the carnival was over, I was working alone in our head office in Gardiner Street. I heard a familiar sound—the song *Something inside so strong* that Dick had used to great effect in his conference speech a couple of months earlier. It was coming from the loudspeakers on De Rossa's white bus. By craning out the window, I could see the bus unloading its balloons and leaflets at their head office, just a few doors down the street. Then the music started again, and the bus came slowly down the street towards our office. As I looked out the window, I could see that De Rossa was sitting alone on the top deck of the bus. As he passed, he looked up and saw me looking down. Slowly and gracefully, he raised two fingers at me, and passed on. "Some day, Proinsias," I thought to myself, "some day."

That Euro election was a triumph for the Workers Party, and just about okay from our point of view. De Rossa topped the poll in the Dublin Euro-election, and also in his Dáil constituency of Dublin North-West. Barry, who had started as the favourite to win a Euro-seat, just grabbed the last one in Dublin, and became our only Euro MP. Otherwise, in the Dáil election, the Workers Party won seven seats, their highest total ever, and we won fifteen, up three.

We were hampered in the election by the fact that it was Dick's first outing since 1987, and the scars of that long night were all too visible. I spent a good deal of the campaign trying to coax him out of Kerry to undertake a national tour, and a lot of time trying to disguise the fact from the media that I failed.

This time, Dick was leaving nothing to chance in Kerry, and he duly topped the poll. But his contribution to the national campaign was very sparse. By and large, the party understood and appreciated that it was vital that the leader's seat be consolidated, but there was some grumbling. Had we not done as well as we did, gaining three new Deputies, that grumbling might have been more intense in the aftermath.

The election was a disaster for Charlie Haughey and for the PDs who lost eight seats. From being the third largest party in the previous Dáil, the PDs were now the fifth. There seemed to be no future for them.

Barry saw it differently. On the night of the count, he declared on RTE that the obvious thing to happen now was for Fianna Fáil and the PDs to form a coalition government. Everyone laughed, but as the weeks went by towards the resumption of the Dáil, it became obvious that forming a government wasn't going to be easy.

Dick made up his mind immediately that he could not be sucked into any talk of government formation. He still had work to do in the party—although we were now in effective control, there were wounds to be bound up. He was totally committed to the party retaining its independence until it was in a position of negotiating strength, and determined not to allow the old coalition splits in the party to raise their heads again.

So he opted out of any serious discussion with other parties, although he did get a kick out of telling Dessie O'Malley and Bobby Molloy, at a meeting, that he felt they had a national duty to help in the formation of a stable government. Instead, he spent some time preparing for the return of the Dáil.

One of the things he did was to consult John Rogers about the constitutional position that would arise if the Taoiseach failed to form a government. John's advice was unequivocal—under Article 28.10 of the Constitution, the Taoiseach must formally resign, although he would then be expected to continue in a caretaker capacity.

John and Dick were actually discussing this very point when Brendan Howlin joined them, and said that he had just met PJ Mara, Charlie's faithful spokesman, in the corridor.

"I presume Charlie will be going to the Park to resign when he loses the vote this afternoon," he had said to PJ.

"Charlie resign? He will in his arse," was PJ's pithy response.

I've always believed that PJ misunderstood Brendan's remark, and assumed that Brendan was referring to another dissolution of the Dáil. I don't believe that Charlie would have consulted PJ in any depth about his intentions that afternoon—or anyone else for that matter. However, whether PJ understood the point or not, his remark constituted useful and fascinating intelligence.

Although we didn't know it at the time, Alan Dukes, who would lead the opposition in the Dáil that afternoon, was receiving identical briefings from his legal advisers.

When the Dáil met, Deputies went through the rituals of voting for three candidates who couldn't win—Charlie Haughey, Alan Dukes, and Dick Spring (Dick was supported in the vote by the Workers Party deputies as well as his own). When the votes were over, and it was clear the House could not elect a government, Alan Dukes (whose right it was to speak first) asked Haughey how he proposed to deal with the conundrum. Watching in the press gallery, I realised glumly that this could be Dukes' big moment.

Charlie simply said that he would adjourn the Dáil for a few days, to enable Deputies to consider the position, and I braced myself for Dukes' onslaught. To my amazement, Dukes agreed with the Taoiseach's proposition, and sat down. The Ceann Comhairle was about to adjourn the House when Dick stood up.

"I would like to seek some clarification from the Taoiseach," he said. "I would be very grateful if the Taoiseach would outline to the House the legal advice he has received in relation to Article 28.10 of the Constitution. As I see it, that Article is very specific—*the Taoiseach shall resign from office upon his ceasing to retain the support of a majority in Dáil Eireann.* Would the Taoiseach read us the advice of the Attorney General on the matter?"

There was an unusual silence in the Dáil (I learned afterwards that that moment of silence had made an extraordinary impact on people who were listening to the proceedings throughout the country on RTE radio. It turned a mundane political set-piece into an occasion of high drama and tension.)

From where I was sitting, I could see Charlie's face. I am convinced to this day that he was totally shocked, that it had never occurred to him that he would be challenged on the point. Unusually for him, he began to bluster.

But if he was chagrined, Alan Dukes was totally discomfited. He too began to shout, trying to recover lost ground by drowning out Dick Spring. But the ground was shot from under him by Garret FitzGerald, who got to his feet and said that Deputy *Spring* was correct, and that he (Garret) had received similar advice back in 1981.

After a few minutes of barracking, Dick proposed a two-hour adjournment to allow the Taoiseach to take advice. It was now as if he was the only voice in the House that made sense, and everyone agreed to adjourn.

When the House came back, the Taoiseach said that he had been advised that there was no particular urgency about the resignation issue, but that, as everyone knew, he would always wish to uphold the "sacrosanct" Constitution—and be seen to do so.

In the interests of providing reassurance, even though it was not legally necessary, he would go immediately to the President and tender his resignation.

Again there was uproar, and again Dick was cool. Instead of trying to score points, he indicated graciously that he believed the Taoiseach was taking the correct course of action, and the House agreed to adjourn for several days.

It was a major turning point in Dick's career. He had a little luck—Brendan's conversation with PJ Mara, Alan Dukes' failure to seize his opportunity—but his innate sense of political judgement and timing were seen to best possible effect on the day.

There's no doubt in my mind that Charlie Haughey fully intended to buck the Constitution, for reasons of ego if nothing else. In a long parliamentary career, Charlie Haughey had seldom, if ever, been bested on the floor of the Dáil. Dick Spring did it that day, and did it with style. What's more, he did it on live radio.

Over the following few weeks, it became clear that there was a new respect for Dick Spring, and Labour, in the air. That was clear a few weeks later, when Neil Kinnock came to Dublin on a party-to-party visit. Everywhere the two men went, they were mobbed. Kinnock, in particular, was a huge hit, and a great personality. Within minutes, he was on first-name terms with everyone, including the chauffeur we hired for the weekend, a lovely man called Tom Conlon.

We had arranged to take Neil and Glenys to the all-Ireland hurling final. It would be nice to report that the GAA went out of their way to welcome a possible future Prime Minister of Great Britain to the home of Irish sport and culture. In fact, there was so little co-operation that the party had to be split up in a variety of different seats.

It didn't spoil anyone's enjoyment of what turned out to be a thrilling final, but the drawback was that it was necessary to make a mad dash to Dublin Airport immediately afterward. I was following the hired car (which Tom Conlon was driving), with Pat Magner and Anne Byrne, and as we approached the airport we all congratulated each other on a successful weekend. Suddenly, the Mercedes in front seemed to lurch forward, and drove up onto the roundabout just in front of the airport, hitting two other cars as it went.

Tom had had a massive heart attack at the wheel of the car, and had collapsed forward, his foot momentarily jammed on the accelerator.

There were five passengers in the car, including Neil and Glenys Kinnock, Dick, and two of Kinnock's staff, Julie Hall and Neil Stewart. All were slightly hurt—cuts and bruises. But Neil Kinnock realised instantly what had happened. He leaped from the car, ran around to the driver's door, and pulled Tom out on to the grass. For what seemed like an age, he pumped his chest and gave him the kiss of life. Then I saw him lie down beside Tom on the grass and whisper urgently in his ear. Dick, meanwhile, had jumped from the car also, and was directing traffic around the accident.

Later, in Beaumont Hospital, I asked Neil Kinnock what he had been doing lying beside Tom.

"Aren't you supposed to say an act of contrition when a Catholic is dying?" he asked me. "I don't remember the act of contrition, but I thought I should say something to ease him."

I never found out exactly what he had said to the dying man. I know that he and Glenys sent a letter of considerable comfort to Tom's widow, and Julie Hall, who had been quite seriously hurt in the accident, also came back to the funeral.

Neil Kinnock lost the next British election, and resigned as Labour leader. I often thought afterwards that if enough people had had the opportunity to witness his presence of mind and his decency, as I did on that occasion, he'd be Prime Minister today—perhaps the first British Prime Minister with a deep and genuine love for Ireland and her people.

In the weeks after Dick had forced Charlie to resign as Taoiseach, naturally some of the more high-minded commentators wrote that there was no real issue involved, just a nice point of constitutional law. After all, what was the essential difference between a caretaker Taoiseach and a real Taoiseach?

As usual, the purists missed the point—or rather, both points. Anyone who has soldiered through referendum campaigns in Ireland knows that the Irish people take their constitution seriously—there has to be a very good reason before it can be messed with. And secondly, a substantial proportion of the people of Ireland—including a great many in Fianna Fáil—had been waiting for a long time for somebody to stand up to Charlie.

One man who had done so, many times over many years, was Michael Mills. Mills had been political correspondent of the *Irish Press* until the FitzGerald/Spring government, on John Boland's advice, appointed him as Ireland's first Ombudsman. Because he was in his mid-50's when he was appointed, the legislation which created the office included a special clause which allowed the age of the office-holder to be disregarded in the event of re-appointment to a second term. In all other circumstances, the holder of the office had to be under the age of 60 on first appointment.

Towards the end of December that year (1989), Barry Desmond invited me out to Strasbourg to see how the European Parliament worked. It was quite an educational experience. In the plane on the way out, at seven thirty on a Monday morning, we were roundly abused by a very drunk Fianna Fáil MEP. When we arrived, I was sent to queue for my expenses, and found myself lining up cheek by jowl with Valery Giscard d'Estaing, who complained bitterly to the woman behind the counter about the current exchange rate.

At lunch on Tuesday, Barry mentioned that he had been talking to Joe Fahy that morning. Fahy was, like Michael Mills, a former political correspondent, but he had worked for the European Parliament for some years. He told Barry that Michael's term as Ombudsman would finish at the end of the year, and that if it wasn't renewed by the Dáil in the next day or so (before the Dáil rose for Christmas), he would be over the age limit for a new appointment.

Barry and I immediately smelled a rat. We went up to Barry's office and I rang Sally Clarke in the Dáil. Sally checked, and was able to tell me that there was nothing on the Dáil Order Paper for the remainder of the week about the office of the Ombudsman. When I asked her where Dick was she told me that he had just gone down to the chamber for the daily Order of Business, where deputies could raise relevant matters to the Taoiseach without notice.

When I explained what I thought was going on, Sally ran down to the Dáil chamber, and handed in a one line note to Dick, telling him to ask the Taoiseach if he had any proposals in relation to the office of the Ombudsman. Without knowing what was going on, Dick asked the question, and the Taoiseach replied that he had no proposals in mind.

When Dick came out of the chamber, and Sally explained what we had discovered, Dick immediately agreed that something was being planned. He checked the legislation, and established to his own satisfaction that unless Mills were re-appointed during the week, it would not be possible to do so. Meanwhile, Barry was doing a little digging of his own in Strasbourg, and discovered from a reliable source that Charlie fully intended to allow the appointment to lapse, and then, when Mills couldn't be appointed, to replace him with Eileen Lemass, a former Fianna Fáil MEP.

It was a mean trick, and somehow typical. Charlie clearly wasn't willing to tell Michael Mills, who had been an outstanding success in his first term, that he was no longer required. He was just going to dump him in a way that couldn't be spotted, and couldn't be undone.

Dick raised the question again the following day, this time expanding a little on the information. When he raised it a third time, we got a phone call from someone close to Des O'Malley, who wanted to know the background. O'Malley, it appears, then went to Charlie and demanded that the re-appointment be made immediately. Charlie, naturally, protested his innocence, and Albert Reynolds, who was Finance Minister, maintained in the House that it had always been the government's intention to re-appoint the Ombudsman. But Charlie had been caught again—and it was Dick who caught him.

That was the first time that Dick encouraged Des O'Malley to do his job as Charlie's watcher-in-chief—but it wasn't the last. Some months later, he found himself discussing the financial affairs of Larry Goodman with O'Malley, who was reluctantly presiding over a rescue of Goodman's beef empire. My role, such as it was, in the affairs of Larry Goodman, went back somewhat earlier, to a very strange night in March 1989.

It was five in the morning, and bitterly cold. I remember reflecting that this wasn't what I had signed on for a few years earlier. Then, I had thought of a life of glamour and intrigue, of smoke-filled rooms and powerful speeches.

I had never envisaged myself sitting in a TD's house at this hour of the morning, taking page after page of notes while others did all the talking.

But I was sitting with brave men. They were public servants. I'm not going to say what branch of the public service, or where they worked, because even to this day they live in fear of being exposed.

But they were sickened by what they had seen and heard— with their own eyes and through the eyes of colleagues in different parts of the country. They had gone to their local

Labour TD with a story to tell—and they had gone to him because he is one of the most reticent and trustworthy men in Ireland. He had persuaded them to tell me their story, on the assurance that Dick Spring would act on the information, and that their identities would never be revealed.

Even though they were willing to talk, they were afraid to be seen. They had come to the TD's house separately—one at two in the morning, and one at two-thirty. They left separately, two and a half hours later. And in between they told stories of wrongdoing in Goodman plants all around the country, in Dublin, Rathkeale, Waterford, Bandon, and elsewhere.

They introduced us to characters and practices we had never heard of, and told us that if only someone with the authority to do so began to look into it, they would uncover a scam of monumental proportions.

What really frustrated them was that they believed there was a "culture of the blind eye" in relation to Larry Goodman and his factories. According to their accounts, local managements in the plants were able to get away with virtually anything, because someone in authority believed in going easy on this particular company.

To my shame, I suppose, I had only the skimpiest knowledge of Larry Goodman prior to this meeting. Agriculture has never been my strong point—in any policy debates we have ever had on the subject within the party, I have always been an onlooker rather than a participant. I knew, of course, that Larry Goodman was regarded as the saviour of the industry, and that his empire, Food Industries, was expanding at a rate of knots. Charlie had already presided over a press conference announcing major business plans for the company.

While I was having my clandestine meeting, a debate was going on in Dáil Eireann about the fact that Liam Lawlor TD, who was chairman of a Dáil Committee inquiring into state-sponsored bodies, had recently been appointed to the board of Food Industries. The debate had arisen because Food Industries was interested in acquiring the state-owned Irish Sugar Company.

Later, I was to learn a lot more about the Goodman empire but for now all I wanted to do was get a few hour's sleep. The following day, I briefed Dick Spring and Barry Desmond about all I had discovered. They were as shocked as I had been, but there was a snag. I had no documentary evidence. There was some coming—I had been told that the Department of Agriculture had imposed a very hefty fine on Goodman, and that they had put it in writing. What's more, I had been promised a copy of the Department's letter within the next couple of days. But I didn't have it yet.

Barry Desmond was fearless. And if any subject under the sun was likely to rise his ire, it was abuse of public money. He had been seething at the lack-lustre way in which the Sugar Company debate was being conducted, and he had some information of his own about practices in the Goodman company. The previous week in the Dáil he had alleged that Goodman companies were already the subject of Garda Fraud Squad investigations—something of an overstatement, as it turned out. Now he felt vindicated by what I had told him and Dick. I didn't know, when I was briefing them, that Barry was going back into the debate that night.

But he did, and he almost blew it. To my astonishment, he announced to the Dáil that Goodman had been fined a total of £1.084 million by the Department of Agriculture. It was true— at least I had been promised it was true—but none of us could prove it.

But if I was astonished at Barry's announcement, I was shocked at the Taoiseach, Charlie Haughey's, instant and emphatic reply. "Let me tell this House," he intoned, "Deputy Desmond is determined to sabotage the entire beef industry with this sort of falsehood."

The following morning, Larry Goodman responded to Barry's remarks as well. "Barry Desmond is anti-business, anti-enterprise, and anti-bloody well everything," he told the nation on radio. And his company put out a formal press release denying absolutely that there had been any fine.

There are moments when you can watch a promising political career going down the drain before your eyes. As far as mine was concerned, this was such a moment. How had I allowed myself to be suckered like that? I had walked Barry Desmond into an outrageous falsehood in the House, for which he was going to have to apologise abjectly.

And Barry Desmond did not take that sort of thing lying down. It was no use my arguing that I had urged him to wait until I had the documentary evidence in my hands. I had promised him that the facts would stand up, and as a result we had slandered one of the most important companies in the country—and made a powerful enemy in the process.

No more than a couple of days later—but it seemed like an eternity—the fax machine beside my desk suddenly kicked into life, and out came a grubby, almost illegible—but thank God, not quite—sheet of paper with the Department of Agriculture's letterhead on it. In the letter, the Department was telling the Goodman company of all the irregularities that had been discovered at their Waterford plant, and that the application of "correction methodology" would result in £1.084 million being withheld from the company.

We had been led up the garden path—not by my original informants, but by the Taoiseach of the country in the Dáil, and by the proprietor of one of the country's biggest companies. I still find it astonishing that they could have been so brazen—so absolutely certain that the full story wouldn't come out.

Barry's allegation against the Goodman company—one of many that were found to be true in substance by the Hamilton Tribunal—was one of the first made in the Dáil. It was made on March 9th, 1989—and he added the information about the fine a week later. It was to be another two years before any serious investigation of the company got under way.

But storm clouds were gathering around the Goodman companies. Unknown to anyone, Goodman was financing his ambitious expansion plans through a complicated series of financial deals, which involved roping in bank after bank. From the outside, it looked as if everything he touched turned to gold.

But eventually, it collapsed around his head. And it was Des O'Malley who found himself in the hapless position of having to bail him out.

O'Malley had sought the job of Minister for Industry and Commerce when he had gone into government with Charlie. It must have come as a terrible shock to him, in August 1990, to discover that he had the choice of saving the Goodman empire, or presiding over the biggest crisis ever to hit Irish agriculture. In any event, the Dáil was recalled on an emergency basis, to rush through legislation that would protect the company from its creditors.

Dick Spring was on holidays at the time, and no more amused than any other TD at having to interrupt his break for the emergency session. As he was preparing to leave home, he got a phone call from a senior bank official, who asked to meet him in Dublin.

At the meeting, Dick was told an incredible story. A meeting of Goodman's bankers had been called by Goodman in London the week before. Over thirty had turned up—banks from every corner of the world.

Most were astonished to see the others there—each thought that they, or at most two or three, were the only ones involved. And more than £700 million had gone west. It was an unimaginable fiasco, and the banking community was convinced that the story would never be told. Dick was given the names of the banks involved, the amounts in each case, and as much of the history of the transactions as could be gleaned.

It was obvious that the Dáil had to be told all this. If they were going to pass legislation to bail the company out, there must be full disclosure. But wasn't that O'Malley's job? Dick went to see him, and found him disconsolate. He knew everything that Dick knew, and was extremely keen to tell the Dáil—but he couldn't. It was his job, as he saw it, to forestall a crisis in the industry, and he had been advised that full disclosure would cause a financial panic. Dick, on the other hand, believed that the passage of legislation was tantamount to underwriting the losses of the company. It simply couldn't be done in ignorance. He made it clear to O'Malley that he was going to tell the Dáil everything he knew. O'Malley didn't exactly give him his blessing—but they parted on good terms!

The speech Dick made in the House caused a sensation. He outlined everything he knew—and he called for the immediate establishment of a Tribunal of Enquiry. That call was ignored for another year, but the Dáil saw another example of Dick Spring's willingness to take on big issues and big interests.

The affairs of Larry Goodman and his companies were to dog all of us for the next few years. Dick Spring went on to be heavily criticised—essentially by Fianna Fáil, but by others too—for refusing to reveal his sources to the Beef Tribunal when he eventually came to give evidence to it.

But some things are never said. Like, for instance, the fact that no allegation made by him based on what confidential sources told us was ever contradicted. Most of the people who spoke to Dick also gave evidence to the Tribunal—and several of them, including some critically important witnesses, were introduced to the Tribunal by Dick Spring. Dick's office undertook a great deal of research at the Tribunal's request— including a detailed account, running to hundreds of pages, of everything that had been said in Dáil Eireann about the beef industry.

No-one cooperated more fully with the Beef Tribunal than Dick Spring did—and if he protected his sources, it was because he promised to protect them. Those who have accused him know full well that had he revealed his sources, the least they would have been afraid of was a campaign of vilification in their workplaces. And they were people whose only crime was that they wanted to see the interests of the public protected.

All of that was still ahead of us at the end of 1989. We'd had a very good year—a good conference, a good election, and Dick had emerged as an outstanding parliamentarian. At the end of the year, he had saved an outstanding public servant from being dumped.

There was one more piece of information to come our way before 1989 ended.

Opening my post one day, I came across a particularly bulky envelope. Inside was a bundle of papers, and it became clear from the context that what I was looking at was extracts from the confidential report of the liquidator of Merchant Banking Limited.

Merchant Banking had been owned by Patrick Gallagher, an admirer of Charlie's. The bank had collapsed in scandalous circumstances, and resulted in very considerable losses to depositors and small savers. Patrick Gallagher himself had subsequently served a prison sentence in Northern Ireland in connection with fraudulent activities. Although a detailed report had been made to the High Court on all the activities of the bank, its contents had never been made public.

But according to these papers, which I subsequently discovered were also in the hands of RTE, the liquidator had found in his report that a number of items in the accounts of the bank had been improperly classified as loans, because they were, to all intents and purposes, gifts. Something around a quarter of a million pounds—a huge sum even then—was involved. They had been given out as loans, but clearly without any intention that they would ever be repaid. No interest or instalments had ever been paid on them, and no effort had ever been made by the bank to recover them.

Among the list of items, I came across the name "CJ Haughey" and an entry for £5,000. The "loan as gift" involved was about ten years old, dating back to the mid-1970s.

I took the papers to Dick immediately. It was his view that whether the sum was large or small—and I had bought a house in the mid-seventies for £11,000, so I regarded it as large—this was an extraordinary position for a Taoiseach to be in, beholden for money to a bank that was involved in fraud.

The money had been paid back by Charlie—but only *after* the liquidation of the bank, when the liquidator had written to him seeking repayment.

Before taking action, however, he recommended that we take a look at some of the other names on the list that I had, to see if we could identify any others. None of the individuals named was familiar, so in the new year I went down to the Companies Office, and looked through their microfilm records to see was it possible to track down the names of any of the companies mentioned.

One of them was a company called Larchfield Securities. Lo and behold, it turned out to be the company which owned the island of Inishvickillaune and some other property in which family members lived. Larchfield Securities was owned in turn, in four equal shares, by Mr Haughey's four children. According to the Companies Office file, Larchfield was heavily indebted. There was a large mortgage on the island, and another one on a house in Wexford. There was no mention in the file of any indebtedness to Merchant Banking—but according to the liquidator's report, Larchfield was down for £11,000.

Dick decided that he would have to go public with this, but that the fairest thing to do would be to bring it to Charlie's attention first. We drafted a letter, outlining everything we knew, and calling on Charlie to make a public statement in the matter. Dick decided it would be only right to go and see Charlie, and hand him the letter personally. I'd have posted it, rather than go through that.

But Dick found Charlie courteous, even affable. He glanced at the letter Dick gave him, and promised to look into the issues raised. There wasn't a hint of hostility.

Charlie wasted no time in replying though. And if his manner in person had been friendly, the one line letter he sent Dick was anything but.

It merely said:

> Dear Deputy,
>
> I read your letter yesterday with disbelief. I categorically reject your outrageous suggestions and find it deeply offensive that you would write to me in this tone.

The contrast between the face-to-face reaction, and the reaction once Dick was out of the room, could hardly have been more complete. In a way, it was decent shorthand for the complex nature of the man.

Dick did decide that the matter would have to be made public, and he gave a long interview to RTE's *Prime Time*. They also filmed both his letter and Charlie's reply for a programme they were making about the whole Patrick Gallagher affair. They built the Haughey connection into their programme, but at the last moment senior RTE management decided that the programme had to be completely re-edited for legal reasons, to remove all references to the relationship between Haughey and Gallagher.

But before that programme was transmitted, we were into another contest, which, among a lot of other things, also illustrated the many facets of Charles Haughey.

6

Beating the Big Guys

There was only one time, in the fifteen years I worked in politics, when I felt the need to drink in the early morning. That was when I worked with Bride Rosney in the campaign that elected Mary Robinson.

I've always prided myself on an ability to meet deadlines, but I have never experienced anything like her talent for meticulous, detailed organisation. She'd never make a general—but the army that hired her as quartermaster would never go short of anything!

During the 1990 Presidential election, and especially during its frenetic later stages, we would meet each morning at seven-thirty, and again last thing each night—sometimes staggering out at one in the morning. No matter how late our meetings would end at night, Bride would arrive first at 7.30 the following morning, with neatly-typed minutes of the discussion the night before. It was after some of those early-morning meetings that I'd find myself wondering if there were any early-opening dockers' pubs nearby!

I never fully understood the nature of Bride's relationship with Mary Robinson—but it was enough to know that anything less than total loyalty to a Robinson cause was likely to result in Bride's unremitting hostility. And we were working in a campaign where she had just one objective, whereas people like me had a number of them.

It was important for us strategically to maintain a close Labour Party link with the candidate, but for Bride that meant ownership. She never understood, or accepted, or cared that Labour would sink with her candidate if the campaign failed. For Bride, Labour didn't matter.

And she was right, of course—even though it lead to some ferocious rows at the time. We didn't set out to win that campaign on day one—not because we didn't want to, but because in the early days that didn't seem possible. That changed quickly—but Bride never believed it had changed.

It started out because Dick Spring was determined to make a difference. In 1983, when Dr Hillery's first term was coming to an end, I had argued strongly that we should insist on running a candidate—in fact I argued for Eileen Desmond as our candidate. It seemed to me at the time—although now I believe the analysis did him a considerable injustice—that Dr Hillery treated the job as a sinecure, and there was no good reason why he should get a second term without an election. In fact, had anyone put up a candidate against him, I don't believe that Dr Hillery would have contested the position.

But we were in the middle of the abortion referendum at the time, and the party was in government, a government that was already struggling. If Labour had decided to contest the Presidential election back then, Fine Gael would have had to contest too, and the chance to divide and conquer the coalition partners would have appealed enormously to the opposition.

In 1989, however, it was Dick who brought up the subject. He believed that Brian Lenihan and PJ Mara had a plan. Brian wanted to be President, and PJ believed that he could engineer a situation where Brian would be unopposed for the job. Brian was the most popular politician in Ireland, and one of the best known. A colourful character, his popularity had been enhanced, if anything, by his brush with death and his dramatic recovery after a liver transplant operation.

The plan was simple. Brian would announce his interest early; flattering and warm-hearted interviews would be arranged; the Fianna Fáil party would nominate him as soon as possible. Other parties would stay away, or would be unable to find candidates of sufficient stature to take on Brian.

Dick Spring always liked and respected Brian Lenihan. But he regarded this plan as an affront. For too long, the office had meant nothing, and it had come to be regarded as the exclusive preserve of Fianna Fáil. He decided that he would have to take steps to ensure that there was an election this time, so that no-one would be a shoo-in.

He laid his ground carefully, consulting the parliamentary party about the advisability of the party contesting the election. Then on the 5th of January, he shocked the nation—and especially his closest advisers—by announcing on radio that he was so determined to see a Labour candidate, he would contest it himself if necessary. Actually, to say we were shocked is understating the case. We were horrified, all the more so when we discovered he was quite serious.

"Why not somebody younger?" he said. "Why not someone with energy, who can make a difference?"

It took a couple of days to persuade him that his place lay with us, and that we should start searching for a serious candidate. For a while we batted around names like Barry Desmond and Mervyn Taylor, but nothing we came up with answered the points Dick had been making about being different and having an impact, especially on younger voters.

To try to put some flesh on the bones of the idea, John Rogers and I wrote a short paper, setting out some ideas about how the Presidency could be revitalised in the right hands. We came to regard this as a sort of job description—Dick even joked at one point that we should consider putting an ad in the newspapers, using the job description and saying "Fianna Fáilers need not apply".

John Rogers swears that it was he who first thought of Mary Robinson. As far as I remember, it was Denise Rogers (no relation to John) who first said to me "if you're really looking for somebody different, why not Mary Robinson?" Denise was one of the hardest working people in Leinster House, fiercely loyal to the party and to Ruairi Quinn, whose secretary she is.

One way or the other, we agreed that John should suss out Mary's interest. Dick's relations with Mary were never great. In the Garret FitzGerald government, it had been widely thought that Mary Robinson would be the natural choice to succeed Peter Sutherland as Attorney General, and indeed Mary had a powerful backer for the post in Garret himself. Dick had never considered anyone but John Rogers, and relations between him and Mary Robinson were very cool after it. They had also had a disagreement about government support for the Institute of

European Law which Mary had set up with her husband Nick. In short, although they were polite to each other, they hadn't really spoken for the best part of five years. Mary's resignation from the party over the Anglo-Irish Agreement in 1985 had been a bitter blow to a government then under siege, and had been taken personally at the time by Dick (and by Garret FitzGerald).

None of that prevented Dick from seeing Mary Robinson as probably the ideal candidate from our point of view—he just didn't think she'd be inclined to listen to him. And indeed, when Mary invited John, Dick and myself to her house in Ranelagh to discuss the proposition that John had put to her, the first encounter was very stiff and formal.

John had been oblique when he approached her first (on Valentine's Day!). He'd given her the paper that we had written and asked for her views. She, I think, thought for a moment that she was being asked for a legal opinion—but it rapidly dawned on her that there was a bigger interest. The "job description" was tailor-made for her.

Others, notably Emily O'Reilly in her book on the 1990 Presidential election, have recorded that Mary was appalled when she read the job description, and realised what was being asked of her. I'm sure that's true, but when I met her for the first time, I was convinced within seconds that she had already made up her mind that she wanted to contest the job. More importantly, I believe that she saw all of its potential—and all of her potential in it. I was to learn over the next six months that the one thing that made her an outstanding candidate was that she knew, in her heart, that she would make a great President.

Mary instinctively knew the difference between power and influence—in some ways she personified it. She had pursued an unsuccessful political career, and yet had exercised considerable influence for change outside politics by carefully choosing legal cases to pursue.

She didn't give away much of her inner certainty at that first meeting. Nick was amiable and welcoming, Mary was brisk and businesslike, and Bride Rosney was dark and unfathomable. I was fairly sure that Mary was deeply interested, and that Nick was supportive. I couldn't figure Bride—the least one could be certain of was that she would want her friend to drive a very hard bargain.

So it proved. Dick wanted Mary to rejoin the party, because he knew—and told her—that it would not be easy to secure a unanimous endorsement of her if she didn't. Mary adamantly refused, arguing that it would make her look like an opportunist. It led to a complete impasse, and there was a period of a couple of weeks when we thought we were going to have to start searching for a candidate all over again. Eventually, after several long and tortuous meetings, Dick acquiesced, and we agreed to go forward with nominating her as an independent person. But we knew, and Mary knew, that it would not be easy.

Emmet Stagg and several others had also been searching for a candidate, and had come up with the name of Dr Nöel Browne. I, for one, was appalled at the idea. I saw him as someone who had little or no respect for the party, and who was likely in any event to self-destruct as a candidate. His days of greatness were, I believed, well behind him, and he had developed into a bad-tempered and curmudgeonly old man.

It all developed into a nasty row, with the left (whose attempted fait accompli with Nöel Browne was defeated) accusing Dick of an undemocratic fait accompli with Mary Robinson. Although once again they muttered about taking legal action against the decisions, at least this time they weren't able to call on the services of Mary Robinson SC!

When Dick rang Nöel Browne, after the parliamentary party had given him permission to put Mary's name forward to the Administrative Council, he explained that he had decided to seek and promote a younger candidate. Browne remained true to form, and hung up on Dick. He then spent the remainder of the campaign taking whatever opportunity he could to sneer at Mary.

Right from the very start, we had agreed that this would have to be a long campaign. We all knew that Mary was coming from behind, and the only way to get her message across was literally to try to visit every town and village in Ireland. She agreed with this approach herself, and was bolstered by a breath-takingly original "blueprint" that she got in the post from Eoghan Harris, which urged her to address such issues as personal appearance, and to confront head-on the liberal issues that might frighten away middle-class rural voters.

One of the ways in which we quickly discovered that this was going to be a different campaign than the many we had run in the past was the first investment we made. That was a £5,000 clothes allowance, set aside for the candidate. Although it turned out to be money well spent, I can still remember the raised eyebrows among the seasoned campaigners who knew about it. We had run many a campaign—in total—for a lot less than we were now going to spend on designer labels!

The history of the campaign has been well documented. I remember the tension, mostly. We never really persuaded the Robinson camp in the campaign that we had her interests at heart. Bride, and her sidekick on the election committee, Peter McMenamin, essentially saw us as losers. Peter, even though he was a member of the party, found fault on a daily basis with every effort that we made. Everything was checked and double-checked, on the basis that it was impossible to trust our competence. People who had never run a successful political campaign spent day after day checking on others who had. There were times when it was difficult to keep my temper.

Ruairi Quinn was our chairman. He saw it as essentially his job to keep the peace between the Robinson camp and the Labour camp—and generally speaking, the easy way to do that was to overrule his own people. If one felt it was crucial to win an argument, in the interests of the campaign and in the wider strategic interests we were pursuing, you had to operate on the principle that you'd better make it harder for Ruairi to overrule you than someone else.

One row concerned the "terracotta rose". I was absolutely determined that the Robinson campaign would use a rose as its logo. I wasn't too concerned about what sort of rose, but I wanted the identification with the party that a rose would represent. Bride, on the other hand, wanted as little party identification as possible.

Nick was the peace maker on that occasion, and produced a basic design that everyone found acceptable. It was a modernistic impression of a rose, painted in three flat brush strokes. However, when he produced the finished artwork, the rose was brown—or terracotta, as Nick described it. In fact, the three brush strokes now resembled a cow-pat rather than a rose.

I hit the roof, and threatened to walk away from the campaign if the Labour Party was going to be treated in this way. We had already agreed to underwrite the costs of the campaign, which were mounting at a frightening rate, and party members had undertaken personal guarantees for a large overdraft. I regarded the introduction of this cow-pat as an insult to the party.

It sounds like a petty enough issue, I know, but the most divisive issue throughout the campaign was this dichotomy between Bride's need for the party, as a vehicle to fund the campaign and nominate her candidate, and her deep distrust of us. We resented it all the more because we were every bit as committed as she and Peter McMenamin to success.

We approached it slightly differently, and that, I suppose, caused part of the problem. I expressed the view, for instance, that this was a three-cornered race, and that our primary objective should be to get into second place, ahead of Fine Gael. My reasoning was simple—in any Irish three-cornered election fought under PR, Fianna Fáil are going to be ahead on the first count. But the winner will be the one in second place— provided they're close enough to Fianna Fáil to make transfers tell. Every Irish election, as a broad rule of thumb, had usually broken down into Fianna Fáil votes and anti-Fianna Fáil votes. The trick is to be the one that is in a position to garner the anti-FF votes.

My stated objective, however, was interpreted, especially by Peter, as meaning that I and the Labour Party would be content to beat Fine Gael. Ever afterwards, the remark about being in second position was used as proof positive that the Labour Party wasn't interested in winning.

To her credit, Mary Robinson herself rose above the squabbling. I don't believe that she entirely trusted us either, but she threw herself into the work. And she couldn't have failed to notice that the party was responding to her.

In the early stages, before the media had begun to sit up and take notice, there would have been no campaign at all without the Labour Party branches who turned out faithfully to meet her. They were impressed, too, by the way in which she had thought out issues, and by the sense that even in those early days she was carving out a new and different role for the office.

Dick tended to stay out of her way. He believed that she preferred not to be seen too much under the wing of a politician, and in any event, that she hadn't especially warmed to him after the disagreements of earlier years. On the Robinson side, however, what they saw as Dick's neglect was resented. They would not have been aware that he was campaigning in his own way, trying to energise the party and help to build up a broader base of support. Instead, they frequently saw themselves as travelling alone.

Little by little, however, the support began to grow—first in the shape of dedicated volunteers, coming in to the campaign office that we set up in Merrion Square, and then in the form of larger and more interested crowds at meetings around the country. Mary herself began to change—not just in terms of the new clothes and hairstyle, which was dramatic enough—but also in the way she reacted to crowds of people. The stiff and formal inflexion that marked her earlier public outings began to give way to a warmer, more outgoing demeanour. You could tell at a glance that her confidence was growing.

We were helped enormously, of course, by the fact that Fianna Fáil were running a campaign of stunning complacency, and that Fine Gael were floundering in their search for a candidate.

In late July, I heard a rumour in Leinster House that Austin Currie was in the frame. My immediate reaction was to believe that if that came to pass, our strategy of looking for second place on the first count was bound to work. I'm a great admirer of Austin Currie, but I just couldn't see how anyone could regard him as electable against Brian Lenihan and Mary Robinson, who in their separate ways had been involved in Ireland's public life for decades.

Greg Sparks and I rang Paddy Powers, the bookie, as soon as we heard the news about Austin Currie, and asked if they had opened a book on the election. They hadn't, but they offered 10-1 against a Robinson win. (I put down £100 there and then. On the day of the count, I got a cheque for £1,100 from Stewart Kenny of Paddy Powers, together with a bottle of pink champagne. He also enclosed a note thanking us for suggesting that a book should be opened. They had lost £30,000 on Robinson, he added, but had won £75,000 on Brian Lenihan!)

Fianna Fáil's complacency was manifested in the way they basically ignored us. Mary made a series of gaffes in a *Hot Press* interview she gave, and compounded them with a radio interview in which she appeared to deny the views she had expressed on the record. In light of what was to happen subsequently, when Brian Lenihan gave two totally conflicting accounts of events, it could be argued that Mary got away with murder—and was helped enormously by the fact that Fianna Fáil basically ignored the controversy.

In fact, by the time Fianna Fáil finally realised that Mary was a serious challenger, it was too late. By the autumn, she had massive momentum behind her campaign.

Once her national bus tour started, it was obvious from the crowds that gathered at every stop—often waiting for several hours to hear her speak—that this was an extraordinary event. People had been starved for choice for nearly twenty years, and they were responding now to that fact. The two big parties, which had basically conspired in the imposition of agreed candidates in the office of the Presidency, were suffering now for their laziness.

We had very little money, and we made up for it with creativity. The posters and slogans that were designed for Mary's campaign were perfect, and the three party political broadcasts that Eoghan Harris prepared were classics of their kind—all the more so because they were made on a shoe-string, and depended entirely on inspired editing and music choices.

The people who volunteered to work in the campaign were unique too, in my experience. I've never met such selfless dedication, nor so many people who got joy and pleasure out of taking on a job that was miles too big for them, and proving it could be done.

But underneath the quality of the campaign, I will always be convinced that there was another thing happening as well, and that Mary Robinson was perfectly placed to tap into it. The politics of Ireland in the previous ten years had seen a number of deeply divisive and embittering moments—the abortion and divorce referenda, the Haughey GUBU scandals. People—even people who had voted against divorce and abortion—wanted a change of politics.

They saw the Robinson campaign as refreshing, as holding up a mirror to something that was a bit less insular and introspective. Her youth and good looks, and her increasing confidence, added to the impression that here was an opportunity to make amends for the divisions of recent years, to look out instead of in.

No-one involved will ever forget the tumult of the last couple of weeks of that campaign. In a way, we were innocent bystanders in the controversy that erupted between Fianna Fáil and Fine Gael. But it had just as wearing an effect on us as it did on the principal actors.

There had been a night, many years before in 1981, on which Garret FitzGerald's government had lost a vote on the budget, and therefore had lost the confidence of Dáil Eireann. He had gone to President Hillery to seek a dissolution of the Dáil—a dissolution which the President would have been perfectly entitled to refuse. Since Garret had lost the confidence of the Dáil, the President could act entirely on his own discretion in granting or refusing the request for an election.

Someone in Fianna Fáil had made phone calls to the President's office that night, to try to persuade him to refuse the dissolution. Brian Lenihan was asked on television if he had been involved in the phone calls, and he denied it.

Why he did so I'll never know—there would have been no subsequent controversy if he had said "Yes, I did try to persuade the President to act on his discretion and refuse a dissolution. What of it?" At least, if there had been a controversy, it would have been academic and of minority interest.

The trouble was that having categorically denied it on television, he was then discovered to have said precisely the opposite to a young student by the name of Jim Duffy—and to have said it on tape. The issue now was not whether the phone calls had been made—but which of the Lenihan stories was true, and which was a lie. One of his own accounts had to be a lie.

Everyone in Ireland, I think, believed that Charlie Haughey had instigated the phone calls, and that Brian had been involved in them.

And Fianna Fáil managed, almost at a single stroke, to create the impression that they were hell-bent on subverting the Presidency, and lying about it in the process.

It was crazy, but it got worse. Events unfolded rapidly to a point where the opposition tabled a no-confidence motion in the Government, and Charlie Haughey was told by his partners in the Progressive Democrats that the price of their support was Lenihan's resignation.

On the day the issue was to be debated in Dáil Eireann, I was in my office, helping to draft the speech that Dick wanted to make in the debate. It was to be the toughest speech he had ever made about Charles Haughey, and in it he used the phrase that Haughey was a virus that had caused a cancer in the body politic. We agonised over that phrase for a long time, until Dick decided that it should stay in.

Although a political opponent of Lenihan's who regarded his position by now as untenable, he was sickened by the fact that Lenihan was Haughey's oldest and closest political friend and supporter. It was Dick's view that Haughey should resign himself, rather than throw his old friend to the wolves to save his skin, and he was determined to get that message across in the strongest language possible.

As we were working on the speech, my phone rang. The person at the other end refused to give me his name, but he said that he was a friend of the army officer who had been on duty in Aras an Uachtaráin on the night that the phone calls were made to the President. When I challenged him about his identity, he gave me some personal details—enough to convince me that he was who he said he was, and that he was likely to know what he was talking about.

According to what he told me, the army officer, on the President's instructions, had taken all the phone calls and refused to put anyone through to the President. One of the phone calls had been from Haughey himself, and included a peremptory instruction to "put me through to the President". When the officer refused, Haughey had told him that he would be Taoiseach again one day, and "when I am, I intend to roast your fucking arse if you don't put me through immediately".

My informant went on to tell me that the President was so concerned at this threat that he subsequently exercised his prerogative as Commander-in-Chief of the armed forces to instruct the Chief of Staff of the Defence Forces to place a note on the army officer's personnel file, to the effect that none of the events of the night in question were ever to be seen as reflecting any discredit on the officer's record, and that everything he had done had been on the express instructions of the President.

I urged the person who had rung me to try to persuade his friend to make a public statement on the matter, or at least to contact us. And I told him that without confirmation from the officer himself, I could not see how Dick Spring could repeat this account in the Dáil. He told me that he would do his best to persuade his friend—in the event, I never heard from him again.

I repeated everything I had been told to Dick, and he agreed that it would be impossible to level such accusations against Haughey, in the highly charged atmosphere that existed, based on an anonymous phone call, no matter how plausible. He did include in his speech a reference to the fact that logs and records undoubtedly existed about all the events of the night, and a demand that they be opened up. They never were, of course.

I watched the debate itself, in the course of which Charlie announced that Brian Lenihan had failed to resign, so he was now sacking him. I gasped with astonishment at one point in Charlie's speech, when he said, his voice breaking with emotion, that he himself had never abused an army officer. His father, he said, had served in the Defence Forces, and anyone who could possibly believe that he would abuse an army officer knew nothing of the deep respect he held for the army!

After Brian Lenihan's sacking, the entirely predictable happened. The tide of public opinion began to swing his way. Opinion polls taken at the height of the controversy put Mary in a commanding position, but as the Lenihan family began to fight back against the humiliation suffered by Brian, there was a palpable wave of human sympathy for him.

Here was a man, who had been to death's door and back, who had given his all to the service of his party, and just when he needed them most they abandoned him. What really cut deep, I always felt, was that not one voice was raised against Haughey in Fianna Fáil. The sacking of Brian Lenihan, the failure to stand by their man, had elevated pragmatism to a high art.

And now he stood alone, and began to climb in the polls. Mary panicked. Throughout the controversy she had remained above it, and when Lenihan was down on the ground, wounded and isolated, she attacked him—and she did it against the strong advice of all those immediately around her. Suddenly our campaign went into reverse. With only a few days to go, we were running out of steam.

On the last Saturday of the campaign, we had arranged a meeting with Fine Gael to discuss a transfer agreement. We had been resisting pressure from them for weeks—they believed that an early transfer agreement might encourage Fine Gael voters "home", while we were determined to stay aloof from any transfer pact until we were certain that Mary was so far in front of Austin Currie that she couldn't be caught. That was another of the areas where there was some tension between us and the Robinson camp—they were so determined to retain independence from party politics that they wanted no formal arrangement. But in the end we agreed, and an announcement was timed for one o'clock on the last Saturday of the campaign. It was going to be the last shot in the locker.

We reckoned without Pádraig Flynn. While Austin and Mary were making their announcement, aimed at encouraging their respective supporters to transfer their votes to each other, Pádraig Flynn was losing the run of himself on Rodney Rice's RTE politics programme. He sneered at Mary, implying that her interest in motherhood was fake, and that he had known her for years and had never known her to express any interest in motherhood.

It was an incredibly crass thing to say, and Pádraig's situation was made all the worse when he was attacked on the programme by Michael McDowell, whose party was in government with Pádraig's. Brendan Howlin was sitting in the studio between them, and wisely left the major portion of the attack to the PD man.

From then until polling day, we sailed through. Pádraig Flynn's intervention had given Mary exactly what she needed at a critical moment—a sympathy vote of the same character as Brian Lenihan's.

Mary Robinson would have won that election if the controversy of the last couple of weeks had never happened at all. Her momentum, before it broke, was unstoppable, and it derived from the fact that she was capturing a mood for change in the country.

She would have won, too, if Brian Lenihan had been trapped in a lie, and not been fired. After his sacking, it began to slip away from her. She might well have lost if, at the last minute, Pádraig Flynn hadn't missed a glorious opportunity to keep his mouth shut.

On the day of the count, in the RDS, I positioned myself in the balcony beside the RTE cameras, and away from the crowd that milled around the stage. I wanted to savour the moment, and it was some moment.

When the returning officer declared that Mary Robinson was declared elected as the next President of Ireland, I found that I was crying, tears of joy pouring down my cheeks. It was one of only two occasions in my life when politics made me cry.

When Mary spoke, in a voice that was stronger than I had ever heard her use before, and using words that were crafted by a genius (not me, alas—I don't know who wrote that speech, but I suspect Eoghan Harris had a lot to do with it), it raised the hair on the back of my neck.

When I saw Charlie Haughey standing on the stage, the famous basilisk stare in place, a rolled up paper in one hand that he tipped into the other in a pale imitation of statesman's applause—the sound of one hand clapping—I laughed out loud. It was some moment, the proudest of my career. We had taken them on, all the big guys together, and we had beaten them. And we had changed Ireland, indefinably maybe, but irrevocably, in the process.

I spoke only once to Mary Robinson after that night. She invited her campaign committee to the Aras for a reception the following February—on Valentine's Day, the anniversary of the day she was first approached by John Rogers. She was gracious and welcoming, and it was a memorable evening. Before we left, she presented each of us with a print of the Four Courts, with a thank you message on it.

And that was the end of any personal relationship. I waved at her when she attended her first rugby international in Lansdowne Road, and she saw me and winked. She and I shook hands on several occasions at state functions, and she always had a kindly greeting. But the relationship between Mary and the Labour Party was, in the end, a professional one. It was business, nothing personal.

It was to be one of the ironies of her career—and Dick Spring's—that their paths would cross in terms of professional relationships—and occasional conflicts—over the next few years. But that couldn't be foreseen in December 1990. All that could be foreseen was that she would make an outstanding holder of her office.

A woman who had retired from public life, with an awesome track record as a lawyer, and a somewhat severe, scholarly demeanour, was persuaded to apply for the job of President, and became the best President we have ever had. It's clear enough that the campaign to elect her had its rows and tensions and difficulties; not all the personal relationships involved ever fully recovered; her term as President was marked by occasional clashes with the executive authorities of the State; she took occasional risks with the constitutional niceties. But she gave life back to the Áras.

I remember some of the slogans that we considered at the start of her campaign, and decided were too risky. Slogans like, "there's enough monuments in the Park already". But the truth was that the office had become meaningless in public life. Mary Robinson has transformed it, by the deceptively simple device of setting out to keep her promises.

I'm very proud of the role that Dick Spring and the Labour Party played in giving the Presidency back to the people (and I don't want to overstate that—it's Mary Robinson who turned the office into the people's Presidency).

I still believe in the notion of a people's Presidency, and I'd love to think that the political parties won't forget some of the promises they made during the most recent Presidential election. We can, and we should, guarantee that the nominating procedure will be changed to ensure that it is a people's choice at every level.

The Presidency is unique for one reason. It is the only post in Ireland in respect of which every citizen has a say. That say shouldn't be arbitrarily limited. The rules surrounding the nomination of the Presidential candidate were drawn up at a time when there was a genuine fear that the office had the potential to become a sort of dictatorship. Those days are gone.

A people's Presidency is achievable. Mary Robinson took the huge first steps, by transforming the office and by using its symbolic powers to bring people in from the cold. That job will only be finished when the politicians face up to the need to ensure that there is always a vigorous, healthy contest, and by allowing citizens of Ireland in future to have a say in picking the candidate as well as choosing the winner.

7

The Year of the Golden Circle

There was no time to relax or celebrate. Mary Robinson's election changed a lot of things, very quickly. Many of them related to the business of day-to-day politics. It undermined Alan Dukes fatally, and put John Bruton into the leadership of Fine Gael. It planted a slowly ticking time bomb under Charles Haughey.

And it marked Dick out as a politician whom the commentators had underestimated. None had predicted the result of the election, and many had scoffed at Dick's choice. Now, there was a sense that he was someone worth listening to whenever he spoke.

And he planned to do a lot of talking, especially to his own party. We had discovered something huge in the course of the Presidential election. There's a lot of joy in winning, and especially in winning worthwhile contests. Dick was determined that the new spirit that was evident throughout the party would be translated into a concrete sense of serious purpose. I was put to work with others in drawing up a new constitution and programme for the party, which he planned to have adopted at the conference in Killarney in April. Again, we left nothing to chance. The Wednesday night meetings were resumed, to ensure that there would be no slippage when we came to conference.

The work that we did on the party programme was *not* aimed at shoving the party to the right. What we tried to do—and succeeded in—was to express the values of the party in language that would enable its appeal to be further broadened. I wanted to hammer home the message that this was about modernisation, and not about a sell-out, and suggested another variation on the leader's speech to try and get it across. We placed two actors in the body of the conference hall, one dressed as a survivor of the 1913 lockout, and the other playing a young woman of the 1990s.

At the appropriate moment in Dick's speech, they were to interrupt him and pose questions about change. So effective were their interruptions that the first time the "old man" leaped to his feet, three loyal, and unaware, delegates made a lunge at him, to fling him out of the hall!

Despite the interchanges with the actors, which placed additional demands on Dick's preparation for the speech, it was the most relaxed performance he ever gave. I had anticipated in the drafting that there would be a lot more than the usual applause, in the aftermath of the Robinson election, and so I had cut the material way down.

Too much, in fact—with ten minutes of broadcast time to go, Dick had almost run out of speech. So he put down his script, and had some ad-lib fun with the delegates, winding them up about the forthcoming local elections. As he pointed out delegations in the hall, and challenged them to double their local election seats, the cameras swung wildly around, the unflappable Walter Harrington, RTE's floor manager, tore his hair out, and the delegates loved it. Afterwards, delegate after delegate came up to me and congratulated me on a brilliant script—"especially the last ten minutes!"

One scripted element of the speech which brought the house down was Dick setting a target for the party, to become the second-largest party in the state.

In the aftermath of the conference, it was seen by some as "Spring being arrogant". It was nothing of the kind. The party had scored a massive victory in the Presidential election, and the way of the party is to sit immediately on its laurels whenever it has done well. Dick was determined not to let delegates do that, but to stretch them a bit further at every opportunity. And he was ready and willing to lead from the front, taking on all comers in the Dáil.

We got the new constitution through, despite some left-wing grumbling about lack of consultation. The grumblers, for once, were justified. Although the new constitution could have been circulated to branches and constituencies several weeks in advance, I had fought hard to prevent it. I was determined to avoid long debates about phrases and sentences, the kind of debate that some people in the party love—and which always manage to make the party look less than serious. The new look and feel of the party—a look and feel that was entirely consistent with its traditional values—had to be accepted in its entirety. Otherwise, it would just look like the old, riven Labour Party all over again.

I think that was the only time I ever argued strongly for what was essentially a denial of party democracy. Although I had something of a reputation in the party for an inability to brook dissent, in general I have always believed that our way of debating issues in public, and our sense that the party belongs to its members, is one of the best characteristics of the party. But building sometimes requires clearing the ground, and if it has to be done, it's best to be done cleanly.

Fine Gael were doing their best to help us. Eoghan Harris and I had fallen out, in the immediate aftermath of the Presidential election, because he believed I had not given him enough credit for the part he had played in the campaign, in a piece I had written in the newspapers. Now he was working for John Bruton, and staged a special conference for them almost immediately after ours. It wasn't one of his more brilliant efforts—in fact it featured an incredibly tacky and tasteless skit, starring Twink. In front of the political correspondents, Twink made fun of an incident of sexual harassment that had been suffered by one of their colleagues, Una Claffey, in Leinster House. Apart from the obvious hurt to someone who had been at the receiving end of a drunken Fianna Fáil TD's attentions, the sketch seemed to show Fine Gael in an extraordinary light. It offended a lot of their own members—and their offence wasn't assuaged by suggestions from the party leadership that they should have a sense of humour.

Within a week, the government was forced to turn head over heels in the Dáil over Larry Goodman. Again Dick led the charge, and this time all the Opposition parties combined, to demand a judicial enquiry into the endless string of allegations against the Goodman company. The government tried to hold out, but once again the PDs demanded that the Opposition be listened to. (In one of the ironies of politics, it was pressure exerted by Des O'Malley that set up the Tribunal which was to bring his Ministerial career to an end.)

It was a particularly humiliating debate for the Fianna Fáil Minister for Agriculture, Michael O'Kennedy, who was sent into the Dáil to rebut all the Opposition arguments, and in the middle of a very drab speech was handed a slip of paper telling him to announce the establishment of an inquiry. I didn't know then that that decision was to occupy a lot of my waking hours for the next eighteen months.

Fine Gael carried the Twink fiasco into the local elections at the end of June, and dropped four points. Fianna Fáil, who had been embarrassed by Larry Goodman's problems and were still totally unsettled after the sacking of Brian Lenihan, got less than 37%, and lost control of councils all over the country.

We went into the elections with a new look, a new party programme, and a highly successful conference behind us. We doubled our seats, and almost doubled our vote. More importantly, key people came through all over the country—people that we had been continuously assessing as likely good Dáil candidates. They were now in pole position.

The perennial cruelty of politics showed in one result. A good friend of mine, Dr Bill Tormey, failed to win a seat. Bill is one of those people who stood by the party in good times and bad, and helped us in ways that no-one was ever told about. He had built up the party in Dublin North-West, moving there when it was a barren wasteland for Labour, and almost capturing a Dáil seat in 1989. Now, when a whole lot of political careers were taking a sudden turn for the better, Bill's nosedived—substantially because he had to cope with a personal bereavement throughout the campaign. He was to go on to be deprived of a nomination in 1992, when he would certainly have topped the poll, and his energy was lost to us.

But that was the only bad news. We had been afraid, in the run-up to the local elections, that the Workers Party would consolidate and even expand on their breakthrough of 1989. It didn't happen, and the results put us back in the driving seat in Dublin.

But the fun, in a sense, was only just beginning. 1991 will probably always be remembered as the year of the Golden Circle—a title brought on by a series of business scandals that occupied the second half of the year. My main memory of 1991 concerns the relationship between Dick Spring and Charles J. Haughey.

As the year went on, it became clear that there were a lot of targets that needed to be taken on in Irish life—and most of the targets had one thing in common—the Taoiseach and his capacity to deny friendships.

As time went by, the exchanges in Dáil Eireann between Dick and Charlie became more and more vicious. A senior and respected academic (with no connection to the Labour Party) contacted us, and briefed us extensively on a series of decisions within UCD, which had led to the university buying a large parcel of land in Blackrock, in County Dublin. The land had previously belonged to Pino Harris, who had bought it from the Mercy nuns, and sold it on to UCD at a large profit.

I had never heard of Harris, but was able to establish quickly that he was a supporter of Charlie's. From the internal UCD documents we saw at the time, it appeared that UCD had not originally intended to buy the land. It was a decision made only at the last minute, and only after the then President of UCD had been told that money would be made available by the exchequer to buy it.

Several things were clear to us immediately. One was that transactions of this kind raised all sorts of questions. The land in question was zoned for education use, and it would have been difficult for Harris to make a large profit unless he could find someone who needed to build an educational institution. And they were thin on the ground.

Again and again we raised this issue in the Dáil. For reasons that have never been clear to me, the media generally didn't take much interest in it, and it never became a *cause celebre* in the same way as other issues. But it did, noticeably, annoy Charlie every time it came up. Eventually, the president of the college told the Dáil Public Accounts Committee that the deal to acquire Carysfort had been initiated by a phone call from Mary

O'Rourke, the Minister for Education, and that he had had discussions with Charlie about it. The money had been given to the college against the strong advice of the Department of Finance.

That didn't stop Charlie denying in the Dáil that he had any involvement whatsoever in the Carysfort deal, and stoutly affirming that he had never had any relationship with Pino Harris. The government was forced to muster all its resources to defeat a Labour Party motion on the issue by four votes.

One issue which did flare into life, and which caused some of the most torrid rows between Dick and Charlie, was the Greencore affair. Greencore was the name of the company that emerged from the privatisation of the publicly-owned Irish Sugar Company. Sam Smyth, Ireland's leading investigative reporter then and since, uncovered the disturbing fact that the minority shareholdings in a company called Sugar Distributors Ltd had been bought by Irish Sugar (which already owned the majority stake) for a sum which generated a £7 million profit for the minority shareholders, sometime previously.

It was claimed that the managing director of Irish Sugar, Chris Comerford, had a financial interest in Sugar Distributors before its sale to Irish Sugar. The obvious and crude conflict of interest put Comerford in the public eye, and led to his resignation. Within days of that, the Greencore board decided to freeze a £1½ million golden handshake negotiated with Comerford. These disclosures rocked the Greencore board, and put pressure on the chairman of the company, Bernie Cahill.

While the public was still digesting this, it was suddenly reported, this time by the *Irish Times*, that the purchase by Telecom Eireann of a new headquarters site in Ballsbridge was under investigation. Over the next couple of days, it emerged that the site had been sold to Telecom for £9½ million by a company called UPH Holdings—who had bought it a short time before for £4½ million. UPH, it transpired, had been set up by Dermot Desmond, a well-known financier, and a 10% share in the company was owned by Michael Smurfit, who happened to be the chairman of Telecom. The chairman of UPH was Seamus Paircéir, a retired chairman of the Revenue Commissioners.

Dermot Desmond's principal activity was as the proprietor of a large consultancy and development company, NCB, and he was well-known as a close associate of Charlie Haughey. His firm had advised Irish Sugar on privatisation, and had been appointed by them to act as their brokers. Haughey denied, in response to questions from Dick in the Dáil, that he and Bernie Cahill had ever met to discuss the appointment, and Cahill confirmed the denial.

NCB had also landed a major consultancy study into the possible privatisation of Telecom, just before the story about the headquarters deal broke. Dermot Desmond's company was engaged too to carry out a study into Irish Helicopters, a subsidiary of Aer Lingus, and John Bruton dropped a bombshell in the Dáil when he revealed that a report prepared by NCB into Irish Helicopters had somehow found its way into the hands of Celtic Helicopters—a rival company which, oddly, was owned by Charlie's son. Suddenly the Taoiseach started denying any friendship with Dermot Desmond.

If they ever had any, Michael Smurfit and Seamus Paircéir lost their affection for Charlie when he went on radio and solemnly intoned that it would be in the interests of public confidence if both men "stepped aside" from their respective positions in Telecom and UPH while the transactions in which they had been involved were investigated. Both men duly obliged, if not with very good grace.

All of this led to scenes of great drama, virtually on a daily basis, in the Dáil. Opposition leaders vied with each other to add to the revelations. It all got too much for some Fianna Fáil backbenchers, who began to issue public criticisms of their leader. It led to a tense parliamentary party meeting in early October.

Charlie faced them down, but not before he had told them that he would review Dermot Desmond's position as chairman of Aer Rianta, and Bernie Cahill's position in Greencore. Desmond resigned the next day, not only from Aer Rianta but also as head of his own company, NCB. Another friend abandoned.

But the controversies refused to go away. Proinsias De Rossa produced correspondence which implied that NCB had earned more than £2 million in fees in the course of a take-over of Irish Distillers by the French company, Pernod Ricard—and it raised again the issue of whether Dermot Desmond could exercise political influence. The ESB admitted that it had spent £166,000 on building a wind-mill "for experimental purposes" on Charlie's private island of Inishvickillaune.

The scene was set for a tense debate on a Dáil motion of no confidence in the government in mid-October. Speaker after speaker lashed into Charlie and the golden circle, and for much of the debate it looked possible that the PDs would switch sides and bring down the government. Mary Harney, for instance, had said publicly that she questioned the viability of their continued relationship with Charlie Haughey.

On the first night of the two day debate, I met Dick and John Rogers in Dick's room in Leinster House. We speculated for a while about what would happen if the government fell the following day, because President Robinson was out of the country. We wondered whether someone ought to get a message to her, about the depth of the crisis.

It was an idle enough conversation, and we did nothing about it. I thought no more of it until I met Stephen Collins the following day. Stephen is a superb reporter, who has a tremendous nose for a story. He asked me if it was true that we were considering sending a message to the President about the crisis, and when I expressed surprise, he told me that a senior civil servant had speculated to him that we might do something like that.

It was a weird coincidence, but at the time, I dismissed it as nothing more.

The no-confidence debate fizzled out, when the PDs found a formula for continuing to vote confidence in Charlie. Day after day, however, Dick and Charlie tore into each other in the Dáil. Dick had earlier secured a denial from Charlie that he had met Bernie Cahill to discuss the appointment of Dermot Desmond's company to handle the privatisation of Greencore. But the *Sunday Business Post* claimed, towards the end of October, that they had in fact met, and had discussed the appointment. Dick tabled more questions.

Before they could be reached, Charlie had to confront yet another motion of no confidence in his own party—the second in a month, together with the motion in the Dáil. Again he won, but this time, people supporting Albert Reynolds began to speak openly about a future challenge.

Charlie went into the Dáil to face Dick's questions about his dealings with Bernie Cahill with two pieces of ammunition. The first was that when he had been asked previously whether he had had meetings with Cahill to discuss the appointment of NCB, he had said that he had had no "such" meetings. He was now prepared to admit that he had had meetings, all right, but never any "such" meetings. Even though it was clear that Cahill had been helicoptered from his home in Cork to Charlie's house in Kinsealy for one of the meetings, it was only routine business—no "such" meeting (no meeting that involved Charlie asking Cahill to do a favour for Dermot Desmond) ever took place.

As incredulity mounted in the Dáil, and as Dick made it clear that he didn't believe a word of it, Charlie intervened to say that he found Dick's attitude surprising. He had evidence from an impeccable source that Dick had intervened in the selection process within Greencore some years earlier, during the 1983-87 government, in a most improper fashion, to secure the appointment of the controversial chief executive, Chris Comerford. Specifically, Dick had telephoned the company on the day the board met to make that appointment, and had called Ruaidhri Roberts out of the board meeting to instruct him to vote for Comerford.

Dick didn't react. He hadn't done anything of the kind, but I believe that it must have crossed his mind to wonder if perhaps one of his colleagues had contacted Roberts and pretended he was acting on his behalf. Sally Clarke and I, listening to the debate on the monitor in Dick's office, heard the charge. Sally, who has total recall of this kind of thing, was immediately convinced it was a lie—but how to prove it? Charlie had mentioned the date on which this intervention had taken place, but it took a few minutes for the date to register with us. As soon as it did, Sally was able to produce Dick's diary for the date, and establish beyond doubt that Dick had been on a camping site in Portugal at the time. We prepared a short statement setting out the facts, and Dick authorised its immediate publication.

He wanted to be doubly certain, though. Ruaidhri Roberts had been the General Secretary of the Irish Congress of Trade Unions, and a Labour appointee to the board of the Sugar company. There was no way of checking with him if he had been approached about the appointment of Comerford, since he had died a couple of years previously.

So Sally rang a number of people, and I rang some more. They were all people who would have been around during the time we had been in government previously. All assured us that they had never phoned Ruaidhri Roberts.

The following day, an odd thing happened. A number of the people whom we had telephoned were approached by a young reporter named Veronica Guerin. She was aware that we had been in touch with them the previous day, and wanted to ask them the same questions we had—in other words, to establish that none of them had, in fact, interfered in the appointment of Chris Comerford on Dick Spring's behalf.

I was staggered, and suddenly remembered the earlier conversation that I had had with Stephen Collins. Somebody had had to tell Veronica Guerin about the phone calls we made (and it was neither Sally, Dick, nor I) just as someone had been able to convey the precise contents of our conversations a couple of weeks earlier to Stephen Collins. The only thing the phone calls and the conversation had in common was that they all happened in Dick's office.

Dick was sufficiently concerned, when I told him my suspicions, that he telephoned the Garda Commissioner. I was invited up to the depot in the Phoenix Park to tell my story, and when the Gardaí heard the evidence, they decided it warranted a discreet enquiry. Garda officers and technical experts were instructed to sweep Dick's Dáil offices and phones on the first available Saturday—which happened to be the second Saturday in November—and I was instructed to accompany them.

Leinster House is locked on Saturdays. Entry requires special arrangements and permission. On that Saturday, however, the House was much busier than usual. A large number of ushers were working. The entire Fianna Fáil parliamentary party was there. So were most of the political correspondents. So was I, accompanied by Garda technical experts.

We all had different purposes. The Fianna Fáil parliamentary party was there to debate the third motion of no confidence in almost as many weeks in its leader, Charles J Haughey. The ushers were there because such occasions can be tense. The political correspondents were there to cover the event.

At one stage, in the course of that long and dreary day, I met Chris Glennon, the political correspondent of the *Irish Independent*, in one of the corridors of Leinster House. He was carrying a kettle, and looking for somewhere to fill it. The one facility that hadn't been laid on was anywhere for the journalists covering the Fianna Fáil meeting to have a cup of tea, so Chris was providing for them.

He saluted me as if it were a normal day, and passed on. I remember thinking that if he had followed me, he might have had an exclusive in addition to the political story that was unfolding in the Fianna Fáil rooms.

The Gardaí found no evidence of any tampering or bugging in Dick's rooms—at least none that was still active. They explained that it was possible to interfere with the phone line without touching the phone itself, and advised me that in future, if any confidential discussion was taking place in Dick's room, the phone line should be plugged out from the wall. I spent a long and dreary day, and it resulted in a story that there was no point in telling at the time.

But the story of that day that was told was Charlie's survival. Scandal had followed scandal in quick succession, but once more, in the early hours of the following morning, he beat off the vote.

He had no way of knowing it at the time, but Charlie's survival that day—by a margin of 55 votes to 22—was to be short-lived. A couple of months later, Seán Doherty was finally to pull the pin from the hand grenade that had lurked in Charlie's pocket for ten years, ever since the tapping of Geraldine Kennedy's and Bruce Arnold's phone. That was the end. But two months earlier, the result on the night of Saturday November 9th must have seemed like a new lease of life.

And although none of us knew it then, Charlie's political survival that night was followed by another stroke of good fortune. Exactly a week after he survived that vote of no confidence, with his political fortunes restored at least for the immediate future, Charlie was still down in the dumps—about money.

So depressed, in fact, that a visitor to his home, the supermarket magnate Ben Dunne, felt he had to do something for him. So he dug into the back pocket of his golf trousers, and handed Charlie bank drafts worth £210,000.

As we all know now, Charlie said "Thanks a million, big fella". The golden circle had come full circle.

8

Top of the World

"Do you accuse my client of perjury, sir?"

When I heard those words, I knew a general election was inevitable—and very soon. They were flung at the Taoiseach, Albert Reynolds, in a strong resonant voice, by Adrian Hardiman SC. He was Des O'Malley's lawyer at the Beef Tribunal.

1992 was the year I became a Tribunal junkie. I spent most of the year there, helping Dick's legal team with research and such advice as I could offer. Not that they needed much—Brian McCracken, Gerry Durkan, and Finbarr O'Malley mastered the complex brief involved very quickly, and Donal Spring, Dick's brother and his solicitor, spent day after day in the Tribunal.

We believed in it. We believed that there was something rotten, not so much in the beef industry, but in the relationship between a certain kind of business and a certain kind of politics, and we were determined to do whatever we could to help root it out.

At the start of the year, Dick took out a substantial personal overdraft and paid retainers to the three lawyers. For the next two years, they devoted themselves virtually on a full-time basis to the Tribunal, and saw nothing more in fees.

From the beginning, Dick was anxious to see the public interest represented at the Tribunal. He never believed that the state's legal team was in a good position to do it, and so the instructions he gave the lawyers involved them in a very wide area of enquiry. We started by compiling a detailed list of all the allegations made, and offering it to the Tribunal. My colleague Marie McHale spent weeks poring through the Dáil record, and compiled a comprehensive record of everything said about beef, every question and answer, every debate and speech, over a five-year period. We gave that to the Tribunal also.

Both Dick and I introduced witnesses to the Tribunal, witnesses who were all examined and cross-examined, and whose evidence was critical to the findings of the Tribunal—and in some cases led to the recovery of large amounts of tax. I gave the Tribunal a detailed account of cheques written to the benefit of a political party—who had written them, the dates and circumstances in which they were handed over, the amounts, the accounts on which they were drawn, and the people to whom the cheques were made out.

All this information was given to me by a reporter, whose credentials were impeccable. He wanted the information in the hands of the Tribunal, but he could not reveal his own identity, for fear of revealing his business and banking sources in turn. As far as I know, the Tribunal accepted the information I gave them in good faith. What they did about it, I never found out.

Mostly, we watched. We saw witnesses come and go, frightened people a lot of them, young people who had been introduced to a world of shady practice and cutting corners, who had been used and then disposed of. We watched as some witnesses came to take the rap for things that had gone on, and while others had their reputations filleted for daring to accuse. We sought out inconsistencies in the stories that were being told, and tried to bring them out in cross-examination. And all the time I became more and more convinced that when this report was finally published, it would be a watershed in Irish public life. I was to be proved wrong—but not for a while yet.

If it preoccupied me, the Beef Tribunal was not the only thing going on. Late in 1991, Dick had set up a small, tight group of people to start focussing on the general election that he believed was imminent. In addition to Sally and myself, Brendan Howlin and Ruairi Quinn attended a lot of meetings, together with William Scally, Greg Sparks, James Wrynn and John Rogers.

We worked hard at planning and preparing, determined that we would be first into the field whenever an election took place. Although an election was not due until 1994, it was clear that Charlie's government couldn't survive, tottering from crisis to crisis as it was.

We didn't know it then, but I was to discover later that on December 5th, 1991, Charlie Haughey had been to see John Major on a secret mission. Charlie's enemies had been routed, and thanks to Ben Dunne, he had plenty of folding money in his pocket. He must have felt, the day he went to see John Major, that the future looked bright. And, although the story of that meeting hasn't been told in detail, it was a historic encounter in its own way.

I imagine that Charlie must have been nervous too. It was the first formal Anglo-Irish summit that he had attended as head of the Irish delegation, since 1981. Back then, it had been Margaret Thatcher on the other side of the table, and even though that meeting had gone well, it had unfortunate consequences.

Relations between Haughey and Thatcher had plummeted in the immediate aftermath of the meeting, and had got a great deal worse throughout the IRA hunger strikes in the North and then the Falklands War. Now, it was necessary to put top-level relations back on a formal and workable basis.

That would have been achievement enough, but Charlie sensed a new and different character in John Major. Straightforward, unpretentious, and unpatronising, he had a grasp of detail and an interest in addressing problems as problems, and not as opportunities for point-scoring.

In a private tête-à-tête between them, of which no formal note was taken, Charlie told Major that he had been taking extensive soundings in the republican movement. There was a mood for peace—to such an extent that a joint declaration by the two governments could well be the catalyst for an IRA ceasefire, and the beginnings of constitutional politics.

Major was sceptical. None of his intelligence reports indicated any willingness on the part of the IRA to give up the gun and the bomb. But Charlie pressed the point home. What would be lost by looking at the possibility of a text? It could be done in secret, and it would never have to be deployed unless both sides developed sufficient confidence that it would do the trick.

There was already a basis, Haughey argued, in the speech by Major's Secretary of State in Northern Ireland, Peter Brooke, which had said that Britain had no selfish strategic, political or economic interest in remaining in Northern Ireland. The principle of consent was there in the Anglo-Irish Agreement, and could even be elaborated upon.

Eventually Major agreed. Telling Haughey that this approach would have to be seen much more as "possibility rather than probability", he insisted on absolute secrecy. To achieve it, he wanted very small groups on both sides, led by cabinet secretaries, and reporting directly to heads of government. Charlie didn't demur—he had no intention of involving his cabinet colleagues (especially Des O'Malley) in any event.

The pace of movement after that meeting, despite Major's scepticism, was surprisingly quick. The two cabinet secretaries, Dermot Nally on the Irish side and Sir Robin Butler, met on December 17th. In early January, John Major gave a secret message to John Hume, which he asked him to convey to "his contacts". That message included a refusal to talk to anyone who advocated or used terrorism, but the implied promise of a "full exchange of views" if violence was brought to an end. It also addressed the developing debate within republicanism directly, by stressing a hope that developments in the European Community would help to achieve a better climate for progress "in and in relation to" Northern Ireland.

What nobody said, but what both sides knew, was that contact with the Provisionals had already been going on for some time. John Hume and Gerry Adams met frequently, usually with Father Alec Reid. Occasionally they had direct contact with Martin Mansergh, the Taoiseach's adviser, who had started work on the text of a possible declaration before Charlie ever went to see John Major.

In January, Gerry Adams responded to the message from Major, which had been conveyed by John Hume. Major hadn't mentioned any possibility of a Joint Declaration in his discussions with Hume, and Adams emphasised that no progress would be possible without both governments being willing to put their names to an agreed text. The process of negotiation was well under way.

It came to an abrupt halt on February 7th, 1992. Two things happened that day. First, Charlie resigned, finally done in by his former Justice Minister, Seán Doherty. It had been coming for a couple of weeks.

Doherty had dropped broad hints on an RTE satirical programme called *Nighthawks* that others in Government knew of the phone-tapping he had authorised in 1981.

His hints had led to some speculation in the media, but not enough to trouble Charlie unduly. Then, just as the media speculation was dying down, Doherty had appeared at a carefully stage-managed press conference in Dublin, to accuse Charlie directly of not only authorising the tapping himself, but of taking possession of the transcripts.

It was the end of the road for Charlie—despite outright denial, his position had finally become totally untenable. Whoever organised for Seán Doherty to break his ten-year silence in the way that they did had succeeded in an Irish coup—and its immediate effect was to make Albert Reynolds Taoiseach.

The second thing that happened on February 7th was that a team of Irish officials—Dermot Nally, Noel Dorr (secretary of the Department of Foreign Affairs) and Seán O hUiginn (head of the Anglo-Irish division of the Department)—travelled to London. They were there to meet Sir Robin Butler and two of his colleagues, John Chilcot (head of the Northern Ireland Office) and his deputy Quentin Thomas.

It was a slightly surreal occasion. There was text on the table, but clearly no point in discussing it. The Taoiseach who had started the process was gone, on the day the text was introduced, and there was no evidence that his successor had the remotest knowledge or interest.

Sir Robin told the group that all he could offer was a good lunch—in the absence of a Taoiseach there was no possibility of further progress. He did say, pointedly, that if the new

Taoiseach wished to raise the matter with John Major, the Prime Minister would be willing to listen.

I knew nothing of this at the time, even though the process that Charlie initiated (for which he's never got any credit) was to occupy most of my life for several years. I did sit in the public gallery on the day Charlie resigned. It was a dignified occasion, and he carried it off well. There was, I think, such a huge collective sigh of relief at his going that none of the Opposition party leaders was inclined to have a go at him.

I have one regret about that occasion—which probably does me no credit. As his own political epitaph, Charlie quoted Shakespeare—Othello's final speech where he says "I have done the state some service, and they know 't; no more of that". I felt he had done himself less than justice, so I scribbled down the next few lines of the speech, and tried to persuade some of our deputies to add them to the record of the House—the lines where Othello goes on to speak of himself as "one who loved not wisely but too well" and compares himself to the base Indian, who "threw a pearl away, richer than all his tribe". I was alone in thinking, however, that these were appropriate additions to Charlie's monument on the day!

I also remember thinking, that day, that with Charlie gone, what were we to do for political excitement? That was a thought I was to live to regret!

His successor, Albert Reynolds, made a bright and impressive start, after a short campaign which had its unseemly moments. He was initially opposed by Bertie Ahern, but Ahern quickly withdrew from the race—not before one of Albert's lieutenants had remarked that people needed to know where the Taoiseach slept at night. It seemed like an obvious and crude reference to the fact that Bertie Ahern's marriage had broken down, and suggested, to those of us watching, that there were undercurrents that were being carefully contained.

Because Charlie was gone, the urgency went out of election preparations, although we didn't stand them down completely. We all remembered that Albert, before he became Taoiseach, had described the coalition with the PDs as "a temporary little arrangement", and it seemed wise to assume that relations would not be good.

However, Albert seemed determined to be different. Before he was confirmed by the Dáil as Taoiseach, he gave a press conference in the course of which he answered, openly and fully, questions about his private wealth—something Charlie had always treated with contempt. His first act after being confirmed was to sack eight of Charlie's Ministers, and promote a number of younger people.

All in all, it looked as if he was determined to make a clean break with the past, and Dick duly complimented him on the fact when he spoke in the Dáil on the formation of the government.

We had our own difficulties—caused by problems in another party. The Workers Party had been in crisis for some time, and Proinsias De Rossa and all of his colleagues in the Dáil, with the exception of Tomás MacGiolla, had started a party of their own, called New Agenda. And according to a spate of rumours that ran around Leinster House, they already had two recruits—Emmet Stagg and Michael D Higgins.

It had been clear for some time that Emmet was unhappy with the direction the party was taking, and especially since he had lost control of the Administrative Council. But the rumours that were circulating about Michael D were a shock.

Pat Magner, Dick and I discussed the possible defection of two deputies, and its consequences. Where Michael D was concerned, Dick decided to take the direct route—something that happens less than it might in politics. He rang him, and asked him was there any truth in the rumours. Michael D was shocked at the question—he had no intention whatever of leaving the party. He did confirm though that Emmet seemed to have his mind made up.

We didn't know whether there was any inducement that might persuade Emmet to stay in the party. And after discussing it, we decided not to try. Within a week, he had resigned from the parliamentary party, and issued a statement criticising what he saw as the right-wing drift of the party as a whole.

A couple of weeks later, he rang Pat Magner. He had had a terrible shock. Not one member of the party anywhere, including in his own constituency of Kildare, had resigned with him. The organisation that he had built up, that he had used as a battering ram in his assaults on the leadership, had decided that its first loyalty was to Labour. The only one who had gone with him was Michael Taft.

When they met, Pat was sympathetic. But, he explained, Spring was a tough, vengeful bastard. Pat just didn't know if he could persuade Dick to let Emmet back in. A few years in the political wilderness, trying to build up an organisation from scratch—and without any funds of any kind—might be necessary. And even if Dick could be persuaded about Emmet, there was no way he was going to welcome Michael Taft back into the fold.

Within an hour, the relationship between Emmet and Michael Taft was over, to such an extent that Taft was refused entry to Leinster House on Emmet's instructions. And Emmet decided to knuckle down to being an outstandingly good Labour Party Deputy.

If we were having problems, the new Taoiseach was already faced with a massive crisis. He had hardly taken office before it was revealed by the *Irish Times* that his Attorney General, Harry Whelehan, had sought and secured an injunction to prevent a pregnant fourteen-year old girl, who came to be known as Miss X, from having an abortion in England.

As the story unfolded, it became clear that the girl was actually in Britain with her parents when the injunction was granted. The girl's parents had contacted the Gardaí, to tell them that a DNA sample would be taken from the aborted foetus, and to ask if the sample could be used as evidence in prosecuting the man who had raped their daughter. This information was passed up the system until it reached the Attorney General, and he had acted immediately, without consulting any member of the Government, to get an injunction against the girl. When the Gardaí told the family about the injunction, they returned home without the abortion.

I was totally incensed at this story. It seemed to me then, and ever since, that there was no moral justification whatever for such an intervention by the state. I identified totally with the cartoon that appeared in the *Irish Times* a couple of days later, which showed a child with a teddy bear surrounded by barbed wire—the 90s equivalent of internment without trial. Even though the Supreme Court was later to find that the Attorney General had acted appropriately within the meaning of his office, I was one of many thousands who found the actions of the state in the X case totally repulsive.

There were others, of course, who felt that the state hadn't gone far enough. The debate that was immediately opened up by the X case was intensified by the Supreme Court judgement issued in early March. The Supreme Court found that there was a real and substantial risk to the life of the young woman involved, because she was in a suicidal condition. Therefore, they found that she was entitled to terminate the pregnancy, within the terms of our existing Constitution.

When we had been in government in 1983, the abortion referendum campaign that had taken place had been one of the most divisive and hate-filled experiences of everyone associated with politics. It had resulted in a provision being inserted into the Constitution which had given an unborn baby an absolute right to life, subject only to an equal right to life of the mother. It was this provision that the Supreme Court had now interpreted as giving the mother a right to terminate her pregnancy when her life was threatened by suicide.

It was a surprising, and yet a humane decision, by the court, and it drove the pro-life movement nuts. The remainder of the year was certain to be dominated by demands for another pro-life referendum, and by conflicting and opposite demands for reform to ensure that, at the very least, young women were not stopped at airports or ordered back from abortion clinics under penalty of the law.

Apart from the human situations involved, it was a legal and political minefield. I can remember in 1992 being involved in endless argument and discussion about the position we should take. I'm very proud still of the major speeches made by Dick Spring and Brendan Howlin on the subject—speeches in which they made clear that the rights of women, especially anyone in a vulnerable situation, could not be trammelled by unfeeling or callous political responses.

In the speech Dick made in the Dáil on the subject, he referred to the fear sometimes felt by a young woman at a time when "something was happening" inside her body. A few days later, on the *Late Late Show*, he was strongly attacked by the popular Father Michael Cleary, a pro-life priest, for comparing, in Father Cleary's words, "a foetus to a thing". I had to send both Dick's written text and the parliamentary record in video form to Gay Byrne before the matter was corrected on the following week's show. In the intervening week, Dick got nearly a thousand letters of abuse.

There was an added personal complication for me in the case. John Rogers was the lawyer who represented Miss X, and it was widely assumed in the media that I would be better briefed than most people for that reason. Despite the fact that anyone who knows John Rogers can testify that he can, and does, make a very sharp distinction between his legal and political work, I came to be regarded as someone who had inside knowledge of the case. In fact, it was a case about which I read everything that was written, because its human aspects obsessed me, and because its political and legal implications were profound. I knew full well that if I asked John Rogers to do me a political favour, and spill the beans on the case to enable us to score a political point or two, he would treat the request with the contempt it deserved.

That didn't stop the media from trying. I got a phone call from an English tabloid newspaper early in the case, asking me to pass on a message to my friend John Rogers. I would be given a blank cheque, which he could fill in for whatever amount he considered appropriate. And all they wanted in return was the young girl's address! At the end of the conversation, I had to ask them which of two particular words they had difficulty understanding.

While the X case gripped us all, the new Minister for Social Welfare, Charlie McCreevy, was announcing wholesale and sweeping changes in the country's social welfare services. Dick had given Emmet the social welfare brief, and he was suddenly swamped by an activist and right-wing Minister. Emmet came to me one day with a press release he had prepared, denouncing a series of cuts in social welfare as "the Dirty Dozen".

I thought it was brilliant—but even more surprising, in its own way, was the fact that Emmet had chosen to consult me, for the first time since his election. From then on, we consulted each other regularly, and gradually I began to see what it was about him that attracted a following. He has immense energy and enthusiasm, and doesn't believe in backing away from any target.

Meanwhile, the Beef Tribunal was continuing its daily drama in Dublin Castle. Seamus Brennan came before it in April, and he was to be followed by a succession of Fianna Fáil Ministers, all denying any responsibility for the various government decisions that had favoured the Goodman company. In July, Des O'Malley, who was still a member of Albert Reynolds' government, withstood several days of strong cross-examination about his claim that the insurance of non-Irish beef for export to Iraq amounted to a serious fraud, and that the policy of confining export insurance to two companies—with Goodman getting the lion's share—appeared to have originated in a conversation between Larry Goodman and Albert Reynolds.

He was followed fairly quickly by Ray Burke, who had been sacked by Albert Reynolds, but who nevertheless described parts of O'Malley's evidence as "dishonest, dishonourable, and disgraceful". This amounted to a direct attack, of a most personal kind, by a government back-bencher on a government Minister, and the political temperature started to rise. Everyone agreed, however, that the key issue in terms of political stability was how Albert Reynolds would respond to O'Malley's criticisms when he took the witness box.

But the Tribunal itself was interrupted, literally in the middle of Ray Burke's evidence, when Burke was asked questions about what had happened in the cabinet room about export insurance. Although, to my eyes, Burke seemed quite happy to have been asked the questions, the state's legal team prevented him from answering, on the grounds of cabinet confidentiality. When the Tribunal protested, it was immediately announced that this matter would have to be dealt with in the courts. From where I was sitting in the Tribunal, it looked as if the state's lawyers had been told in advance that the Tribunal would be challenged all the way to the Supreme Court if they tried to enquire into any discussions in the privacy of the cabinet room.

Within days we were plunged into a bizarre situation, where the Beef Tribunal, which had suddenly seemed to be getting to the heart of the matter, had to be adjourned. It could enquire into everything that happened outside the cabinet room, immediately before and immediately afterwards. It could examine every bit of paper that went into the room, and every bit that came out. It could look at every proposal and every argument and every decision—except the ones that were made verbally, behind closed doors. I thought at the time that it was a crazy situation, and it made me begin to wonder about the mindsets that were pursuing it.

I must have been wrong, because in September the Supreme Court ruled by a majority that not only did government have the discretion to preserve cabinet confidentiality, they had an absolute obligation to do so. Ireland thus became the first country in the world where if you wanted to hatch a criminal conspiracy with absolute impunity, the best thing to do is get yourself elected to government first!

All of this was contributing to the daily raising of tension between the government partners, although a lot of the political commentators were still predicting that the government would run its course. When Des O'Malley remarked publicly in September that the PDs wouldn't be forced out of government by Fianna Fáil, it was seen as further confirmation that they were determined to stay the course.

I saw it as evidence of the pressure he was under—I had been convinced since watching his evidence to the Beef Tribunal in July that he was preparing to make an honourable departure from the government. It would have happened in September, I believe, if the legal challenge on cabinet confidentiality had not delayed the proceedings of the Tribunal.

Throughout all this, Dick was making strong and wide-ranging contributions to the Dáil, on the X case, on Northern Ireland (where an attempt at talks had begun and foundered in the course of the year), on cabinet confidentiality, and a range of other issues. The climate of the country was changing rapidly, as political shocks were exacerbated by a sense of national disappointment and disgust, when it was revealed that Ireland's most popular Bishop, Eamonn Casey, had fathered a son seventeen years earlier, and was making financial contributions to his education from diocesan funds.

Throughout it all, as the government began to disintegrate, and as petty sniping between government partners became the order of the day, Dick's stature as a person of integrity grew perceptibly. The only worrying feature of it was that his evident popularity didn't seem to be translating into the kind of support for the party that we had been hoping for. We were still stuck at 12% in the polls nationally, although behind the figures, there were a lot of encouraging signs that many of our candidates were making considerable local impact.

In Dublin, for instance, Ruairi Quinn had emerged as the key figure in putting together a "civic alliance" that forced Fianna Fáil out of control of Dublin Corporation. All our Councillors, many of them young, were making an impression on the Dublin radio stations. In fact, during that period, we concentrated an awful lot of effort on ensuring that the two new Dublin stations hardly ever had to run a news bulletin, any of the eighteen hours a day that they carried news, without having a Labour Party statement available for them.

My assistant, Sinéad Bruton, and I were often the first in to Leinster House in the morning and the last out in the evening. We perfected a system of reacting quickly to breaking news—and we would often do it in the name of one deputy in Dublin and a different one in a rural constituency. It wasn't unusual for essentially the same statement to go out in four or five different names, all carefully targeted for local advantage.

By late September, most of the candidates who would run in the general election had been chosen by their constituencies. More than that, they'd all had their photographs taken, and a new, larger than usual poster had been printed for each of them. Every constituency was ready with several thousand copies of a standard leaflet, so that they could start canvassing within minutes of the election being called.

Every candidate who wanted it had been through a three-day course of media training, and all had been supplied with handbooks of questions and answers about every conceivable issue. We had chosen a complicated campaign slogan, but one which we felt reflected the mood of the country—Justice into Economics (to reflect continuing anger at cutbacks in social welfare and other essential services) and Trust into Politics (our answer to the golden circle and the beef and other scandals). Work on a manifesto to reflect the themes we had chosen was well underway.

We were ready—never more ready. "We're so bloody ready," Dick said at one of our Wednesday night meetings, "that if this government lasts another year, we'll have peaked too soon."

Albert Reynolds solved that problem for us.

There had been huge public interest in Charlie Haughey's appearance before the Tribunal. Watching it from the edge of the lawyers' table, I had marvelled at the magisterial way in which he had peered down his nose at his questioners, dismissing all allegations or suggestions of impropriety as the work of small minds. It was to be the last time that Charles Haughey emerged with credit from a public appearance, his style if not entirely his reputation still intact.

Nobody expected Albert Reynolds to adopt the same demeanour when he took the stand. He had developed a series of mantras to describe himself—"I am what I am, what you see is what you get, like it or lump it, good bad or indifferent"—and these would come tumbling out, often in the same sentence, whenever he was under any questioning, in the Dáil or in the media. His style was plain, no nonsense, and matter-of-fact. This would be a more down-to-earth performance. But still, as Taoiseach, he would have to be careful. It wouldn't, we thought, be likely that he would be offering any controversial evidence.

Albert had other ideas. He had clearly been smarting about Des O'Malley's evidence for some months—that was a side of Albert I was to get to know a bit better in later years!—and almost from the moment he settled into the witness box, he tore into O'Malley. The assembled public was treated to the spectacle of the Taoiseach of the day calling one of his most senior Ministers dishonest and reckless, and repeating it several times for the benefit of anyone who mightn't have heard it.

Not that he got it all his own way. We all wondered how O'Malley's own lawyers would respond when it was their turn to cross-examine Albert. It wouldn't be easy, we reckoned—you have to treat the Taoiseach of the country with some measure of respect.

But if Adrian Hardiman felt respect, he took care to hide it. For more than a day he tore into Albert, starting with his very first question, when he bellowed at Albert that the Taoiseach had accused his client of perjury ("that's your word for it," was Albert's reply). This was no mere lawyer's theatrics—there was no doubt that Hardiman would not have gone after Albert the way he did without explicit instructions from Des O'Malley. By the end of the day, the audience in Dublin Castle was reeling, and the two men at the centre of the storm were at war.

Then Albert seemed to back off a bit. He let it be known through spokesmen that he was only responding in kind to O'Malley's provocation, that he had to draw a line in the sand about his own personal integrity, which O'Malley had challenged, that there was no need after all to break up the government. But his essential charge remained, and he refused to withdraw it—the figures that O'Malley had used in his own evidence to the Tribunal were deliberately inflated, and his evidence was therefore dishonest. O'Malley couldn't stand for it.

And so, probably a year before it was necessary, Albert brought the government down. An opposition vote of no confidence became inevitable, and the Dáil hung on Dick's words more than any other as he spoke in the debate.

The speech he made then was to be quoted against him again and again in the next few years. He attacked the Fianna

Fáil Party strongly, and Albert Reynolds with it, for cheapening and debasing politics. At the end of a period of three years when the poor had been made to bear the brunt of every cutback, while a golden circle of business fat-cats had emerged, and one scandal had followed another; at the end of a year in which government Ministers had accused each other of perjury, while a fourteen-year old rape victim had had the power of the state used against her, it was a logical speech to make.

But it had another logic too. Dick said in that speech that it was impossible to see how anyone could support Fianna Fáil unless they underwent the most radical transformation. He was never to be forgiven for finding himself in a situation where it was impossible to live up to that statement.

Fianna Fáil wasn't ready for the election that was now upon them—in fact they were in a state of shock. Neither were the PDs. Only one party had done as much preparation as was possible. And only one party had a leader whose standing was as high as it could possibly be. That was us.

Within days, Pat Magner, who was in charge of Dick's national tour, was reporting back from the road that Robinson was happening all over again. Crowds were coming out of nowhere to meet Dick everywhere he went. He wasn't making speeches, just working the streets, and there was an enthusiastic welcome in every part of Ireland.

I was doing what I always do during an election—living on coffee and cigarettes in head office. I have a superstition about elections—I've always been convinced that if I ask anyone for a vote we'll lose the seat. In fifteen years in active politics, I never once knocked on a door to ask anyone to vote for the party. I couldn't do it now to save my life.

Once the election starts, I hardly ever leave my desk. I work phones all day and into the night, dealing with the media and with the constituencies, trying to harass and cajole, endlessly trying to present the best possible stories to keep morale as high as possible.

And I've always been lucky in elections too—lucky to be surrounded by the best possible people. Sally Clarke, Marie McHale, and Sinéad Bruton worked eighteen hour days during that election, never allowing the sun to go down on an unsolved problem. Marion, Angie, Jackie and Dermot in head office were heroic in keeping every constituency in touch all the time.

The first breakthrough was when I got a call from Dave Moynan in Kildare, who had always been loyal to Emmet, and a brilliant constituency worker. He was complaining about the allocation of Dick Spring posters that had been sent to Kildare.

"But you got the same as everyone else, Dave," I told him.

"It's not nearly enough," he said. "You've no idea how big Spring is here."

When I hung up, I knew we were on to something. Dick going down big in Kildare!

It was the same everywhere. Willie Penrose, another canny operator, scrapped all the leaflets we had supplied, and put out one that simply said "Penrose—Dick Spring's man in Westmeath"—in a constituency where we hadn't seriously contested for a seat in decades!

Being the third party in Irish politics has one major drawback. Television loves presidential contests. All the television concentration in an election campaign is on the Taoiseach and the alternative Taoiseach. Everyone else, no matter how good their campaign, gets squeezed.

I had watched it happen in every previous election since television began to play a role. It makes good campaigning much harder—because the essential secret of a good campaign is to be central to the action. No matter what your message, you can't get it across effectively if you're being marginalised.

This time we had a plan to deal with that. We were determined to be a central part of the action from start to finish, and we came up with the idea of a third potential Taoiseach. Since the media wouldn't buy the idea that we were seriously going to pass out Fine Gael in the course of the campaign—and the early polls gave no indication of achieving the gains we would need—we decided to launch a demand that the office of Taoiseach would be rotated in any coalition arrangement that would be considered after the election.

This idea was to be floated, in a considered and detailed speech, in the middle of the campaign—after we had time to measure the progress we were making, and just long enough before the end to give any tiring troops an extra fillip.

It wasn't a new idea—Alan Dukes had suggested something similar in the context of a possible coalition between Fine Gael and Fianna Fáil after the 1989 election. It hadn't been taken seriously then, because the notion of those two parties coalescing was seen as preposterous. But the fact that Alan Dukes had floated it, we figured, would make it harder for Fine Gael to shoot the idea down now.

But John Bruton had ideas of his own to float. He didn't waste any time—or any energy consulting us—before announcing that after the election, he would put a rainbow coalition together, involving Fine Gael, Labour, and the PDs.

Within days, Dick was being asked to react to this proposal everywhere he went. He was annoyed, and regarded the idea as presumptuous. Our support for any such arrangement, conceived without any consultation and involving parties with whom we had fundamental ideological differences, could never be taken for granted, he warned.

But the question kept coming up, and eventually Dick decided, pretty well on the spur of the moment, to trump it. In response to a question from an RTE reporter in Waterford, he said that he would expect the idea of a rotating Taoiseach to be part of any coalition deal he would strike on behalf of the Labour Party.

We held our breath. This wasn't the way the idea was supposed to come out. It might be too easy for the media to dismiss it, if it seemed like a top-of-the-head idea. There was a chance it would be seen as arrogant.

But within days, the first opinion poll that had a chance to measure support for the idea found that a great many people thought that Dick Spring would make an ideal Taoiseach. And his ratings, and suddenly ours, were surging ahead.

Barry Desmond wasn't contesting this election, because he had decided to concentrate on Europe. Instead, he served as our national director of elections, and did a superb job. The first difficult decision of the campaign fell to him.

One of the constituencies where we had been unable to find a candidate was Clare. But at our campaign meeting one morning, Ray Kavanagh told us that the constituency had come up with both a candidate and a slogan. The candidate's name was Moosajee Bhamjee, and he was a South African Indian psychiatrist. There was a stunned silence around the table.

"Can I ask," said Barry, voicing the question the rest of us were afraid to ask, "is it fair to assume that we are talking about a black man?"

"Well," Ray said, "I think in South Africa he'd be called coloured."

"And tell me," Barry pressed on, fingering the note that had been faxed up from Clare, "can it really be true that the Clare constituency is proposing to use the slogan 'A vote for Moosajee Bhamjee is a vote for change'?"

When he was assured it was, Barry looked around the table. "I think we'd better say yes," he told us, "if only so we can claim to have produced the understatement of the campaign!"

But if we were worried about a backlash, it never came. Throughout the campaign, it became clearer and clearer that Dick's integrity was the only issue that mattered to the electorate. Our manifesto was greeted with universal approval, and everywhere he went, Dick was greeted with the sort of acclamation that we had become used to in the Robinson campaign.

Most of our candidates, even though they had a fair bit of experience as councillors, had never run in a general election before. There were all the usual fights and arguments—people demanding more of Dick's time, people complaining that they weren't getting enough exposure on television. Sinéad Bruton, who ran the press office for the campaign, did a superb job of ensuring that none of the rows became public, and coped with a far larger than ever before volume of press interest.

Two things happened just before polling day that confirmed we were on a roll. The first was that Fianna Fáil imported a negative campaign expert from Saatchi and Saatchi, and launched a vicious series of advertisements, all aimed at us, claiming that we were on the point of taxing everything that moved. Their ads relied on an old policy document that had undergone all sorts of changes in the interim, but they were enough to panic some of the Dublin constituencies particularly. We had to spend the last penny we had on counterattack ads, drawn up virtually overnight.

Then the "great debate" took place on RTE, between the Taoiseach and the alternative Taoiseach, Albert Reynolds and John Bruton. Both men performed sturdily, but there was a palpable sense that the real man was missing, and that the contest, for the first time in the holding of such debates, was largely irrelevant. After the TV debate was over, I rang Dick at his home in Tralee to find out what he thought of it—it was the only television he had sat down to watch since the start of the campaign. Kristi told me that within two minutes of the start of the debate, he had fallen fast asleep in his armchair. I told her that was all I needed to know!

From the moment the campaign began, and once the early canvass returns were available, I became convinced that we might just break 30 seats. Sinéad and I discussed the possibility endlessly, and did all sorts of combinations to demonstrate how it might happen. But I refused to allow it to be said publicly, insisting all the time that our target was the 25 seats that had been called for six years earlier as a long-term target for the party.

I was furious when Ruairi Quinn said on radio, for instance, that he believed it would go over 30. Twenty-five would be an important psychological barrier for us, and setting the bar too high publicly was only inviting commentators to write off success as a disappointment.

Despite my allergy to canvassing on the doorsteps, I had a habit, for as long as these things were allowed, of standing with Sally Clarke outside the polling station at the Technical School in Bray on the day that votes were cast. I had been absolutely certain that we were going to win the Presidential election in 1990 because of the experiences I had there—people going to extraordinary lengths to tell us of their intention to vote for Mary Robinson.

This time it was the same. People by-passed the Fianna Fáil and Fine Gael canvassers, and instead of taking our Liam Kavanagh leaflets, stopped to talk to us about what a great campaign it had been, how great Dick Spring was, and that "he was going to stand up to that shower". I went to bed that night knowing with absolute clarity that change was in the air.

On the night of the election count there was a huge party in the Riverside Centre on Dublin's quays. Twelve Dublin Labour TDs were there, up from three in the previous Dáil, most of them brand new to national politics, and most of them poll-toppers. They were cheered to the echo when their names were called out. Dick Spring arrived from the Kerry count—where he had buried the ghosts of 1987 with a whopping victory—and I thought the roof would lift off.

But the biggest cheer was reserved for the announcement, very late on, that Clare too had voted for change. Moosajee Bhamjee became the thirty-third Labour Deputy elected that night. As someone remarked, Dáil Eireann, which had elected many a cowboy in its day, had finally elected an Indian.

We were on top of the world. We had done the impossible, and done it by systematic hard work and planning. When I told Dick that nothing could stop us now, he grinned.

"Don't you believe it," he said. "The real problems start tomorrow."

9

Meeting Albert

I woke the morning after the 1992 count with an unmerciful hangover, but also with a mounting sense of excitement. We could do it. We could put an anti-Fianna Fáil rainbow coalition government together—although not the one John Bruton had envisaged.

Ever since the Workers Party had arrived on the scene, they had posed a threat to Labour. Throughout Dublin, although virtually nowhere else, they had built solid bases in constituencies we had neglected, or where we had made a mess of things. The history of the WP, in some ways, was built on showing us how it could be done, especially in working-class areas of the city.

They had had their own troubles, especially with internal machinations of various kinds, and their problems had resulted in a great deal of media hostility. As a party, they were viewed with the utmost suspicion. But individual members of the party had managed to transcend that, and were universally regarded as among the brightest of Dáil performers.

Within Labour, reaction to the WP, or Democratic Left as it had now become, ranged from envy for their discipline and coherence to outright hatred, arising from individual incidents in the past. They were at their most dangerous when we were in government—constantly sniping at anything we tried to do.

Now, suddenly, there was a chance to end all that. But it depended on one thing. In Dublin South Central the count was still going on. Eric Byrne, for Democratic Left, was engaged in a titanic struggle to take the last seat from Fianna Fáil's Ben Briscoe—a decent man and a good TD, who had made the classic mistake of telling his constituents that this election would be his last hurrah.

If Byrne were to win, it would mean that Fine Gael, Labour and Democratic Left would have 83 seats between them. More importantly, the left in such an arrangement would have almost fifty per cent of the government seats. Fine Gael had lost nine seats in the election, and were down to 45. A bloc of 38 left-wing seats would put us in the most powerful negotiating position that the left in Ireland had ever seen.

There was another option, that morning—the original Rainbow, as proposed by John Bruton, would have a total of 88 seats (the PD's, even though their vote had fallen in the election, had won ten seats). But that option would mean that the conservative element of the government would have 55 seats to our 33. The odds against implementing any serious element of our programme would be immeasurably shortened. Fine Gael and the PDs already agreed about a great deal of budgetary strategy and social policy—we would be fought every inch of the way every time we tried to increase spending on such areas as health or housing.

And we would not have the numbers in cabinet. A FG/Labour/DL coalition could yield seven left-wing cabinet seats, against Fine Gael's eight; a FG/Labour/PD coalition could give us as few as five against their ten.

In addition, the PDs were the only party who had deliberately set out to target us from the start of the election campaign. Des O'Malley had never missed an opportunity to have a go—including making the prediction that Michael D Higgins would go mad if he were ever to serve in government. It was clear to me, the morning after the election, that if the PDs saw us as potential government partners now, it would only be for the sake of making up the numbers.

I rang Dick (who seemed to have a more manageable hangover than mine), and we went through the only options that occurred to us. The one thing we didn't discuss—because it never crossed our minds!—was the possibility of doing a deal with Fianna Fáil. In the last few days before the election, Fianna Fáil, who had previously run a lack-lustre effort of a campaign, had mounted an all-out assault on us. They obviously had a lot of poll data that indicated how well we were doing, which led to their importation of the Saatchi and Saatchi specialist in negative campaigning. It was probably the first serious instance of negative campaigning in Ireland, and it had left a bitter taste. As far as we were concerned, Fianna Fáil could lick their wounds—we wouldn't be troubling them.

And they had plenty of wounds. The campaign had been a personal disaster for Albert Reynolds. He had been almost universally blamed for causing the election in the first place, and had been pilloried throughout the campaign for his occasionally unfortunate way with words—using the word "crap" in interviews, for example, or announcing an intention to "dehumanise" the social welfare system. It was clear, even from television pictures, that his forays among the electorate were attracting the smallest crowds any Fianna Fáil leader had ever had. The result had been the loss of ten seats, and the smallest Fianna Fáil vote since 1927.

With 68 seats, they were 15 short of a majority in the Dáil. It looked as if Albert Reynolds had lost his only chance to be elected Taoiseach by the people.

Not that I cared. The one item on my agenda that morning, once Dick had agreed, was to track down Pat Rabbitte, and find out if he would be willing to meet me. He was, and we arranged to meet in the Braemor Rooms in Churchtown.

We met at noon on the Sunday morning after the election, and by the time I left him, two hours later, I was satisfied that if it were up to him, we would put a centre/left coalition together in no time. I told him, with Dick's full authority, that we were anxious to bury the hatchet in respect of the past enmity between our two parties, and that above all we wanted to have nothing to do with the politics of the PDs. I also told him that if we started a process between us, we would operate in good faith from start to finish. He warned that it was not a subject around which the leadership of his party was totally united, but undertook to come back to us quickly.

We made our first mistake then. Because we wanted a centre/left government, our next port of call should have been a private contact with John Bruton. We should have tried, right from the beginning, to ensure that he was at least open to the possibility of doing business with DL—a prospect he had ruled out during the campaign, though not as vehemently as the PDs had.

But John Bruton had annoyed everyone in the Labour Party, by seeming to take our participation in his choice of rainbow for granted. Even in the aftermath of the election, which was just as disastrous for Fine Gael as it had been for Fianna Fáil, there was no hint of acknowledgement that the situation had changed. Instead, he was almost triumphalist, still operating on the assumption that he would be the next Taoiseach—and that we would do the decent thing.

That triumphalism was evident to us a few days later, when Dick got a letter from him, inviting him to join negotiations on government formation with the Progressive Democrats. Two things seemed evident from that letter. First, it was clear (to us at any rate) that Fine Gael and the PDs were already talking. And second, there were going to be a number of pre-conditions to negotiation. We would have to accept five years of budgetary parameters, and the distribution of power and responsibility within government on the basis of party strength.

This letter, coming as it did from a party which could not claim, by any stretch of the imagination, to have received a resounding mandate from the people in the election, infuriated us. By the time it arrived, we were already in discussions with the DL. Brendan Howlin and I had been deputed by Dick to meet Pat Rabbitte and Des Geraghty, and the shape of an agreement was already emerging between us. They were somewhat suspicious of our intentions, it has to be said, and the documents they were producing were a good deal longer than we felt we had time for. Besides, after the long count in Dublin South Central finally ended, Briscoe had just held on to his seat. It meant that the best "our" rainbow could muster was 82 seats—and that would mean a very difficult time in government. But nevertheless, we had committed ourselves to negotiating in good faith with DL, and we were determined to see it through.

It could have worked better, had Fine Gael and ourselves been more open with each other. Pat Magner and Maurice Manning opened up a line of contact with each other, but both sides, by then, were suspicious of the intentions of the other.

Meanwhile, unknown to all of us, Ruairi Quinn and Brian Lenihan were having quiet chats. They were to make a substantial difference, later on.

Matters between us and Fine Gael got a lot worse when, eventually, a meeting was arranged between John Bruton and Dick. It was scheduled for the Constitution Room of the Shelbourne Hotel on Sunday morning, a week after my meeting with Pat Rabbitte.

The day before Dick and John were due to meet, Barry Desmond and Nora Owen were among the panellists on Rodney Rice's *Saturdayview* programme (the same programme where Padraig Flynn had shot himself in the foot during the Robinson campaign). Naturally, the programme focussed on the various manoeuvres taking place around the formation of a government. Nora expressed considerable confidence that the meeting between Dick and John would go well, and graciously acknowledged that Dick had all the makings of a fine Tánaiste, adding for good measure that some of the Labour Deputies would make good Ministers too.

This was too much for Barry, who announced that the principal purpose of the following day's meeting would be to enable Dick to put some manners on John Bruton. As a precursor to a delicate piece of negotiation, it wasn't terribly well judged!

As it happened, the meeting the following day was uncomfortable. Peter White, the Fine Gael press officer, and I remained outside the door throughout, and I think we can both testify that it was a good deal calmer than some of the discussions Dick and John used to have in the days of the Garret FitzGerald government. But it was clear from occasional glimpses inside that neither man was particularly enjoying the encounter. When they came out, the media could see that both men were extremely grim, and that very little progress, if any, had been made.

Both Peter White and I were caught up by then in the need to score points off each other. When I overheard Peter saying to one of the journalists that the Constitution Room of the Shelbourne was an obvious venue for a Fine Gael meeting, I couldn't resist pointing out that we had paid for the hire of the room. It was that sort of pettiness that I think made it clear to the shrewd observers around that this relationship wasn't going anywhere in too much of a hurry.

Peter also reported to the media that Dick had stayed on his feet throughout the meeting, and it was generally interpreted that he had been lecturing John. In fact, after the physical strain of the campaign, Dick's back was in almost constant spasm, and it was more comfortable to stand. But it added to an impression of hostility—when in fact what we felt was irritation.

As I drove Dick away from the Shelbourne, I noticed that his hands were shaking. When I pointed it out, he acknowledged that he was still very tense.

"It had to be done," he said. "I told Bruton as straight as I could that he was impossible to work with before, and I couldn't see any sign of change. From now on, I don't work with people who always have to have their own way—there has to be give and take."

Little did we know!

Dick suggested that he and John Bruton should meet again, this time to discuss the document we had by now agreed with DL. Although it was a much more amicable meeting, John's agenda was the establishment of tripartite negotiations involving the PDs rather than DL. He did say at the second meeting that he was not personally opposed to the idea of a rotating Taoiseach.

His objections to the involvement of DL were no longer based on ideological grounds, but instead on the fact that he couldn't sustain an argument in favour of a minority government when a majority government was possible, if only we would agree to work with the PDs.

We ended up going through the motions of a meeting with Fine Gael and the PDs. We were represented by Ruairi, Brendan Howlin, and Mervyn Taylor. Des O'Malley, Bobby Molloy, and Pat Cox represented the PDs—and took the opportunity to protest at how unfairly labelled they had been. They were totally pragmatic on issues like privatisation, they insisted—to describe them as a right-wing party was only a travesty of the truth. And as for all that stuff about Labour being impossible to work with, and Michael D Higgins going mad in government, and so on—sure that was just the old guff that you had to use during election campaigns!

We decided eventually to put an end to the shadow-boxing. We had a document that we had agreed with the Democratic Left, and it represented a very sizable element of the platform on which we had fought the election. In fact, it was a very radical and comprehensive document, covering a wide spectrum of social and economic policy issues. But it was useless, if it was never going to be implemented.

So we decided to take an initiative, and sent it to the other parties in Dáil Eireann who would have responsibility for voting in the election for a Taoiseach. That election was due to take place in the Dáil on Monday, December 14th.

I argued initially that we shouldn't include Fianna Fáil among the parties who would be invited to respond to our document. Ruairi, on the other hand, was adamant that every party had to be included. Eventually, we compromised. Albert Reynolds was leaving for the EU summit in Edinburgh early on Friday. It was probably going to be his last act as Taoiseach, and it would require all his time and attention, because he had committed himself in advance to securing a doubling of Ireland's contribution from the EU. I reckoned that if we sent our document late on Thursday, he would have no time to respond until after he had come home. That would give John Bruton, I thought, a day or two to come to his senses.

Besides, I felt, there were elements in our document that Fianna Fáil couldn't possibly accept. They had announced during the election campaign that they intended to sell both of the state banks—we were proposing a state-controlled third banking force. They had spent the years in government drastically cutting back on local authority housing investment, to a point where it had come to a virtual standstill. We were proposing massive investment in that area. They had ignored all of the so-called "liberal agenda". We had wide-ranging proposals for family planning reform, another divorce referendum, and decriminalisation of homosexual acts. There was a lot more—so much so that I found it hard to see how, even if Fianna Fáil responded at all, we were ever going to find common ground.

So no-one was more surprised than I was when a reply was received from Fianna Fáil within a few hours of our document being dispatched.

What I didn't know was that Martin Mansergh had read the arithmetic too. In the immediate aftermath of the election, he had approached Albert Reynolds, and pointed out that at least the mathematical possibility existed that a Fianna Fáil and Labour government could be put together. Albert had given him *carte blanche* to prepare something, in case of an approach, and Martin had spent the preceding two weeks—when otherwise he would only have been clearing his desk anyway— researching all of our positions, and writing the kind of response that we were sure to find attractive.

I've always suspected that what he was actually writing was the kind of document that he would like to see in action himself. As I came to discover later, Martin Mansergh has much more in common with European mainstream social democratic values than some members of the Labour Party—and certainly than a lot of members of the party he worked for so diligently.

It was all there, in the document we received. A third banking force, reform of confessional legislation, significant investment in social services. Anything that we were likely to find contentious in their policy position was simply dropped.

I was horrified. There is an old door in Saint Patrick's Cathedral around which a legend exists. The legend has it that the door separated two feuding families in medieval times. One of the family members, tiring of the feud, broke a hole in the door and stuck his arm through. He reasoned that the other family would either clasp his arm in friendship or cut it off. It was, according to the legend, the end of the feud and the start of a new relationship.

Fianna Fáil had broken a hole in the door, and their arm was sticking invitingly out. What's more, we were being invited to grasp it—or cut it off—as soon as Albert Reynolds returned from Edinburgh, the following Sunday afternoon.

There's a myth about politics that some political parties are media driven, and others are policy driven. We all like to think that we belong in the latter category, but the truth is that every political party wants to pursue a policy line—but also wants to know how the media will react to it. The media, and especially the print media, think they form opinion. But they form opinion first within political parties, who regard them as the most critical sounding board. It's a matter of degree—there are times when the best thing to do with the media is to ignore them completely, and get on with doing what you believe to be right. But a lot of the time, sensible politicians will take soundings first.

That's what we did on this occasion. It was immediately clear, from a visit to the political correspondents' room in Leinster House, that we would have a lot of explaining to do if we rebuffed this policy-friendly approach out of hand. The pol. corrs. were intrigued by this development, and clearly expected it to be followed through.

So a meeting was set up, for Sunday afternoon, December 13th. The manager of the Berkeley Court Hotel, Jack Donnelly, offered a private room—which subsequently turned out to be the penthouse suite. When we got there, Jack told us that the previous occupant had been Tina Turner—references to steamy windows during the meeting between Dick and Albert sprang to mind!

We also arranged a separate room in the hotel, and Dick asked some of the people closest to him to make their way there quietly. We met there in the early afternoon, and for several hours we discussed the pros and cons inconclusively. Barry, Ruairi, and Brendan were there. So were John Rogers, Pat Magner, William Scally, Greg Sparks, James Wrynn, and myself.

When we established that the Taoiseach would be accompanied only by his Press Secretary, Seán Duignan, it was agreed that I would accompany Dick, so that I would be meeting Albert Reynolds for the first time. As we left to meet Albert in the lobby of the hotel, Pat Magner called after us, "Break a leg, Dick!".

I think I expected to meet someone with the hunted and hang-dog look of a politician who had been under immense pressure for several months. There was no doubt that since the election campaign, the knives had been out for Albert Reynolds—both in the media and in his own party. If he couldn't do a deal with Dick Spring, he'd be gone in a week. He needed us a lot more than we needed him.

The first revelation was how bright and breezy he was, like a man without a care in the world. He had just arrived back from Edinburgh, where he had astonished everyone by announcing that he had secured £8 billion in structural funds over the next few years. He had gone there expressing determination that they would be doubled, which would have yielded a figure of six billion.

Either it was a negotiating triumph, or he had considerably exaggerated his success. But why would he do that, since he was on his way out of office?

One way or the other, he was in high good humour as we took the lift to the penthouse suite, and as the meeting began. He and Dick retired to the dining room of the suite, and sat around a long table, while Seán Duignan and I disported ourselves in comfortable arm-chairs around a mock fire.

In his book about his experiences in government, Seán has described how his impression at that meeting was that I was already fully reconciled to the notion of a government with Fianna Fáil, and only really wanted to discuss logistics with him—like how we could get rid of Padraig Flynn, for example! It goes to show how impressions differ.

I found him, unusually, very down in the dumps. Seán is one of the most gregarious and charming people you're ever likely to meet, but he had been through hell in the previous few weeks. As he regaled me with stories about how one thing had gone wrong after another during the election campaign, until finally the Taoiseach and leader of Fianna Fáil had found himself entirely alone, with only Seán Duignan for company, I found myself working at cheering him up.

He was already resigned to going back to his job in RTE, and not looking forward to it, because he assumed that he wouldn't be allowed to be involved in reporting politics. I told him that there was bound to be something better around the corner, and that Dick Spring thought so highly of him that he'd be happy to see him continue as Government Press Secretary if a deal was done. All in all, I suppose I did a good job of creating the impression that we were there to do business—even if that wasn't my aim.

In reality, I was by now confused and ambivalent. On the one hand, I could see the full range of possibilities that would open up on the policy front—essentially because I regarded Fianna Fáil as utterly pragmatic, and unlikely to get in our way too much. On the other, the vision of Albert Reynolds in the witness box at the Beef Tribunal kept appearing in front of my eyes, and it made me deeply uneasy each time I thought of it.

While Seán and I were talking in the comfortable armchairs, I could see Dick and Albert, through the glass doors that led to the dining room, in deep and intent conversation. Albert seemed to be doing most of the talking, but there was clearly no animosity. I couldn't, unfortunately, hear what was going on.

It lasted for an hour or so, and then we went downstairs in the lift, to be greeted by a battery of cameras. Albert looked chirpy, and this time Dick looked a little hunted. Both made non-committal noises to the cameras, and I took Dick to the room where his friends and colleagues were waiting.

I was surprised to see that Donal, Dick's brother, had arrived to join the meeting—he seldom participated in policy or strategy discussions with others, although Dick often consulted him alone, frequently late at night.

Dick slumped in a chair at the head of the table, and took a few minutes to compose himself. Then he told us that Albert was very anxious to do business, and could see no possible obstacle in the way of it. Albert had emphasised, again and again, that what he foresaw was a different kind of coalition, one that would be very much based on partnership.

This wouldn't be a case of a small party being tagged on to a larger one for the sake of making up the numbers. It would instead be the first time that two large parties had got together, and everything we did would reflect that new reality.

It was encouraging stuff—and it was, I thought, perfectly tailored to meet Dick's mindset. I remembered the remark Dick had made to me after the Shelbourne Hotel meeting with John Bruton. "What else did you talk about?" Ruairi asked.

"We talked about Northern Ireland," Dick said. "I promised him I wouldn't elaborate, but you can take it that there are real possibilities there. The other thing he told me was that I was getting a briefing that Des O'Malley never got!"

That was all he told us about Northern Ireland. But I was watching him closely, and I knew that whatever he had been told he had found intriguing.

They discussed the £8 billion in European funds also, and the possibilities of major new investment in infrastructure and in education. But clearly, the pitch that Albert made had been centred principally on delivery, by a new-style government of a kind never seen before. There was more than a touch of deathbed conversion about it.

When he had finished, Dick asked for views around the table. There was silence for a few minutes, and I realised that everyone in the room was tense. This was a defining moment for all of us. I looked at Barry, and thought I knew what was going on in his mind. Barry had always been strongly anti-Fianna Fáil, throughout his entire career. Now, because of his commitment to the European Parliament, he would play no role in whatever government emerged. He knew that a difficult decision had to be made, one way or the other, and he was struggling with it—the first time in my life I ever saw Barry in doubt.

John Rogers spoke first, and passionately. He emphasised the fact that Albert Reynolds remaining as Taoiseach did not appear to be the result anticipated by the electorate. We had campaigned for change—how could we find ourselves supporting the same Taoiseach?

William Scally, who spoke before I did, expressed what I felt. While he largely agreed with John, he said that he could envisage circumstances where the mould could be broken, but that the Beef Tribunal was a time-bomb ticking under a potential Fianna Fáil and Labour government. On balance, he said, a decision to open negotiations with Fianna Fáil was likely to be highly dangerous.

I supported that view, and said that I would prefer to see a four-party coalition if necessary. At the same time, I admitted to being attracted to the policy possibilities that existed, and said that I didn't relish the thought of John Bruton being Taoiseach, after all our memories of the 1980s.

Barry, when he spoke, was emphatic, but, unusually for him, subdued. Fianna Fáil would never change, and we had no place in any relationship with them. But he accepted too that a relationship with Fine Gael and the PDs was likely to deliver a lot less. Barry cared passionately about the social policy aspects of government, and he still remembered the rows that had taken place in the 1980s about health and social welfare spending. He shuddered to think about Des O'Malley being in charge of social welfare at any time in the future.

Ruairi was just as emphatic as Barry, saying that this possibility opened up an undreamed of chance to get a radical policy agenda through. He also told us about his discussions with Brian Lenihan, and emphasised that Lenihan and others in Fianna Fáil would be very supportive of Labour policies. Brendan seemed opposed to opening discussions with Fianna Fáil, but again, he was doubtful of concluding successful negotiations with the others. On balance, he said, he thought a Fianna Fáil link was likely to be more stable than a four-way arrangement.

Pat Magner and James Wrynn both referred to what could be done by a government in which Fianna Fáil was a willing partner—and a government that would have a huge majority. James pointed out that Fianna Fáil in government were perfectly capable of working to implement the changes they would frustrate in opposition. Greg Sparks agreed with that view, while Donal Spring wondered aloud about how Dick's own people in Kerry would ever be persuaded to accept that Fianna Fáil were no longer the enemy.

As Dick went around the table, it became clear that his advisers were divided down the middle. As the discussion went on, the option of a four-party rainbow began to gather strength in our minds. It was not an option that had been seriously debated before, but it began to emerge, I thought, as something that might well have to be taken seriously.

At the end of the discussion, Dick asked each of us to express a view, for or against the opening of discussions with Fianna Fáil. In my recollection, Ruairi, Brendan, Pat Magner, Greg Sparks, and James Wrynn voted for. Barry Desmond, Donal Spring, William Scally, John Rogers, and I voted against.

Although our vote was expressed as a "for or against Fianna Fáil", it was clear that those who had voted against favoured, as an alternative, the four-party rainbow.

Five against five. We had always prided ourselves as a group on an ability to give coherent advice when it was required. On one of the most crucial issues we ever had to decide, the party leader was effectively on his own. At least he knew that whatever he decided, there was no-one in that group who would let him down. But I don't imagine that was much consolation at that moment.

"Thanks a lot, guys," was all Dick said when the five-five figure became clear. "That's a big help!"

For several hours after that, we carried on the discussion, and ended up having a meal in the hotel. In the course of our discussions, one thing that did emerge was the fact that the Dáil was meeting the following day, and there was no prospect of electing a Ceann Comhairle. In some ways, if that happened, it could provoke a bigger crisis than failure to elect a Taoiseach. The Dáil had failed for a period of weeks to elect a Taoiseach in 1989, and the sky hadn't fallen in. But if the House couldn't elect a chair, it would be entering totally uncharted territory.

Dick was fairly sure that if we wanted to, we could elect one of our TDs—Liam Kavanagh was the obvious choice—with Fianna Fáil support. It emerged during the discussion on the point that Ruairi had also discussed this issue with Jim Mitchell of Fine Gael, who was clearly keen on the job.

The strong consensus of the meeting—the only consensus we managed that day—was that it would be totally unwise to seek Fianna Fáil support for one of our candidates before any decision had been made on entering into discussions with them. It would look immediately as if we had been bought and paid for.

The alternative was to allow the outgoing Ceann Comhairle Seán Treacy—who had resigned from the Labour Party in high dudgeon in the 1980s and had been hostile to us ever since—to retain the position. We all swallowed hard and agreed that that was the right way to go.

On the main issue, we got no nearer to offering crisp advice, and it was clear when we went our separate ways that Dick was troubled.

The following day—14th December 1992—was ironically the tenth anniversary of the day that Dick had become Tánaiste in Garret FitzGerald's government. Again that day, after Seán Treacy had graciously accepted the post of Ceann Comhairle from a grateful House, Dick was nominated for the office of Taoiseach, along with John Bruton and Albert Reynolds. All three were beaten.

The atmosphere in the House was loaded. A number of the Fine Gael people present couldn't resist jeering the Labour benches, and I thought some of our people were going to lose their tempers. Proinsias De Rossa and the other DL deputies supported Dick's nomination, and they had a few words after the House was adjourned. De Rossa, I think, understood the difficult position Dick was in—in any event, there was no recrimination from them during the day.

Later that evening, Dick called Pat Magner and me into his office. We knew immediately what was troubling him.

"I'm going to give John Bruton one more chance," he said. The remark was aimed primarily at Pat, who favoured doing a deal with Fianna Fáil. But he immediately concurred—if that was what Dick wanted to do, he'd have Pat's full support.

Sally Clarke put John Bruton on the phone to Dick, and they had a short conversation, which seemed from where I was sitting to be cordial enough. Dick asked him about the rotating Taoiseach idea, and John said that that was simply unacceptable to his Parliamentary party. Then Dick raised the idea of a four-party coalition, and again John said that his party was totally opposed to doing business with DL.

"Is that your final word, John?" Dick asked. It was.

"In that case," Dick said, "I'm going to do what I have to do."

(That conversation caused a minor controversy some time later, when Dick referred to it in a speech. John Bruton disputed Dick's account, claiming that Dick had got the date wrong and had misreported the content—that Dick, in effect, had made no reference to the four-party coalition. John was right about the date, but my memory, sitting listening to Dick's end of the conversation, is as set out above.)

That night, the Parliamentary Labour Party approved, with some misgivings, the opening of negotiations with Fianna Fáil. Almost immediately, Fine Gael and the PDs broke off all contact with us, saying—quite fairly from their point of view— that they had no interest in being involved in a Dutch auction.

The options were clear—either we succeeded in making an agreement with Fianna Fáil that we could stand over, or we crawled on our bellies back to Fine Gael and the PDs, to accept whatever they offered. In other words, there was now no option.

Could we have handled it differently? The answer to that is yes, of course we could. We could have opened better lines of communication to Fine Gael immediately after the election, and set about persuading them that the electorate had given a mandate for a significant left-wing input into government. Maybe they would have listened, and maybe not. We allowed ourselves to be deflected by their attitude, and especially by their complacency in the aftermath of the election. And we were to pay a heavy price for that in due course.

The irony is that we had campaigned, hard and effectively, for left-wing values in that campaign, and for fundamental political change. The only one who seemed prepared to listen to that message was the target of a lot of our campaign, Albert Reynolds.

Sometime in the course of the following couple of weeks, I remember meeting Jim Downey, the distinguished political journalist. He told me that he had met some senior Fine Gael people in the bar of Buswells Hotel, and they were giving out yards about the Labour Party. In the course of the conversation, Jim asked them if they could remember the names of the nine Fine Gael Deputies who had lost their seats in the election a few weeks previously. They could remember three or four, no more. That story summed up for me how little Fine Gael had learned from the electorate in that election.

I will always believe that the bigger mistake was made by Fine Gael, which got no mandate in that election. Fianna Fáil responded to the demand for change—Fine Gael didn't. And although I, and many others, had to swallow hard at the notion of forming a government with Fianna Fáil, it was the right thing to do as the options unfolded.

Four years later, a political folk wisdom had formed, one that was impossible to disturb. When people looked back on 1992, they saw a Labour Party that had campaigned against Fianna Fáil, while secretly plotting to get into bed with them. Nothing could be further from the truth—but it's easy enough to see how the perception formed.

There was one other way that we could have saved ourselves later grief. We could have used Ruairi's secret line of communication with Brian Lenihan to send a message to Fianna Fáil, letting them know that if they wanted to do business with us, they'd have to get a new leader.

There was little doubt at the time that the electorate had reacted massively against Albert Reynolds rather than his party, and the perceived need for change could well have been largely met by a change at the top, as well as the change in policy direction that undoubtedly occurred.

Would that have been an honourable way to proceed? I've often wondered. I toyed with the idea in the aftermath of the election, but I never put it forward because I didn't believe then that it was the right thing to do. Most of us had watched as the PDs took one scalp after another in the course of their relationship with Fianna Fáil, and we were conscious of the fact that we would never allow that to happen to us. I know that Dick Spring felt strongly that Charlie Haughey should have resigned himself rather than sack Brian Lenihan, and I came to believe that the days when one party interfered, for its own sake, in the affairs of another had to end.

Mind you, there were times in the next couple of years when I regretted keeping my mouth shut!

10

Building a Partnership

It was early in January, and there had been no respite since the election. Just before Christmas, Dick had given his evidence to the Beef Tribunal, and it had been a source of worry and distraction.

It was an entirely unsatisfactory occasion. Dick had submitted a lengthy witness statement to the Tribunal, which outlined what he had known and how he had known it. It repeated the allegations that Dick had made, and pointed to the evidence already before the Tribunal which supported those allegations. Although his statement had refused to name his sources, it made it clear that all of those sources had been independently interviewed by the Tribunal. And it stood over the allegations.

Every other witness had been led through his or her own witness statement by the Tribunal's legal team. As well as giving the witness a chance to settle into the witness box, it enabled them to make their case under direct and straightforward questioning, before being subjected to cross-examination. In Dick's case, for reasons I've never understood, this procedure wasn't followed. Instead, the Tribunal more or less put it to Dick that he had nothing to add to his statement, and no hard evidence to support his allegations, before leaving him open to cross-examination.

Dermot Gleeson, who was then Senior Counsel for Larry Goodman, had a field day with Dick. As Dick got more and more uncomfortable, he challenged him again and again to produce evidence for any of his allegations. Without revealing sources, it wasn't possible to answer in any satisfactory way. Dick was also under the constraint that if he offered pre-emptive opinions about Albert Reynolds, it would jeopardise the negotiations that were going on intensely as he sat there.

As it happened, none of the allegations Dick had made about the beef industry concerned Albert Reynolds specifically in the first place, apart from his role as a member of the 1987 government. None of that stopped Fine Gael from sneering at Dick, especially for refusing to reveal his sources.

When the Dáil met on January 5th, with our negotiations still going on, John Bruton really got stuck into Dick. Fine Gael had unearthed the speech he made before the election, and were now throwing it back in his face. Dick was annoyed—but we had to agree that if the shoe were on the other foot, we'd have done the same to them.

Meanwhile, our negotiations were agonisingly slow. They were basically situated in a number of rooms in Government Buildings. Every day, our three negotiators, Brendan Howlin, Ruairi Quinn, and Mervyn Taylor would meet their counterparts, Bertie Ahern, Noel Dempsey, and Brian Cowen. Generally speaking, issues would be put on the table by our side, and Fianna Fáil would organise responses. These would then, when they had been hammered out by the politicians, be passed to the drafters downstairs.

The drafters were Greg Sparks and myself on the Labour side (frequently helped by David Grafton), and Martin Mansergh, principally, on the Fianna Fáil side. Occasionally, we would get together to hammer out a point, and in the end, Martin and I worked on the language of the document for several days. The economic scenario underpinning the agreement involved Greg and William locking themselves away for a couple of days to hammer out sufficiently flexible language.

But in the main, we operated through reams of paper. Within days, we discovered that we were actually negotiating with the civil service. Although we never met a civil servant, the members of the Fianna Fáil team were all still government Ministers. Every time we would put forward a sentence or an idea, back would come position papers which had all the hallmarks of having been prepared in government Departments. There was little or no sign, apart from one or two issues, of any personal input from the Fianna Fáil members of the government.

It was that fact, more than any other, that made for long and tedious negotiations. Greg and I found it immensely frustrating to be negotiating for change, against a highly gifted and talented organisation that was totally rooted in the status quo. I had seen it before, but more than once, Greg exploded at the fact that the civil service could give you forty pages overnight on why something shouldn't be done, but found it impossible to help you to do it, even after it had been agreed at political level.

It seemed to suit the Fianna Fáil Ministers to let it run that way. I had no doubt that if they wanted to, they could put their feet down and force the civil servants into a different gear. But they preferred, instead, to put us through our paces. Gradually, it dawned on us that this was the Fianna Fáil way. They simply didn't believe, in normal circumstances, in second-guessing civil service advice.

For generations, they had allowed the civil service to make the basic decisions, while they dealt with the political impact of decisions. This process of change was as much a challenge to their culture as it was to our patience.

It convinced us that drafting an agreement was one thing, implementing it would be another. I began work on a separate document, to be discussed between Dick and Albert Reynolds, about the implementation mechanisms that would be necessary.

It was into the middle of this work that Des O'Malley dropped his bombshell. At a private meeting with Dick on January 5th, he told him that he had evidence that privileged documents, prepared by his Beef Tribunal legal team, had been delivered to Fianna Fáil headquarters. What was more, this information had come to O'Malley because one of the state's lawyers, Gerry Danaher, had boasted about it to one of O'Malley's lawyers, Diarmuid McGuinness.

Dick Spring knew implicitly that if such a conversation had been reported by Diarmuid McGuinness, then it had happened. McGuinness, although a lawyer for O'Malley, was a member of the Labour Party, and had actually worked closely with Dick during the New Ireland Forum in the mid-1980s. He was a friend of Dick's, and a totally honourable and professional lawyer.

Dick was staggered by this revelation. As a lawyer, he knew how serious it was for papers of this kind to be allowed to fall into improper hands. As a politician, he knew what would happen if the media and the Dáil came to believe that anyone in government had been involved in espionage or sabotage in relation to O'Malley's legal position at the Beef Tribunal.

But what to do? O'Malley had told Dick, at the end of their conversation, that he would be making an oblique reference to the incident in the Dáil that afternoon. It was clearly meant as a warning that Des O'Malley was now watching Dick Spring. But the information, although Dick had no doubt about its truth, was entirely third hand—hardly a basis for scuttling negotiations on the formation of a government.

We thought initially about ringing Diarmuid McGuinness to try to get his account of the story, but realised that that would place him in an entirely invidious position. He couldn't, ethically, talk to Dick about his dealings with Des O'Malley without O'Malley's permission.

One of the curiosities about the story, as told to Dick, was that the conversation between the two lawyers had taken place on Christmas Eve, yet O'Malley had not come to Dick about it until January 5th, two weeks later and just as the negotiations were coming to a conclusion. Why the delay? Was it possible that O'Malley had decided to wait until we were further advanced in our negotiations?

Whatever O'Malley's motivation, Dick decided that he was not going to have references made to the matter in the Dáil before he took action. He consulted the only two lawyers around, John Rogers and Mervyn Taylor, and their advice was unanimous. He should take the story immediately to Albert Reynolds, and demand a thorough investigation.

Dick went to see Albert, who told him he was shocked at the discovery. Together, they decided to ask the Attorney General and the Garda Commissioner to investigate the matter fully.

Naturally, the story broke within hours, and there was quite a controversy. O'Malley was somewhat crestfallen to discover that an investigation was underway even before he referred to the matter in the Dáil—it was clear he hadn't expected Dick to react quite so fast.

As a controversy, the story ran for a while, and ended up with Danaher being slapped on the wrist by the Bar Council. Dick's speed in initiating an investigation before the allegations became public ensured that no mud stuck to him.

It had one sequel that made me wonder. About a day after the allegations were reported, I met Seán Duignan on his way to the political correspondents' room. He showed me a statement he was carrying from the Attorney General. It said simply that the Attorney had investigated the matter fully, and was satisfied that no wrongdoing had occurred.

It was clear from the way Seán answered my questions that the Attorney had not interviewed all the participants involved in the controversy, but had spoken only to the state's legal team. I told Seán that I felt that was no way to conduct an investigation, and if that was how things were, he'd land us in trouble sooner or later.

Within a couple more days, the agreed government programme was finished. I believed strongly, as I still do, that it was an agreement to be proud of. There was a huge Labour input, not alone in terms of policy but in also in terms of initiative, negotiating, and language. It was also fresh, and easy to read. In overall terms, if implemented it would change the policy direction of the previous five years radically, from a conservative and tight-fisted approach to a definite social democratic one. But it couldn't be challenged on the grounds of recklessness either. Between the parties we had struck a very good balance on the critical issue of fiscal responsibility.

The document was quite vague on the subject of Northern Ireland. I had a long discussion with Martin Mansergh in the course of the negotiations, and while he was giving nothing away, he spoke strongly about the need for a flexible approach. When I consulted Dick, he told me to go along with the language, and that I would be fully briefed on all its hidden meanings in due course.

Martin had also written a peroration at the end of the document, which was sent to me for discussion. I rang Martin and told him that I didn't want to change a word of it, except to suggest that the last sentence be separated out to stand on its own. It read, as far as I remember, "In all that we do, we will try to reflect the spirit of the Irish people at its best". After my initial doubts, I believed by now that we had a real chance to make a huge difference.

I was particularly proud of a few specifics in the agreement. First, the language of partnership, which was radically different from everything that had gone before. That section of the agreement was one in which the civil service had no input that I'm aware of, and it was strong and clear. It fully reflected the breakthrough that we'd made, and can't have been all that easy for Fianna Fáil to swallow.

Second, there was a written guarantee that Irish neutrality would not be changed without a specific referendum.

When this issue was raised in the negotiations, the Department of Foreign Affairs had supplied the Fianna Fáil negotiators with documentation that, although carefully written, made it clear they were horrified at the proposal. We had had a long struggle to get the language we wanted, and made many a comment about the faceless bureaucrats in Iveagh House—comments that I hoped hadn't been repeated back when I met most of them later! The Department did strongly welcome specific commitments we insisted on in relation to aid to the developing world, designed to change some of the most shameful policy cuts of previous years.

Third, there was strong language under the heading of disability, a subject in which I have had a life-long interest. We had made financial commitments in this area in the course of the election campaign, and I was disappointed when we couldn't get Fianna Fáil agreement to put a hard-and-fast figure for investment into the final document.

But we had also advocated a Department of Disability in our manifesto, and in the discussions about cabinet formation between Dick and the Taoiseach, that had been broadened into a Department of Equality and Law Reform, with an understanding that it was to be a Labour Ministry.

Fourth, we had a new section in the agreement, under the general heading of "Strengthening our Democracy". It contained a number of radical proposals for reforming the institutions and for cleaning up what were widely perceived to be defects in the system—the sort of defects that had allowed a golden circle to flourish.

In respect of one issue under this heading, we ran into a brick wall. It was one of the few policy areas that had to be referred upwards to be discussed by Dick and the Taoiseach, because the Fianna Fáil negotiators had no room to manoeuvre. That was the idea of a Freedom of Information Act, to which the Fianna Fáil side (and their civil service advisers) were implacably opposed. We settled in the end for a written commitment to examine the need for legislation. It was to be a couple of years before Albert Reynolds decided there was indeed a need.

The other main policy area that was left to the two principals was the Beef Tribunal. It was clear that the Tribunal would report at some time during the administration of this new government, and there was no knowing what it would say. I believed—wrongly as it turned out—that the contents of that final report would be the most difficult issue we would have to deal with. Dick shared that view, and secured an agreement from the Taoiseach, to be written into the overall document, that the government would accept the report and honour all its recommendations and implications. We thought we were lighting a fuse—but we had no idea what was at the end of it.

Throughout all the negotiations, Dick never publicly dropped the idea of a rotating Taoiseach. None of the commentators believed it was possible to secure, and Fine Gael in all their statements jeered at Dick for abandoning it—even though they had indicated total unwillingness to entertain the idea themselves.

The reason Dick refused to publicly acknowledge defeat on the issue was simple—he was determined to secure the largest Labour presence ever seen in an Irish government. We had thirty-three deputies out of a potential government strength of 101. When it came to the division of cabinet seats, that gave us an mathematical entitlement to 4.9 seats, as compared to Fianna Fáil's 10.1. Dick had served in government before, and he believed passionately that a 2:1 ratio would give Fianna Fáil an immediate psychological advantage in relation to decision-making. Although it was widely assumed that we would end up with five seats to their ten, Dick was determined to go at least one better. For that reason, he mentioned the rotating Taoiseach to Albert Reynolds every time the subject came up.

From the outside, that sort of argument can seem like a row about perks and trappings. It was nothing of the kind. We went into those negotiations with a different attitude about power to the attitude we had previously—we were hell-bent on effecting real and lasting change.

Some months before the election, I was having lunch in Bewley's in Grafton Street with William Scally and Brendan Lynch. Brendan is an economist, with extraordinary insights and a lot of conviction. He wouldn't always be a person you would turn to for political advice, but I've never known his economic forecasts or judgements to be wide of the mark. He made a remark at that lunch that stuck in my mind, and was to have a major influence on how we set out to approach the next four years.

We were talking about power, and how it could be used to make lasting change. Brendan pointed out that in the past, Labour had always gone for Ministries that enabled politicians to be busy with projects. The net effect was that Labour always found itself in government, at worst in a defensive mode because it went for spending Departments; at best in a busy but dependent mode—waiting for the people who really handled the levers of power to deliver the resources for their projects.

This time, if we were going to effect lasting change, we had to have our hands on the levers. That meant a number of things. We had to be strong and cohesive in the cabinet room, a team with enough players to cover every subject. We had to look at the Ministries where the change would come from, and not settle just for the "caring" Ministries we had always gone for.

We had to be part of the economic engine of the government as well as the social engine.

That raised the issue of the Department of Finance. It was clear from the outset of Dick's discussions with Albert Reynolds that we could have Finance, or Foreign Affairs, but not both. There have been many who have argued ever since that Dick should have chosen Finance, and there is a lot of justice in the argument.

He felt himself that he would not have made a good Minister for Finance—he has always struggled with economics—and he was absolutely convinced that it was essential, for reasons he wasn't able to explain to us at the time, that Labour would have a major input into Northern Ireland policy. Had he taken Finance, which he could have, his involvement in Northern Ireland would always have been at second-hand. So we compromised, and Dick decided to seek a Junior Minister in Finance who would have a strong role in economic policy.

I had been pushing for some time to try to inject some new imagination into government, through a reform of government Departments and the creation of some new portfolios. I claim credit for essentially designing three new government Departments—Equality, Arts, and Enterprise and Employment. I strongly believed that these could be seen as new engines for change, and would give us access to areas that would enable political creativity to flourish. The Department of Enterprise and Employment would also give us a major economic input.

The other area where lasting change is not only possible but essential—the area of greatest investment in the future—is Education. If I ever had the opportunity to be a member of an Irish government, I would want to be Minister for Education, and I was determined that we would appoint the first Labour Minister for Education in the history of the state. When I raised the subject with Dick, I was surprised to discover that not only had he already discussed it with the Taoiseach, but Albert Reynolds had agreed.

In general, it didn't appear that the Taoiseach was unduly bothered about which portfolio we got, once the total number was agreed. He couldn't deliver the combination of Finance and Foreign Affairs, and there was considerable resistance from within his own Department to the creation of a Department of Arts and Culture. He did admit to Dick that he didn't personally care too much about the subject, but it had been a preserve of the Taoiseach's Department ever since Charlie's day. Charlie had always seen himself as Ireland's foremost patron of the arts, and gathered all the institutions under his own aegis, the better to operate like a latter-day Medici. It led eventually to some frank exchanges, at the end of which Albert surrendered his status as a renaissance man.

The final element of the deal was agreement on mechanisms for implementation. Originally, the system I had designed provided for each Minister to have a European-style *Chef de Cabinet*—but to our surprise, there was immediate opposition from the Cabinet Office. It transpired that the relevant civil servants felt threatened by the title.

Eventually, it was agreed that each Minister would have a Programme Manager, with the specific task of monitoring the implementation of the agreement as far as their Department was concerned. The Programme Manager assigned to the Taoiseach would chair weekly meetings, at which progress on all legislation and other commitments would be systematically reviewed.

Dick Spring had served as Tánaiste before, and had discovered that the job of Tánaiste in a multi-party government, to be done right, requires a massive overview. The leader of the minority party has to be in command of his own brief, but also has to understand what's going on in every other Department before decisions come to be made at the cabinet table. In many ways, he or she must have the same breadth of understanding as the Taoiseach—but the Taoiseach has a hundred or more civil servants to help him do his job.

So it was agreed to establish an Office of the Tánaiste, with a small group of civil servants to carry out specific functions, notably to take responsibility for the initiatives in the "broadening democracy" section of the new government programme. There would also be a legal adviser and a policy adviser, and the Programme Manager would operate out of the office too.

We were assigned a number of rooms on the second floor of the Taoiseach's Department to accommodate the Office. In later years, the legend grew that the Office of the Tánaiste was housed in some mythical and utterly luxurious building somewhere in Dublin. We often wished it were so!

And so, finally, the deal was done. And not before time— storm clouds were beginning to gather, both inside and outside the party.

One of my jobs during the negotiations was to give regular briefings to the political correspondents about progress. My instructions were to keep them fully informed, but not to break any confidences! As a result, some of the sessions in the pol. corrs'. room were testy affairs. It became almost an anti-news story to be reporting that "negotiations continued today". Most evenings, I was pressed for something that helped the story along, and tried to oblige.

The one area where I couldn't help them, but it came up most days, was the identity of the likely Labour Ministers. There were two reasons I wasn't able to help them. First, Dick would have killed me if I floated names before he was ready. And more to the point, because he didn't make up his mind until the end, I didn't know the names anyway. Any guesses I'd make would be no more than that.

One name that was regularly floated was that of Jim Kemmy. It was logical, because he was the party chairman, and was something of an icon for the left. It was, I think, conceived by journalists analysing possibilities and probabilities, and quickly developed by the well-oiled Leinster House rumour machine. Jim Kemmy, however, believed that I had floated his name, even though that was untrue. The name of Jim Kemmy, and others, just added to the intrigue surrounding the end of the negotiations.

I was to discover afterwards that Jim Kemmy desperately wanted to become a Minister. When his name appeared in print and on the airwaves, he thought that he had secured a job, and never approached Dick to make a case for himself. I don't know whether Dick would have changed his mind about the team he had put together if Kemmy had approached him.

The bottom line was that Jim came to believe that I had put his name about as part of a Machiavellian plot to undermine his candidacy, and he never forgave me for it. It contributed too to a frosty relationship between him and Dick Spring that lasted a long time. While it never undermined Jim Kemmy's loyalty to the party, it gave him occasional pleasure to be slightly mischievous over the following difficult years.

In the world outside the negotiations, big trouble was brewing over the state of the currency. Although most of the trouble was well outside Ireland's control, and had been going on since Britain's "Black September" some months previously, pressure on the punt mounted disastrously over Christmas and in the first few days of 1993, after the ending of exchange controls. It was essentially a European problem, but commentators naturally singled out the absence of a government as part of the reason for the increases in interest rates that began to drive up mortgage costs in the early part of the year.

This was the beginning of the media onslaught that didn't let up for another four years. It was irresponsible, particularly of the Labour Party, to be holding up the formation of a government in the face of the currency crisis. What were we doing, after all, except playing around with silly ideological premises and holding out for the spoils of office? It was suddenly long past time that the Labour Party did its duty and put a government together.

Dick recognised the signs, as did I. The "media" was doing it again. Everything we did in opposition had been fully supported by the commentators and the experts. But Labour fighting for implementation of policy, instead of recognising its natural place as a mudguard for some other, bigger party, simply wasn't acceptable.

And now, too, the media was waking up to the fact that Fianna Fáil and Albert Reynolds were going to remain in government, with our support. It wasn't what they had supported us for, and they were realising that they didn't like it.

Around this time, I spoke to a senior person in the *Irish Times*, and asked why there was so little understanding about what we were trying to achieve. I believed that the policy direction we were outlining for the next few years was momentous, and I couldn't understand why it was being judged only on the narrow criteria of who our partners were.

"You have to understand," I was told. "We regard the Labour Party like the daughter to whom we've given every advantage. We've put you through the best finishing school, we've taught you etiquette and decorum and how to entertain our visitors in the parlour. And now you've gone and married the boy from the wrong side of town, when there were some nice polite boys from good schools to choose from!"

It was because we saw it coming that Dick warned the party, when it gathered to debate the programme in the National Concert Hall, that there would be no honeymoon for this government. Pat Magner said to me after that conference that, in fact, this was a very modern marriage. The screwing would come before the honeymoon!

But the conference, for the first time in the party's history, endorsed the proposition to go into government with Fianna Fáil almost unanimously. The motion was moved by Dick, and seconded, at Dick's request, by Emmet. One or two delegates spoke against—one, from Carlow/Kilkenny, warning that if you lay down with dogs, you'd get up with fleas. Overall, the mood was one of keen anticipation.

On the way out of the hall afterwards, Dick turned to me and said, "That's answered something I've always wondered about. The party isn't full of anti-coalitionists after all. They were just anti-Fine Gael all along!"

That night he began to finalise decisions about cabinet members and staff. Some of the staff choices were immediate— he had always depended on William Scally, and there was never any question that anyone else could serve as his senior policy adviser. Sally Clarke has always been indispensable to him too, and she moved from Leinster House to be Dick's personal assistant in Government Buildings. He asked me to think about the other positions—and it was implicit that I could have whatever post I wanted.

When I thought about it, I realised I didn't want any of the jobs that were available. There was a general assumption in the media that I would become deputy Government Press Secretary. But I had done that job before, from 1983-1987, and I was convinced that too partisan an approach to the job was potentially damaging. I strongly believed that we should look for a professional journalist, someone likely to be respected by his peers and trusted by his new political colleagues.

Then there was the post of Programme Manager. Again I was fairly sure that that was a job that needed a systematic, managerial approach. I am good at meeting deadlines, and good at getting a job done, provided I do it myself. The skills of delegation, direction and organisation have always eluded me. We needed someone who had those skills in abundance.

Where the first job was concerned, I recommended John Foley. John was a senior political journalist with the *Irish Independent*, highly respected on all sides of Dáil Eireann for his thoroughness and professionalism. He had a reputation for fairness, although no-one would ever describe him as sycophantic. He just called it as he saw it, straight as an arrow.

Dick was delighted, and authorised me to approach John. John, on the other hand, was totally shocked, especially when I told him about the seven days a week and the sixteen hours a day. It's tough being a journalist, coping with four-day weeks and six weeks holiday a year. It's not an easy transition to politics.

But he was also intrigued—John had been reporting politics for a good many years, and now here was an unparalleled opportunity to see it from the inside. I knew immediately that he would accept the offer.

As Programme Manager I approached Greg Sparks, again with Dick's enthusiastic approval. I had first met Greg in the mid-1980s, at a time when I was anxiously seeking the job of General Secretary of the party, against Ray Kavanagh and Bernard Browne.

Greg approached Dick and me at a function, and told Dick very firmly that Ray Kavanagh was the obvious man for the job. Then he went scarlet when Dick introduced me to him!

If our relationship didn't get off to the best possible start, I was impressed when Greg was one of the first people (and one of the very few) to offer to help Dick, in a voluntary capacity, immediately after the 1987 election, at a time when we were at our lowest ebb.

From that moment on, he applied his considerable energy to every task he undertook—and he took a few risks as well, especially when he offered to be one of the people who guaranteed the finances of the Robinson campaign. He had also built a successful professional practice as an accountant, and was clearly someone of high management calibre.

Finbarr O'Malley was the obvious choice as Dick's legal adviser. A razor-sharp mind hidden behind a diffident and sometimes sardonic personality, Finbarr had unlimited talent as a draughtsman. He had designed a number of pieces of legislation for us in opposition, and was to go on to be a major contributor to the ethics legislation and the freedom of information legislation that we enacted.

When I presented my recommendations to Dick, he said, "they're all great—but what are you going to do?"

I told him that I knew that something was happening in relation to Northern Ireland, and I wanted to be involved in it. So it was agreed that I would go to work with the faceless bureaucrats in Iveagh House about whom I had been so scornful.

That was my contribution—Dick's was a lot more difficult. He had had very little choice about his cabinet colleagues in his first government—people had largely selected themselves on the basis of seniority. This time, he was determined to pick a team—people who would be loyal and who would deliver. Above all people who would work together, and stick together through thick and thin.

It's often been said since that he picked people from both wings of the party to try to neutralise the left. While that was part of his motivation, I believe he actually approached the job as if he were back as captain of a football team, picking people for positions, trying to find horses for courses.

Mervyn was surprised to be approached. He had acted as one of our negotiators at Dick's request, but he believed that his time to serve in government was over. He was taken aback to be asked to build a Department from scratch, but went on to develop a genuinely historic record.

If Mervyn was surprised, Michael D Higgins and Niamh Bhreathnach were astonished. Secretly, I think they were both equally surprised—and Michael D was disappointed—that the portfolios they were offered weren't reversed. But both accepted with alacrity and commitment.

Brendan was the one who took the most persuading. He didn't want to be Minister for Health, a portfolio that he had shadowed with considerable distinction for four years. Dick had to tell him there was no option, but he was the most reluctant Minister.

Not so Ruairi, who was thrilled with the challenge of Enterprise and Employment. He had always wanted a big economic Ministry, and now he was in charge of one of the largest Departments of state, in terms of its scope, that there was.

I think Dick found the Junior Ministries much harder to fill—because there was more disappointment involved for those who didn't get the call. People like Liam Kavanagh, Seamus Pattison, and Michael Ferris had stuck by Dick through thick and thin, and they found being overlooked very hard. Some were very bitter for a long time afterwards—others took it as a necessary part of politics that close friendship didn't guarantee promotion.

Some were even disappointed at being elevated. Eithne FitzGerald and Joan Burton had both performed well in the election—Eithne spectacularly so—and looked forward to senior positions with some anticipation. Both were chagrined to discover that they would be occupying Junior Ministries only, although both went on to do outstanding jobs.

The real surprise packet was Emmet Stagg. The man who had been a thorn in Dick's side since the day he was elected never expected to be part of his team. We even thought that he might refuse an offer. But he didn't. As we walked back down the corridor after his meeting with Dick, the new Minister for Housing turned to me.

"You know," he said, "if the shoe had been on the other foot, I don't think I'd have given Dick a job. I guess that makes him a bigger man than me."

That was a proposition that would be tested soon enough.

11

Partnership at Work

There's something to be said for being a government adviser, when you're tucked up in bed in a luxurious suite, and Edward Scheverdnadze is sleeping two doors away.

When Foreign Affairs told me we'd be staying in a guesthouse in Bonn, as guests of the German government, it didn't sound too promising. But Petersburg is no ordinary guesthouse. It is the German government's residence for distinguished visitors—staffed all year round whether it's full or empty.

Ireland's foreign policy is run and administered by a total of about a thousand public servants, scattered all over the world. The Department of Foreign Affairs accounts for about half of one per cent of government expenditure.

On the other hand, a thousand people are employed by the *protocol* section alone of the German foreign service. They spend more on hospitality than we spend on the total implementation of policy. So when you land in Germany as a guest of the government, you are pampered every inch of the way. There were six of us—Dick Spring and five civil servants, and when we landed in Bonn, there were six BMWs, each with a driver and protocol officer, to greet us. We were driven directly to Petersburg, which is an enormous villa on one of the hills overlooking the city, and each of us was ushered to a palatial suite for the night.

The only other guests were Edward Scheverdnadze and his wife, who were enjoying a short holiday at the German government's expense. We, on the other hand, were there to do business. Dick was having his first meeting with Klaus Kinkel, the German Foreign Minister. We were approaching the moment of final decision in relation to Albert Reynolds' £8 billion pounds, and it was already clear that not every member of the European Commission agreed with Albert's calculations.

But at least we were doing it in style. I remember lying in bed that night, after finishing off the rather pleasant German white wine that had been thoughtfully left beside my bed, and thinking back to some other nights that weren't perhaps quite so glamorous.

Like the time in the mid-1980s when Pat Magner, William Scally, John Rogers and I went down to Tralee for a meeting with Dick in the middle of some crisis or other. Dick had arranged rooms for us in a hotel just outside the town—but they had forgotten to tell him that even though they would let us have the rooms, the hotel had been closed all winter.

We were each assigned a huge, freezing room. After we had hung our clothes in the reeking wardrobes, we went in search of something to eat, only to discover that there was no dining room, no kitchen, and no service. And no bar either. About eleven o'clock, we drove into Tralee in search of something to eat, and although I deny it to this day, my colleagues tell me that I advised them in favour of a particular chipper—an up-market place, I assured them, that even served coleslaw!

There's no doubt—times change when you're in government. But not always that much. It began, a few months before Petersburg, in a way that was startlingly familiar.

"We're going to meet the men who gave us fourteen good reasons last week why the punt shouldn't be devalued," Dick announced. "They want to give us the eighteen good reasons why it has to be devalued now."

We were at the first meeting of the Labour Ministers. It was a Wednesday morning at nine o'clock—and it was to be the start of a pattern that never wavered for the next four years. Every day the cabinet met, no matter what the weather or the circumstances, the six Labour Ministers would meet in Dick's room in Leinster House. They were joined each week by Eithne FitzGerald, and by William, Greg, John Foley and myself. Over the years, the only change in that routine would be if there was a crisis—then, sometimes, the meetings would happen at eight o'clock, and because Leinster House wasn't open at that hour, they would be transferred to Iveagh House.

Each meeting would begin by discussing the cabinet agenda. Greg would report on the meeting of Labour advisers and Programme Managers that had taken place the previous evening at four-thirty—another part of the unwavering pattern—and would highlight any areas of the agenda that we thought were likely to cause difficulty. We would normally spend half of each of those meetings discussing non-agenda items of particular importance, so that there was a range of views feeding into the Ministers.

From the very beginning, the agenda was crowded. It's the first rule of government that the management of events can fill the entire day, to the exclusion of everything else. We were determined to avoid that—to ensure that while every event and crisis was dealt with, there would also be room for initiative.

Almost the first thing that Greg did, when he started work, was break down the programme for government into its component parts, item by item and Department by Department.

With his colleague and chairman, Donogh Morgan in the Taoiseach's Department, they devised a reporting system that enabled weekly monitoring of the programme to be put in place. And each week, meetings of the Programme Managers across the system of government kept the pressure on for change and reform.

Inevitably, though, events tended to dominate our Wednesday morning agendas. The Celtic Tiger was hiding somewhere beyond the horizon when we went into government—in fact we arrived in time to put a tough and unpopular budget in place. And the Taoiseach and Tánaiste, together with the Minister for Finance, had to deal with difficult decisions on devaluing the punt within days of coming to office.

As I said, there was a strong sense of déja vu about it, where Dick was concerned. He had only been Tánaiste for a few days ten years earlier when identical decisions had to be taken. This time, however, he had a good deal more confidence when it came to dealing with the mandarins involved—and it showed in the questioning.

The meeting between the Ministers and the mandarins lasted a couple of hours, and the Ministers enjoyed putting the senior public servants through their paces—getting them to explain why all the reasons against devaluation were now no longer operable, and why the policy they had strenuously opposed a week before had now become essential.

In the end, Dick asked, "So you're telling us that this is entirely unavoidable and the only course of action?"

"Yes," he was told. "If we don't do this now, it will create huge economic, monetary, and fiscal problems."

"And what if it doesn't work?" he asked.

After a moment's silence, the answer came back.

"Then, Tánaiste, we will have a political problem!"

(Once, in opposition, I had prepared a script for Brendan Howlin, who was impatiently waiting for it in the Dáil chamber. I asked Michael Ferris if he would deliver it to him in a folder—but when Brendan opened it, all he found was the slip of paper I had inserted, with the single line "you're on your own, you bastard!" written on it. Because it was a joke, Michael had the real script in his pocket. But mandarins have more subtle ways of telling politicians they're on their own!)

The first couple of weeks in government fulfilled Dick's promise to the delegates in the National Concert Hall—there was no honeymoon. Oddly enough, though, the series of long meetings that were necessary to finalise the budget and deal with the devaluation served as a bonding agent for the government as a whole. Even though we were immediately taking flak, there was a feeling of being up and at it.

If that was true in government, it was a good deal less true in the parliamentary party. Looking back on it later, I realised that we had made one fundamental mistake. Everyone who had been involved in building up the party and in forming the government had gone off to work for the government. The parliamentary party, many of them brand new Deputies, had been left to fend for themselves. It took several weeks to sort out office space and proper facilities, and in the interim, a feeling of alienation began to grow.

Ita McAuliffe, who has worked as the administrator of the PLP for a number of years, and is one of the most efficient and loyal people I know, told me afterwards that those were some of the worst weeks of her career. She handled the transition magnificently, but that didn't stop a number of the TDs from feeling that we were having a great time, and they didn't matter. Added to the disgruntlement that some were feeling about being passed over for promotion, it generated communication difficulties that in some cases lasted throughout the entire period of government.

Some of them actually began to crow a bit when we landed ourselves in trouble over the cost of Programme Managers, advisers and other staff. That was predictable—but none of us knew how long it would last, nor how vicious a good deal of the media reaction would be.

It was Geraldine Kennedy of the *Irish Times* who started it— not for any vindictive reason, but because, on a quiet news day, she had gathered up the answers to a series of parliamentary questions, and totted up the cost of the new staff. It was expensive—more than half a million pounds a year—and even though it was almost an entirely policy-oriented group of people, it caused a massive outcry.

What did the most damage were a number of staff who were, in fact, very badly paid—Niamh Bhreathnach's daughter, Dick Spring's sister, and Emmet Stagg's cousin.

Cliona Ferris, Niamh's daughter, had worked for her mother for a number of years in a totally unpaid capacity. When Niamh became a TD she employed Cliona as her secretary—something hundreds of TDs had done before her. A few days later, Niamh was a Minister, and Cliona was automatically moved on to the Department of Education's payroll, at the bottom of the secretarial assistant's pay scale. She was hard working, bright, and totally dedicated to her mother's constituents. Yet her name began to appear in newspapers as if her appointment was the ultimate in nepotism.

In some ways, it was worse for Maeve, Dick's sister. Maeve has provided an indispensable service to the people of North Kerry for as long as Dick has been a TD, as his constituency secretary. It was widely, if not universally, known by the media. But when it was reported in the newspapers first, after Dick became Tánaiste, her married name was used. That was simply because the civil servant who had compiled the parliamentary answer had used the name on Maeve's payslip. But it looked as if we were trying to hide her, by using her married name as a subterfuge. It was a silly mistake, but it added to the air of sleaze that some in the media were beginning to develop.

Emmet, as a Junior Minister, was entitled to employ two civilian drivers, as every other Junior Minister was. One of them was an unemployed relative, who had also worked for him in a voluntary capacity in opposition—the sort of person it is difficult to overlook when you are in a position to give out a job. Mind you, Emmet did his—or our—cause no good with his aggressive answers to some of the questions raised about the appointment.

The storm that broke over our heads about these appointments shook all of us. In the course of one discussion about what we should do, Niamh offered to resign her portfolio—she would rather do that, she said, than subject her daughter to any more of the harassment she had been receiving. Cliona was young, and earning £200 a week, but the newspapers were full of snide references to her as if she were milking the system for all it was worth.

Dick was furious and wouldn't countenance talk of resignation, although it was clear that the references to his own family hurt deeply. Maeve was highly respected, and a model public servant—albeit an unestablished public servant, with no security or promotion rights—and the treatment of herself and Cliona by some in the media went far beyond anything that was fair or reasonable.

The controversy eventually simmered down, although it never went away. In fact, controversy of a similar kind flared up later in the year, when Dick stayed in the Waldorf Astoria Hotel in New York during his first visit to the United Nations.

The hotel was chosen by the Department, essentially because it would put Dick in the same hotel as President Clinton and we were anxious to have an opportunity to meet him.

But someone close to Fitzpatrick's Hotel in New York rang the Irish newspapers and sold them a line that an Irish hotel wasn't good enough for Dick Spring. After an exhilarating and exhausting week in New York, where Dick met (and impressed) an astonishing array of people, we arrived home to find that he was now accused of arrogance and self-indulgence for staying in New York's most luxurious hotel. The image of Dick as a jet-setter was firmly established, and would be replenished every now and again by stories about the use of the government jet.

It was all extraordinarily unfair. The most striking feature about Dick, to those who have worked for him, is that he doesn't give a damn about his surroundings. The only demand I ever heard him make in respect of furniture was for a harder chair, because he can't sit comfortably in a soft one!

When he arrives in his office, he starts working out of his briefcase, and he doesn't stop until he's finished. He could be in a shed or a palace—it wouldn't make a huge difference.

But that didn't matter—the Labour Party has always been painted as being in love with the trappings of office, and here was more evidence. It was to hang around our necks for four years.

There was a deeper point to it as well—a fairer point that should have sunk in before the controversies started. But it didn't. It took the tax amnesty to bring that more fundamental point home to us—that we had to practice what we preached.

To this day, I can't put my hand on my heart and say that I know where the tax amnesty came from. It didn't surface in our negotiations, and it wasn't part of the budget discussions. What I do know for sure about it was that it was opposed by the Department of Finance and its Minister Bertie Ahern.

Most of the Ministers and their closest advisers were uneasy about the amnesty. It didn't feel right to be offering an inducement to tax evaders—especially large-scale tax evaders—to try and generate some revenue. Some, like Colm O Briain (who had gone to work for Michael D. Higgins) argued strenuously against it at our weekly meetings, on moral and ideological grounds. Others were more pragmatic.

The truth was that they were difficult times, in budgetary terms. Ministers with ambitious spending plans—and Ministers committed to implementing radical social policy changes—needed the money, and their eyes glistened each time they thought of a windfall, like the £200 million that the amnesty promised.

Two people argued consistently and strongly against the amnesty from the start. One was Bertie Ahern, the other was William Scally. At private meeting after private meeting, William pointed out what should have been obvious. In accepting the idea of a tax amnesty, we were cementing the contrast between the high moral tone of our politics before the election and a sudden drop in standards afterwards.

The furore caused by the employment of relatives was a spurious and unfair contrast—in truth there was no nepotism or corruption involved. But it had nevertheless created an impression. Whatever our motivation in agreeing to an amnesty for every sleazebag in the country—and we would undoubtedly be attracting hot money and possibly ill-gotten gains—we would be fatally undermining our credibility as a party of standards.

Dick agreed with William. But there was a complication. The one thing that had become clear, as the debate went on in government, was that the Taoiseach was strongly in favour of the amnesty. The Taoiseach and his Minister for Finance, both members of the same party, were on opposite sides of the argument. If Dick took sides with one of them, that would end the argument—whoever he sided with would win.

Dick decided not to take sides. He believed that the arguments put forward by Bertie Ahern had already got a majority in the cabinet, and there was no need to expend political capital on a confrontation with the Taoiseach. It would be infinitely better if the amnesty were quietly buried without any difference emerging, this early in the life of the government, between the partners.

On the day the cabinet was to make a decision on the amnesty, Greg Sparks reported to the meeting of Labour Ministers that, unusually, he had had a phone call at one in the morning from Bertie Ahern. Bertie was absolutely resolute, Greg reported, and determined to ensure that the amnesty didn't go through. He had wanted Greg to tell him that the Labour Ministers would support him, and Greg had done so.

Three hours later, the cabinet adopted the amnesty Bill. As far as I know, no arguments were put forward on behalf of the Department of Finance, and none of the Labour Ministers insisted on a point of principle. None of us knew what had happened. But the amnesty that the Minister for Finance opposed was put into effect a few weeks later by the Minister who opposed it.

What William had predicted came to pass. The Labour Party, in particular, was branded as having lost interest in the politics we used to practice. From that moment on, we were fair game for every critic who wanted to attack *our* standards. And we brought it on ourselves.

The evening the government adopted the amnesty, William wrote to Dick, tendering his resignation. Although I never saw the letter, Dick told me that he wasn't offering to leave, but actually resigning. Dick was distraught at the prospect—not because it would add to the public controversy, but because of his respect for William as someone of the deepest principle. He had misjudged the depth of William's feelings, just as we had all misjudged the extent to which whoever wanted the amnesty was prepared to exert pressure to get it.

It was no easy decision for William Scally either. He had given a lifetime's effort to the Labour Party, and had served a number of party leaders through thick and thin. It caused him intense pain to leave, and he wanted to do it quietly, without causing any trouble for the party. But he saw the tax amnesty as a fundamental betrayal of everything the party he had grown up with ought to stand for.

And more—it wasn't even necessary. We didn't need to raise money that way—all the signs were already present (at least to economic experts) that strong economic growth was around the corner. Nobody would have suffered in the end if we declined the thirty pieces of silver.

Dick was determined not to let him go. And in the end, William was persuaded to withdraw his resignation. But it was a bitter lesson. In future, if a core issue demanded it, both sides had to understand fully what was at stake. There could be no more shadow-boxing—if something was wrong, it was wrong.

At the end of the day, though, it has to be said that the tax amnesty did not sour relations between the parties. It made us wonder—wonder why anyone wanted it so badly. And it made us doubt ourselves and our judgement.

But there was precious little time for reflection, or to regroup and take stock of the situation. Almost as soon as the tax amnesty issue was resolved, in the most unsatisfactory way possible, another crisis blew up. And this was one where the Taoiseach's credibility was on the line, and the Tánaiste's job was to save it.

There had been some doubts about Albert's £8 billion in EU funds since the moment he had announced it, after the Edinburgh summit. At the press conference at the end of the summit, Albert had rounded on one journalist, John Downing of the *Irish Independent*, who knew his way around Brussels and had asked for a detailed breakdown of the figures.

But in the various trips we had made backwards and forwards to Brussels throughout the first half of the year, it had become clearer that the Commission had a much smaller figure than £8 billion in mind. And Albert wouldn't accept a penny less.

In Germany in June, Klaus Kinkel had promised to be helpful. But it was equally clear that he felt that £6 billion would represent a considerable victory for the Irish—as indeed it would have been had the hurdle not been set a lot higher the previous December.

Although the December summit had agreed to a doubling of Structural Funds in the overall, there had been no hard-and-fast agreement on how it would be shared. Spain, Portugal, and Greece were arguing strenuously that they had got a lot less than Ireland in the past, and therefore should get more now.

Our calculation of £8 billion was based on an assumption—not an agreement—that Ireland's slice of the larger cake would represent the same proportion. But others, with a better case than ours, had their eye on the cake too.

Dick had surprised the June Foreign Affairs Council—the monthly meeting of Foreign Ministers from each member state which made all the decisions (except those reserved for summits of Prime Ministers)—by exercising an effective veto on the implementation of the whole package until Ireland was satisfied. That in turn had led to threats by others that if Ireland didn't back off, more than one country could exercise a veto.

So there was a lot at stake when we set off for Brussels on July 20th—so much so that an RTE crew came to Dublin airport to film our departure. The word from Brussels was that Bruce Millan, the EU Commissioner in charge of Structural Funds, wasn't prepared to agree to a penny more than £6 billion. Ireland was going to have to capitulate.

Dick's officials were worried. They had done remarkable, even heroic work, in maintaining Ireland's case. But now it was down to political decision.

The team was led throughout those negotiations by Noel Fahey, the Department's assistant secretary in charge of economic policy, and Padraic McKernan, Ireland's Permanent Representative in Brussels. They were as different as chalk and cheese—Noel with a permanently worried air, always surrounded by reams of paper; and Padraic who created the impression almost of a conspirator, who would glide people into corners and emerge with another favour granted for his country.

But they were an incredible team—both men of powerful intellect and an unparalleled knowledge of the European institutions and their methods. They were assisted by David Cooney, another extraordinary young diplomat who went on to play a remarkable role in the peace process.

On this occasion, because of the high stakes, the team was augmented by a senior official from the Department of Finance, Michael Tutty, who had constructed a good deal of the mathematical calculations we were relying on. Paddy Teahon, the Secretary of the Department of the Taoiseach, joined us to keep a watching brief on behalf of his political boss, and also to twist any arms he could find (Paddy has an amazingly pleasant way of doing that). It couldn't get any more high-powered— even though we all felt that it wasn't really necessary for the Department of Finance to be riding shotgun on us.

It culminated in a long night of tough negotiation—and an incredible performance by Padraig Flynn, Ireland's unique Commissioner, who, immediately on our arrival, appointed himself as mediator between the Irish and the rest of Europe. It was the first time I ever saw him in action, and it was an unforgettable sight.

EU negotiations are like no other. Mostly you sit crowded together in a small room, the Minister and his entourage, without food, coffee, or even drinkable water, waiting for developments, while officials scurry backwards and forwards among the participants.

On this particular night, it was Pee Flynn who had given himself the job of scurrying, and it was us who had to sit and wait. Occasionally, action and decision would be called for— and then speed was crucial.

"D'ye know what rough trade is, lads?" was Flynn's opening gambit. "Because ye're in for a lot of it tonight!"

We had an idea what rough trade was—not something you'd normally associate with genteel negotiations over the share-out of structural funds. Dick Spring knew that it meant a relentless ganging up on the hapless Foreign Minister who was holding out against the rest, and he made his first crucial decision of the night, by asking Flynn to arrange for the other Ministers to gather in their meeting room upstairs.

I didn't go up for the impromptu speech he made to the other fourteen, but Noel Fahey did. When he came back down, they were all a bit tense. Dick had told his Ministerial colleagues, in no uncertain terms, that rough trade wasn't going to work. He would stay as long as necessary, and wasn't going to be either bent or broken. If they wanted the matter resolved, they knew what it would take.

When Dick left the room for a minute, Noel Fahey turned to me.

"Now I know what it's like to be lining out for a tough match with Spring as captain," he said. "And I'm glad I'm on our team."

That was around eleven o'clock. For the next six hours Dick Spring disappeared from time to time, as a relatively friendly sighting was made in the corridor, to catch people on a one-to-one basis and gradually build a base of support.

The rest of us sat, occasionally being given a new set of figures to work on, and a new vision of Pee Flynn in full flight.

In the late evening, Michael Tutty came to see Dick. He explained that he had an exam the following morning in Dublin, which would be one of the final stages in a masters degree. He wondered how the Tánaiste would feel if he made a dash to the airport to catch the last flight home.

"I wouldn't ask normally, Tánaiste," he said, "but it's clear that nothing is going to happen tonight, and I won't be needed to do any calculations."

Dick looked at him coolly, and asked what use the master's degree would be after Michael's transfer to Cavan. It was Michael's first exposure to Dick's sense of humour, and he nearly had to be picked off the floor. When he was reassured by Dick for the third time that it was only a joke, and that he could go home and sit the exam (which he subsequently passed with flying colours), I was left in charge of the calculator, to my horror.

Every now and again, Commissioner Flynn would make a grand entrance to our room, to give a progress report, always in the most flamboyant language possible. After one of his eruptions, and when he had swept out again, I heard one of our senior diplomats murmur, "I've lost him surely—I've lost the only playboy of the western world!"

In the course of the night, I gradually became familiar with hitherto alien concepts like mecu and becu. All the figures we had to use were in millions and billions of ECU in 1992 prices, and as the man with the calculator, it was my job to convert them into Irish pounds at current value. By the end of the night I knew the formula by heart.

Eventually Pee Flynn burst in again. He sat beside me and slapped me on the knee.

"Quick!" he said. "Quick! 9.2 becu—'92 prices. What is it? Quick!"

I was unnerved by the intensity of this apparition, as I suppose I was meant to be. But I still managed to tap the figures into the calculator, and after checking a few times, discovered that we had now got to £7.85 billion—as close to our target as made no difference. We all agreed.

"I'll tell you what you do now Dick," said Pee. "You ring Albert, and tell him it's our judgement that's the best we're going to do, and ask his permission to shake hands on it."

"I don't think so," Dick replied. "I'll ring Albert and tell him we've taken it as far as we can. But if I think it's a fair deal, I'm not going to be asking for permission to shake hands."

"Begob," said Pee, "I like your style!"

It was now five in the morning. After Dick rang the Taoiseach at home in Dublin, and told him what he was going to do, I was put on the phone to give him the exact figures.

It was the first time that I was exposed to Albert Reynolds' sharpness and alertness. It was five in the morning, and we had just been through one of the longest and roughest days I ever remember. I had been working with a set of figures all night, and he had just been woken from his bed in Dublin. At least, I assume he had been asleep—maybe he'd stayed up to wait for the call. As I was to discover later, he thought little of staying awake all night if necessary.

But he quizzed me backwards and forwards, asking me to recite the conversion formula that had been used, and apparently checking it against a formula he had developed himself, before pronouncing himself satisfied that at least the arithmetic was right. "Good man," he said, before going back to sleep the sleep of the just. You wouldn't think that this was a deal that might make or break his reputation.

The only thing left to do was to shake hands with Jacques Delors. Dick wanted a witness to the transaction—because there'd be nothing in writing. The Commissioner stepped forward.

"The Tánaiste may not be of My Party," he announced. "But he's Tánaiste of My Country. Commissioner Pee Flynn will be proud to be his witness."

Immediately, Joe Brosnan, the Commissioner's *Chef de Cabinet*, leaned forward and whispered urgently in his ear. Commissioner Flynn spoke again, his tone if anything more melodramatic than a moment previously.

"Commissioner Pee Flynn cannot do what he just said he would," he announced grandly, and as if we should have known what he was going to say. "The Commissioner has taken an oath that precludes him from bearing witness on behalf of a member state. Ye had better get yourselves another witness!"

And he swept out of the room, like Anew McMaster on a bad night.

Dick went and shook hands with Jacques Delors—witnessed by Paddy McKernan and Paddy Teahon—and the night of the £8 billion was over.

We were to get a fourchette—and its upper limit would be the £7.85 billion that was agreed. Fourchette, we all decided, was a two-pronged fork in French, and there was no doubt in our minds that we'd get the higher prong.

A couple of days later, when I was drafting something for the Tánaiste's speech to the Dáil about the occasion, I fell to wondering whether there was an English equivalent of the word fourchette. I looked it up in the dictionary, and there indeed it was (and is—page 465 of the Concise Oxford Dictionary, 1992 edition): "a thin fold of skin at the back of the vulva". I decided to leave it out of the Tánaiste's speech!

It taught me a lot, that night—about standing your ground, about how to build a base of solid support from nothing, about how to make a judgement call and act on it. They were the things Dick Spring did, and he never put a foot wrong. Albert Reynolds trusted him that night, and didn't interfere—but he was sharp, and totally in touch. These were two men who knew their objectives, who knew how to get there, and who respected each other's toughness and judgment. They were bound to make a great team, despite everything.

And they would need to, with some of the other things that were going on.

12

Peace Work

"We are very serious about this project ... we accept the
integrity of BAC's seriousness ... we have accepted
concepts which form no great part of our traditional
vocabulary ... what is required is a package which
creates a political dynamic for irreversible change and
whose objective is the exercise of the right to national
self-determination ... "

For the first time in my life, I was reading a private letter
written by the Provisional IRA to the Taoiseach, and it chilled
me to the bone. It was unsigned, ending merely with the Irish
word "críoch", but there was no doubt about its provenance. It
had been transmitted by a priest to a senior adviser, and it was
a response to first, tentative drafts of a Joint Government
Declaration which the IRA had seen.

There were things about the letter I didn't understand. What
did BAC mean, for instance? It was explained to me that BAC
was short for Baile Atha Cliath, and was the Provos' way of
referring to the Irish government.

But that wasn't what I found chilling. The letter was written
a couple of weeks after a bomb had ripped through the centre
of Warrington in England, injuring dozens of people and killing
a three-year old boy, Jonathan Ball. Another twelve-year old
boy, Tim Parry, had died on a life-support machine five days
later.

On the day Tim Parry had died, five Catholics had been
killed in Derry and Belfast in UDA shootings, bringing the
number killed in Northern Ireland to an average of more than
one a week since the start of the year. The murders, and
especially the murders of two little boys, had provoked an
enormous emotional reaction throughout Ireland.

It was a significant turning point in terms of the revulsion that people throughout Ireland felt, towards paramilitary violence and towards the IRA in particular. And in the middle of this, I was being invited to be part of a group that would work towards bringing them in from the cold.

I struggled with this concept for several days, as I think Dick had struggled before me. It flew in the face of everything we had done and said and believed about Northern Ireland throughout my involvement in politics. For years we had argued about the need to marginalise men of violence. The 1983-87 government had briefly considered internment as an option, and had made the political gesture—led by Dick—of instituting a boycott of elected Sinn Féin representatives.

Although he had taken a central part in the negotiations that led to the Anglo-Irish Agreement, Dick had argued, in 1988, for the suspension of the operation of the Maryfield secretariat because Unionists found it oppressive and threatening. He had been widely criticised for that stance at the time, but it was an idea that had been adopted later, and led to the involvement of Unionists in the abortive Brooke talks of the early 1990s.

In other words, our whole approach—in common with most members of the Dáil—had been centred on the notion of a strong constitutional centre with the capacity to exclude and marginalise paramilitaries. Over several sleepless nights, I had a crisis of conscience about what was now proposed as a major switch, both in strategy and, I believed, in principle.

And yet there was a logic to it that was inescapable. Twenty-five years of trying to marginalise men of violence had failed. We were no closer to peace at the end of a whole series of political initiatives, which had occupied the energies of successive governments, than we were at the start. People were still being killed, and there was no end to the killing in sight.

I came to the view, in the end, that the IRA could not be defeated. That meant one thing, to my mind—that it was only going to be possible to make peace with an undefeated IRA. If there was to be compromise, then hateful as it seemed, it had to be a compromise that would appear honourable to them. There had to be an effort that would see things from their perspective—not a "Brits out" campaign, but a new approach that would enable an appeal to be made to better instincts.

As I read the briefing papers I had been given, and thought about the issues involved, it began to seem to me that it was necessary to look more through the eyes of people who saw themselves as willing to *die* for Ireland, and resist the urge to attack them as people who were willing to *kill* for Ireland.

What did that make me? I've never, as far as I know, been a nationalist. I'm proud of my Irishness, and never wanted to live anywhere else but Ireland. But I've never been gripped by "the national question", nor had any interest in the unity of the country. When a leading loyalist said to me some months later that he was never going to give up any of his Britishness in order to make me feel more Irish, I was able to tell him honestly that I would feel less Irish, not more, if my love of my country had to be expressed in him giving up his.

So as far as I was concerned, this was never about unity. The process of 25 years, and the new process I was being invited into, was about stability and peace. I *was* convinced—and always have been—that an Ireland at peace would be a totally different place to live in and invest in. I believed strongly that if peace and stability could be achieved, it would unleash a new dynamic throughout the island. That—and above all the possibility that people would stop killing each other—would make any serious effort to approach the issue of peace worthwhile.

When I began to think of it in those terms, it made sense to me. I could no longer see any issue of principle in seeking to draw people in from the cold—especially if republican leaders wanted to arrive at political, rather than violent, ways of pursuing their aims. There was no issue of principle, provided government did not compromise fundamental democratic rules, or find itself telling lies.

And, in Dick's view, there was another bottom line. Both governments had to work together. He was determined that there should be no situation in which the Irish government would find itself taking sides with terrorism against the British government. That didn't mean that the British government always had to get their way—Dick believed that months of hard and tough bargaining lay ahead, and he had no illusions that the British approach to negotiation was always highly-principled and ethical.

But it was fundamental to him that a democratically elected government had to be dealt with openly and honestly. In the meantime, he believed that it would be necessary to prepare people for a change in direction—even though it would have to be done subtly. His first step was to emphasise how large a priority he attached to Northern Ireland, and why.

In Dick's party conference speech in Waterford, 80 days after he had become Foreign Minister, he read out a list of names. He read them simply, without introduction. It took a few minutes for the delegates to realise that these were people—ranging in age from 19 to 58—who had died violently in Northern Ireland.

A strange, almost eerie, silence fell over the hall as the list of names continued, and it was obvious that the reading had made more of an impact than any passionate rhetoric could have.

He then added the names of Jonathan Ball and Tim Parry, and mentioned Julie Statham—a young girl who had taken her own life in despair at the murder of her boyfriend—to bring the total dead in the first three months of the year to 27.

The list was a shocking one, the more so because people had forgotten all but the most recent names. It brought home the horror of the continuing situation to many delegates—including many who had become accustomed, and numbed, over the years to the endless recitation of violence.

Dick went on to tell the delegates that he had deliberately sought the job in Foreign Affairs in order to do what he could to bring that litany to an end. And he ended that section of his speech by declaring that he was prepared to sit down anytime, anywhere, with any politician or public representative who believed in exclusively democratic and political means to peace. From the reaction, there was little doubt that he had the unequivocal support of his own party.

Dick knew, when he was making that speech, that changes in Northern Ireland strategy had been developing for some time. We already knew, from the briefings we received, that the history of change went right back to the talks between the SDLP and Provisional Sinn Féin in 1988.

Those talks, which had essentially ended in failure, had nevertheless introduced key concepts to the language of nationalism—notably the notion of self-determination and how it might be expressed, and the idea that the British were neutral in relation to Northern Ireland. Neither concept was agreed, but a debate had begun.

The essential features of the debate were twofold. If the British were neutral, and seen to be neutral, then whatever historic justification may have existed for an armed struggle was no longer valid. If the Irish people chose to express their right to self-determination by accepting the principle of consent within Northern Ireland—by accepting that the future of Northern Ireland should be a matter for its people—who would have the right to gainsay that expression?

The debate had been renewed in October 1989 when two priests, Father Alec Reid and Father Raymond Murray, had taken it on themselves to write to John Hume, Gerry Adams and Charles Haughey. Their letter (written with the support of Cardinal O Fiaich) relied heavily on the idea that the Irish nation's right to self-determination could be expressed in a democratic strategy for political, social, and economic justice in Ireland.

Father Reid in particular carried out nearly two years of shuttle diplomacy between the principals involved, seeking to develop the idea of a democratic programme, supported by both governments. John Hume and Gerry Adams had begun meeting again in 1991, and after some time, Martin Mansergh had become involved. The work they were doing began to crystallise into a draft Joint Declaration.

This was the idea that Charlie Haughey discussed at a meeting with John Major on December 5th 1991—a couple of weeks after he had defeated the final vote of no confidence put forward by members of his party, and shortly before his past caught up with him.

The new Taoiseach, Albert Reynolds, had taken the issue up with John Major immediately on arriving in office. At a summit meeting in early February 1992, he persuaded Major to allow work to continue between officials on a text—even though Major was unwilling at that stage to allow any hint that he might be prepared to consider any concession to men of violence.

Work did continue, under Albert Reynold's direction, and within a month or so, Martin Mansergh gave a possible draft Joint Declaration to Father Reid.

In June 1992, the Provisionals sent back a draft of their own—and this time it incorporated a lot of the language that Mansergh had used. It seemed that the Provos were moving towards acceptance that their struggle was with their Unionist neighbours—and that therefore a process of reconciliation was now something they had to look at.

The pace quickened with a number of speeches made by leading Provisional Sinn Féin spokespeople. Although these were reported in the media as interesting, they were much more important when viewed through the eyes of those who had been operating behind the scenes.

All these speeches referred to changes in republican thinking, including the need for "an all-embracing and durable peace process".

Exchanges went on about forms of language over the following months, and they culminated in the note that arrived in the Taoiseach's hands a couple of months after Dick took over in the Department of Foreign Affairs.

Just before that note arrived, John Hume had met Gerry Adams, and the meeting became public knowledge. The government was forced to issue a cautious, non-judgmental statement. Just after the note arrived, a huge IRA bomb exploded in the heart of the City of London, killing one man, injuring scores, and causing a billion pounds worth of damage.

That was the background against which we were plunged into the peace process. It was still embryonic, especially in the sense that there was relatively little government engagement with it. The process was going on in the background, but so far, on a basis that could be turned off if it was going nowhere. All but a very few senior officials and politicians were totally unaware of it, and were to remain so for another six months.

Officially, the line was one of no contact with Sinn Féin—although as we were to discover in detail later, the British government had their own direct line of contact well and truly open. Despite the fact that the process was a secret one, it had nevertheless already opened up for discussion many of the concepts that have become the cornerstones of progress. And of course, the key strategic shift—from exclusion to inclusion—had already been accepted at the top in the Irish government, and explored, if not yet accepted, by the British.

John Major's British government was totally hamstrung by its parlous voting position in the House of Commons, which made them dependent on Unionist support. His policy was essentially one of containment, through a process of trying to engage constitutional parties in talks. The continuing, and even escalating violence, made any open discussion of a new way forward impossible for him, and risky for the Irish government.

But work had to be done. It was going to be done at official level, through a liaison group of Irish and British officials, reporting to Sir Patrick Mayhew and to Dick Spring. Dick decided that I should be a member of this group.

It had taken me some time to be accepted in the Anglo-Irish Division of the Department of Foreign Affairs. There were three key people. Seán Ó hUiginn ran the section, David Donoghue was his number two, and Declan O'Donovan ran the Maryfield secretariat. The first time I met them, especially Seán, I realised that I was an outsider, a member of a highly dubious species, likely to leak all their secrets and incapable of being trusted. Not that they weren't polite and welcoming—they were—but their reserve was total.

It contrasted with the more open and genuine welcome I had got from Noel Dorr, the Secretary of the Department, who had briefed me fully on the work of the Department and given me the run of the place. I had known Noel slightly in his days as Ireland's Ambassador to London, but more particularly I knew of his legendary reputation as an analyst and draughtsman.

I was made welcome too by the Tánaiste's Private Office staff. Niall Burgess, Mary Cusack (who was later replaced by Lavina Collins), Theresa Tuite and Gerry Staunton were all people who turned out to be incredible resources for Dick Spring. Totally non-political, their professional loyalty was absolute, and they were all incredibly competent. We struck up a strong friendship which, I hope, has lasted to this day.

The story was essentially the same throughout the Department. They had never had a political adviser before who was interested in policy, and it made them nervous.

They began to realise quickly enough that it could be an advantage to have someone who generally had open access to the Tánaiste, and who understood where the Tánaiste's interests were likely to lie (I didn't tell them that when Dick chose to, he could keep his own counsel from me just as much as from anyone else). And it was useful too to have an in-house person who carried a reasonable degree of weight around the system generally. Almost immediately after arriving in the Department, I was able to help sort out some problems in relation to their annual estimates, and it helped to put me in good standing.

But Anglo-Irish was a tougher nut to crack. It took a good deal longer to win the trust of people, part of whose job is to be paranoid. As I was to discover myself, Anglo-Irish relations is the hardest school. It involves skills of negotiation and language, history and theology, philosophy, psychology, and endless patience.

And you have to be able to hold your drink. Most of the drudgery in Anglo-Irish relations is in the set-piece occasions— highly stilted and formalised meetings where people make prepared speeches. Most of the work gets done late at night, over a meal or with a drink in your hand. I was to come to know and appreciate the meaning of the term "dining for Ireland" very well over the next couple of years—although there were occasions when another hangover for Ireland seemed like too high a price to pay for peace!

Gradually, I became accepted by the people in the Anglo-Irish Division. In a way, it was the Provos' letter—and a major disagreement about it—that brought us together.

With the letter, the IRA had sent a draft of a Joint Declaration that they would be prepared to accept. It was important, because in accepting it the Provos indicated a willingness to accept "exclusively ... peaceful, political means". Their acceptance of the draft implied too, their willingness to countenance the principle that self-determination by the people of Ireland "must be achieved and exercised with the agreement and consent of the people of Northern Ireland".

But it was clear from the text that in return, the British government would have to accept that self-determination inevitably would have to take the form of agreed independent structures for the whole island, within an agreed time-frame. Clearly, this was impossible—especially given the difficult situation in which John Major had to live and work. But it also placed a question mark around the whole issue of consent—in the scheme proposed by this language, Unionists would be invited to agree to independent all-Ireland structures and nothing else.

Clearly, although the language demonstrated a huge degree of change in republican thinking, there would be a great deal of work to be done before a text was likely to emerge which would bridge the large gap that still remained.

That wasn't Albert Reynolds' view. Early in 1993, he conceived a plan that involved flying to London without any further ado, under the pretext of taking in a West End show, and presenting himself at 10 Downing Street—catching John Major on the hop, and persuading him to adopt this document in its entirety.

He didn't tell Dick about this plan—in fact, we found out about it by accident, from an official with whom the logistics were discussed. Dick's immediate reaction was that it was a crazy idea, which would not have survived any discussion in government. John Major would have had no choice but to reject the document out of hand if it were presented to him as a *fait accompli*—and couldn't possibly accept all of its terms in any event.

Dick went to see Albert, and effectively stopped him from going. By way of persuasion, he told him that if he went down that road, he'd be on his own. This was a document that we would have to assess carefully ourselves, and use as a basis for negotiation. But we couldn't, in the middle of intense violence, try to force the British government to accept a *fait accompli*. It just wouldn't wash—and if they rejected it in principle, how were we ever going to get its terms examined?

Albert didn't like it, but he didn't go. The document was sent to the British government a few weeks later as an Irish government draft—which it was, since it had originated from Martin Mansergh in the first place. It went on to undergo significant change in negotiation, but nevertheless to become a crucial building block in the overall process.

But Dick's "you're on your own" remark appeared in print subsequently (in Seán Duignan's diary among other places), in a way that suggested that Dick never supported Albert to the extent that he should have. He did—even when it involved telling Albert things he didn't want to hear.

It left a bad taste between the Taoiseach and the Tánaiste. Albert didn't appreciate being given advice by a novice to the process. Before too long, however, Dick discovered for himself what it was like to be on his own.

The Inter-Governmental Conference—the monthly set-piece meetings between the two Governments—was a rather routine affair when Dick took it over. It operated to a set agenda at each meeting—a tête-à-tête between the Foreign Minister and the Secretary of State to start, followed by a security session which involved the Justice Ministers and the police chiefs from both jurisdictions. The rest of the meeting was taken up with a plenary session, which tended to be a very dull affair. The last half-hour of the plenary was usually taken up with agreeing a communiqué—which was always fought over, even though it usually didn't vary very much from meeting to meeting.

In many ways, the process was quite arcane. All the work the officials did was described as "ad referendum". Literally, that meant that no agreement arrived at official level was valid until it had been politically endorsed. In practice, it meant that the work of officials could be freely disowned whenever necessary.

Even the officials on both sides had a language of their own. If we wanted, for example, to put an idea forward just to see how it would travel, it would be incorporated in a bit of paper known as a "non-paper". The British had their own word for that—anything totally unofficial was written down on "angel paper". It was clearly understood between us that nothing ever got elevated beyond non-paper or angel paper status unless we had political clearance on both sides to do so.

That way, an Irish or British suggestion, provided it was clearly non-paper or angel paper, became the property of both sides once it was made—but if either side threw it in the bin, it disappeared.

Discussions at the Inter Governmental Conference were bedevilled from the start by a difference of approach between the two governments. The British government was forever seeking to get the all-party talks that had been abandoned in 1992 re-started. For our part, we were now firmly embarked on a process aimed at getting everyone into those talks. This would be argued out at meeting after meeting, and occasionally caused exasperated exchanges between Ministers.

At one meeting of the Inter-Governmental Conference, for example, Michael Ancram, who was Sir Patrick Mayhew's politically astute deputy, explained in great detail that his government had a new idea—to invite all the parties (the constitutional parties, that is) to take part in a new initiative. He kept referring to this initiative as "British-organised multiple bilaterals". I passed a note up to Dick pointing out that the acronym for this initiative was BOMB, and when Dick mentioned it, Michael was momentarily flummoxed. Noel Dorr helpfully suggested that we should call it instead "A Long British Engagement Round the Table"—ALBERT for short. The general laughter allowed the subject to be changed.

Once the liaison group of officials reporting to the Conference started to work on pieces of text, of the kind which might ultimately form a Joint Declaration, the plenaries at the Anglo-Irish conferences started to get much more interesting. It wasn't so much that text was argued about in the plenary sessions—it was more that it became a good place to judge the amount of political resistance we were going to get to ideas that were being discussed at official level. The body language at those meetings was the thing most worth recording.

The body language between Dick Spring and Patrick Mayhew began to heat up quite a bit around the end of May. The heat was caused by President Robinson.

She was planning a trip to Belfast in mid-June, and when her itinerary was supplied to the British (as it had to be), they went mad. Among the President's engagements was a visit to West Belfast, where she would be attending a reception for local community activists. Gerry Adams was on the guest list. It was not on as far as the British were concerned, and in letters and phone calls, Sir Patrick told Dick so very bluntly.

The issue was eventually discussed at cabinet, and the view was unanimous. The meeting with Adams was unwise—it would be exploited by the Provos for propaganda purposes, and it would needlessly damage relations with the British—just at a time when we needed the best possible relations if we were going to negotiate anything meaningful. The irony was that our efforts to bring Sinn Féin in from the cold were going to be jeopardised by President Robinson's efforts.

There was a dilemma, though. Under the Constitution, the President needed the permission of the government to leave the state. No Irish government had ever accepted that a visit to Belfast was a foreign visit in that strict constitutional sense. It had seldom, if ever, arisen before in the case of the Presidency anyway. To take a view on the issue of permission for the President to go, therefore, would raise difficult issues of Constitutional principle.

At the end of the government meeting, it was agreed that there would be no question of issuing an instruction to President Robinson—especially since it would be immediately seen, anyway, as a capitulation to British pressure. Instead, Dick was authorised to go to Áras an Uachtaráin on behalf of the government, to discuss the visit with the President, and to point out the downsides surrounding one item on her itinerary.

On the day the cabinet met, Dick was due in London that evening for a meeting of the Inter-Governmental Conference, and there was immense pressure for a decision from the British government. He went straight from the government meeting to Aras an Uachtaráin, and from there to the government jet.

When he came on board the jet, he told us that the meeting had gone well. The President had undertaken to consider all the points he had made, and it had been agreed that they would meet again the following day. In some ways, that was better, from his point of view, than an immediate decision, because it would enable him to get through the meeting in London by deflecting discussion until the President's pending decision had been made.

So we flew to London in a relaxed frame of mind, and arrived at the Irish Embassy in Grosvenor Square in time to have a last minute preparatory meeting. In the middle of the meeting, Joe Small, our Ambassador in London, was handed a note, which told us that Downtown Radio in Belfast was quoting a spokeswoman for the President as saying that the controversial visit was going to go ahead as planned.

Dick was furious. It seemed unconscionable that an agreement to meet again the following day would be pre-empted in this fashion. And it resulted in a very angry meeting in the Northern Ireland Office.

They had heard the same reports as we had, and were demanding explanations. Despite Dick's inner feelings, he took the position when dealing with Sir Patrick that Ireland's President had every right to go to Belfast and the British had no right to be trying to lay down pre-conditions.

At one point in the meeting, things got nasty, and there was a broad hint from the British side that they could not take responsibility for the President's security. Dick looked Sir Patrick between the eyes, and told him that if this visit was cancelled on security grounds, he would be issuing a public statement making it absolutely clear that the British government were unwilling to guarantee the safety of the President. The issue wasn't raised again.

When Dick went to the Aras again the following day, he was assured categorically that no-one had issued any statement on behalf of the President—but he was also told that she had made her mind up, and was going ahead with the visit in the absence of a direct instruction from the government.

The mystery of where Downtown Radio had got its perfectly accurate information was never resolved. And one other mysterious thing happened. In media briefings that started to come out from government sources—no-one knew who!—the whole affair was portrayed as a disagreement between Dick and President Robinson.

There was no mention of the fact that he was representing the government, or that he and the Taoiseach were in full agreement. If Albert would have been on his own in flying to London earlier, someone made sure that Dick was on his own on this issue. I couldn't help but admire the symmetry.

There was little time for investigation or recrimination, however. While we were busy the following month, trying to negotiate Albert's £8 billion in Brussels, John Major was having European difficulties too, specifically when it came to trying to get the Maastricht Treaty passed by the House of Commons. When the Unionists, who had earlier argued against the Treaty, supported the government, suspicion grew on our side that Major had done some kind of deal with them. We were assured by Sir Patrick that nothing could be further from the truth—and he also dismissed allegations being made by some Unionists that his government had been in secret contact with the IRA for some time.

Although negotiations continued on a possible Joint Declaration, the pace was somewhat desultory for several weeks. It was then that John Hume dropped his bomb-shell, in a way that nearly scuppered the whole process.

Late in September, just before he went to the United States, he implied that he had handed over a report of his discussions with Gerry Adams to the Irish government. Quite why he did so I have never known, but the remarks caused chaos. For a week or more, the newspapers were full of speculation—and the speculation wasn't about whether we had received anything, but what was in it. Hume/Adams was born, to hang around the Anglo-Irish end of the peace process like an albatross.

There was no Hume/Adams. Or, to be more correct, the extraordinary and remarkable work that John Hume had done had put the Irish government in a position to send a draft document to the British, with some prospect that it would lead to a ceasefire. But that document had gone three months earlier—and it had been sold by the Irish government, and accepted by the British government, as an Irish government proposal. There was no other way it could be done.

It was immediately made clear by the British government that they would have no truck whatever with any document that had Gerry Adams' fingerprints on it.

This was a hypocritical gesture in many ways—especially when we discovered a few weeks later that the British government had been talking to the IRA for months. But it was the only position that would keep John Major in 10 Downing Street—where we wanted him.

Fortunately, no formal question was ever raised by the British about the provenance of the document they already had. It proved the wisdom of not rushing off to London back in April, because then the document would not have been presented as ours.

I've never been in any doubt that the British government knew the background and history of the document, but they chose to make a distinction between the draft Declaration, in their possession before John Hume went public, and a mythical document known as Hume/Adams.

But it took some doing to keep them interested at that point, and a lot of courage, especially on the Taoiseach's part. Speaking in Bodenstown, he poured cold water on the Hume/Adams process. While describing the work that John Hume and Gerry Adams had done as important, he said bluntly and forcefully that the two governments had to build a framework for peace on their own terms. It wasn't well received by his own—but he did it because it was necessary.

Dick and Albert and John Hume had a frosty enough meeting in early October. It led to the *Irish Times* reporting the details of a document that John Hume had allegedly handed over to them—even though they had seen nothing!

But if relations between all the parties were strained at the start of the month, by the end of October the mood throughout Ireland was one of untold despair. That despair was alleviated only by one thing—an act of statesmanship by Dick Spring, in one of the peace process's darkest hours.

In the middle of October, the IRA issued a statement saying that it supported the Hume/Adams process and that it could provide the basis for peace. A week or so later, they seemed to send a different, more typical message.

It is a Saturday afternoon on the Shankill Road in Belfast. A small fish shop, called Frizzells, is busy because it's lunchtime. One of the customers has no place there, because he is an IRA man, called Thomas Begley, and he is carrying a bomb.

When it goes off prematurely, it blows two members of the Frizzell family to pieces, together with eight other people, including a seven-year old girl who's clutching her mother's hand. Thomas Begley is killed instantly too.

As the smoke clears, and the full horror of what has happened is revealed, the whole of Ireland is convulsed. Feelings of horror, shame, and revulsion are everywhere. But above all despair. For many weeks now, there has been a growing feeling that, perhaps, some sort of breakthrough is possible. Perhaps whatever is going on between John Hume and Gerry Adams has the seeds of peace in it.

And now the IRA has sent what seems like a definitive answer. As the days go by, six people are killed in individual acts of retaliation, and in what seems like the most grotesque two fingers to the principles of peace, Gerry Adams carries Thomas Begley's coffin.

Members of the Dáil gather on October 27th, to try to express the horror they are all feeling. What can be said? Is there nothing to do but condemn? Is there no way hope can be kept alive?

Dick decided that we had to try to keep hope alive. We worked through the night on a short speech, one of the most important he ever made. It outlined six democratic principles— not new in themselves, but a bringing together of the different strands of the peace process in one place. Easy to read, and easy to understand. Self-determination, consent, freedom from coercion and violence, and an open invitation to talk—even to those involved in the most recent horror, if only they would put away the bombs.

There was a drafting error in the speech—it seemed to imply that unionists would be able to block change even if they became a minority within Northern Ireland—and we had to correct that. But the speech as a whole made an extraordinary impact. It was welcomed across the board—even by the leader of the Unionists, Jim Molyneaux. The British government made it clear that they would be willing to discuss the principles at a forthcoming summit. That was a coded way of saying that the negotiations on a draft Declaration were back on track.

Hope had been revived—and it survived even the next atrocity, a few days later, when two loyalist gunmen opened fire on the Rising Sun bar in a small town called Greysteel, in County Derry.

It didn't solve all the problems, by any means. At the Brussels Summit at the end of the month, John Major insisted again and again that he could make no progress while "Hume/ Adams fingerprints" were still visible. He and Albert and Dick had several meetings—one of them in the amazing residence of the British Ambassador, a massive house built around a courtyard in the heart of the city that had been in British possession during the Napoleonic Wars.

The sessions between Albert and John Major were tense, but they resulted in Dick and Albert agreeing to "take the fingerprints off the process". This was done in the communiqué after the summit, and a couple of days later Seán Duignan was sent out to tell John Hume publicly to "stand back" while the governments got on with it. In some ways, it was a small price to pay if the outcome was going to be successful, but John Hume was deeply hurt by it, and it led to a lot of difficulties, especially for Albert Reynolds.

He had to come home to face an Ard Fheis where there was a strong feeling that the government had let Hume down. He had to make a strong speech saying that there was no question of betraying nationalism, and appealing to John Major to take his courage in his hands. I believe that Albert Reynolds had some low days in the immediate aftermath of that Ard Fheis, and probably felt more lonely then than at any other time in the process.

We were having our own troubles—and I was learning a little bit about political loneliness too. The six principles, that had done so much to help the process back on the rails, had never been written down anywhere, other than in the speech Dick had delivered in the Dáil. Sean Ó hUiginn suggested that we should incorporate them into a working paper that we were preparing in the Department, a paper that was intended to be used in fleshing out the language of the Joint Declaration at some stage in the future. The working paper was updated to reflect the six principles as a sort of preamble.

Very few people had seen that paper. It was a document intended to build on a Declaration that had not yet been agreed, and therefore it had very much a contingency status. But it was circulated to a few very senior officials, and one or two members of the cabinet.

One of them, in an act of gross irresponsibility, gave the paper to Emily O'Reilly, who was then the hard-working political correspondent of the *Irish Press*. In the process, they gave her a major exclusive, and poisoned relationships within the government, and between the governments, for a long time afterwards.

The finger of suspicion pointed at me. I was one of a small number of people, outside the cabinet room or the senior civil service, who had got the document. I had good relations with a number of people in the media, and indeed spent a lot of my time talking to them about the peace process, and Anglo-Irish relations in particular.

But not for the purposes of betraying secrets, or weakening Ireland's negotiating position. I was horrified and angry when I realised that it was being widely, and wrongly, assumed—including by many of the political correspondents—that I had leaked the document to Emily O'Reilly.

I was also among a number of people who were interviewed by the Gardaí about the leak. For three hours one Saturday morning, they questioned me, politely but firmly, in my home, and I made a detailed statement.

There was no outcome to that investigation, in the sense that no-one was ever charged with the leak. Therefore, no-one was ever exonerated either, and I carried around the burden of assumed guilt for quite a while. I even went to the lengths of asking Emily O'Reilly to tell Seán Duignan, without revealing her source, that I wasn't it. She did, and I was very grateful—but I don't think Albert Reynolds believed it. My own boss never doubted me, however, and that was all that mattered as far as I was concerned.

There were two reasons I was angry about the leak. First, it was immensely damaging to trust—it made senior British officials wonder about what they were dealing with. And it gave them a negotiating edge. For a long time afterwards, every time a sensitive subject came up, the name of Emily O'Reilly would be bound to surface—as a kind of code for "you can't trust the Irish".

But secondly, all through that period I was engaged in secret and sensitive work. The publicity associated with the leak put me at risk—not a lot, but enough to jangle my nerves now and again.

In 1985, when the Anglo-Irish Agreement was being negotiated, the Irish government had kept in close touch with the SDLP and other nationalist politicians. It had assumed that the British government was bringing Unionist opinion along—but that was a wrong assumption. Part of the reason for the unionist hostility to that agreement had been the way in which they had been totally excluded from the process by their own government.

Dick was determined that, in so far as we could help it, that wouldn't happen this time. So, in every spare moment, he and I went North, always in secret, and visited everyone who would talk to us from the Unionist community. More often, I travelled around Northern Ireland alone, meeting clergymen, community workers, trade unionists, and others.

On one occasion, shortly after the Emily O'Reilly leak, I was driving down a lonely country road near Hillsborough, when a motor bike tucked itself in behind me. Over several miles, I became more and more paranoid, speeding up and slowing down, indicating to the left, doing anything that would shake it off. Eventually we came to a wide stretch of road and the motor bike overtook me and sped off into the night. It was a few minutes before my heart stopped thumping!

The first time I drove to Belfast, I got hopelessly lost and had to stop and ask for directions—not realising until I had walked into a shop that I had stopped in the middle of the Shankill Road! As it happened, the people inside couldn't have been more friendly—although they were intrigued by the fact that I was the first Dubliner who had ever been in their shop.

I got to know the homes and houses of Unionism very well in those weeks, and was treated with the most incredible hospitality and courtesy everywhere I went. Even when, on one visit, I was being shown some of the sites where the Shankill Butchers had dumped bodies, I was treated in a totally open way.

I was helped enormously in paying these visits by two people, Brian Fitzgerald and Chris Hudson. Chris was a trade union official in Dublin who had been very active in the Peace Train. He had a wide range of contacts in Northern Ireland, including the leadership of the smaller loyalist parties, who weren't known in the Republic at all at the time. Brian, who was the Labour TD for Meath, had also established a lot of contacts among unionists, even though he was an unashamed and direct nationalist in his views. They respected him for his honesty and bluntness.

The first time I met the leadership of the loyalist parties, Brian accompanied me. That way, had the meeting become public, we would have been able to describe it as a party-to-party encounter.

That first meeting took place in the run-up to the Downing Street Declaration, and therefore long before any ceasefires. I couldn't, strictly speaking, have gone at all if I was going as a government representative.

We had agreed to meet in a neutral and secret venue in Belfast, and I knew that Gusty Spence and David Ervine would be there. I didn't know what to expect. I had a vague memory of Gusty Spence—the first man sentenced to life imprisonment in the troubles for murdering a Catholic—as a hard man, wearing military gear and cradling a rifle in his arms. I was totally unprepared for the twinkly-eyed, pipe-smoking and avuncular figure who greeted us when we arrived for the meeting.

I've seldom been as impressed by anyone as I was by those two men. They had been through a crucible of violence, crime, and punishment—and they had come out the other end determined to end violence once and for all. There was a sense about them that not only had they learned a lot in prison, but had been uplifted—perhaps even redeemed—by their experiences. I came away from two hours discussion with them convinced that these were genuine peacemakers.

They argued strongly that if there was going to be a Joint Declaration between the governments, it must be in a form that loyalism would recognise. In addition to enshrining consent (which I assured them it would) they pressed for the inclusion of a set of principles about discrimination, which formed the core of their own political philosophy, and which had been published as part of their party literature. They had already given these to the Reverend Roy Magee, a remarkable Protestant clergyman who was working with them and speaking to the governments. I took the principles away with me, and they subsequently found their way, almost completely unchanged, into the text of the Downing Street Declaration.

(There was one minor change in the loyalist principles before they were inserted into the Downing Street Declaration. One of the principles called for the right to equal opportunity in all social and economic activity, "regardless of class, creed, or colour". The issue of gender was left out, and I changed the phrase to "class, creed, sex or colour". It enabled me to claim credit, if nothing else, for putting sex into the Downing Street Declaration!)

Meanwhile, we had made significant progress on the text of a Joint Declaration. There was a large measure of agreement at official level, and the governments seemed to be moving ever closer towards agreeing a document. Then the British dropped another bombshell.

There was astonishment at every level of the Irish government when, on November 25th, the British handed in a new text, one that no-one had ever seen before. This was after months of slow and painful work towards an agreed text. What was worse, the British were coming to Dublin Castle, for a summit meeting on December 3rd, clearly believing that in this new text (which would have produced an unrecognisable Declaration) they had played a trump card.

In our analysis, they were, at the very least, trying to buy time to appease Jim Molyneaux, and they knew that it would take months of intensive negotiation to reconcile this new text with the document that was all but agreed—and was as close as we could get to a Declaration that the Provos would at least recognise.

Dermot Nally, who was Secretary to the government, is the mildest of men. He was known throughout the length and breadth of the Irish civil service as a man of both wisdom and experience, and as someone it was impossible to ruffle. When I saw Albert Reynolds having to calm him down, at a meeting to discuss strategy in relation to this new text, I knew that we were going to be in for a bumpy few days.

"It's unforgivable!" Nally raged. "Who do these people think you are—the Prime Minister of Togo? They can't be allowed to ignore months of detailed negotiation, and tell us that we have to start all over again just because they click their fingers!"

It was agreed that our mission would be to get the new British document off the table in its entirety. No ifs, ands, or buts, as Albert would say—no fall-back position, no compromise. We were going to the summit to talk about one document only, and it was not going to be a unilaterally introduced British document.

In other words, with the world's media gathered outside, all of them expecting to be told about progress towards an agreement, we were going to say to the British—we do the deal our way, or it's no deal. Either they backed off, or we had the biggest crisis in Anglo-Irish relations since Mrs Thatcher's "out, out, out" speech. It was the kind of strategy that needed a man who was prepared to bet his house and everything he owned on one roll of the dice. But, fortunately, we had just the man for the job.

The meeting took place in the room in the Castle just beside the James Connolly Room, so-called because it was there that Connolly was treated for his injuries the night before he was shot in 1916. The two delegations were seated on either side of a Queen Anne table, and Albert got right to the point.

"You're making a fool out of me, John'" he said, "and I won't have it. We'll do no business on the basis of this thing." And he threw the British paper into the middle of the table.

"What are you suggesting?" Major asked him "Surely we have the right to table important new ideas ..."

"I'm suggesting bad faith, John," Albert snapped. "And we'll do no business that way. We go back to the document we started with, or we're outta here now."

John Major had been toying with a pencil as Albert spoke. At the use of the words "bad faith" the pencil snapped in his hands. He looked down at it, bemused, and then looked up at Albert.

"I think we should talk privately," he said. He was pale, his lips tight.

"Grand so," Albert grinned, and I realised with a start that he was enjoying this.

They disappeared into an ante-room, just the two of them. A half-hour passed. Normally in such situations the rest of the delegations relax, and mingle with each other, waiting for the principals to return. This wasn't one of those occasions.

Eventually the door to the ante-room opened, and Albert came out, saying to the nearest British official, "he wants to see ye inside". I happened to be standing nearest to the door when Albert emerged, and I said "How did it go, Taoiseach?"

"It wasn't too bad," Albert replied. "He chewed the bollix off me, but I took a few lumps out of him!" He grinned, as always, but he too was pale, and tense.

When John Major returned, it was as if nothing had happened. It was agreed, without any further discussion, that work would resume on the text that was already in hand. Some desultory work was done on some of the paragraphs, before the meeting ended with an agreement to finalise the text as rapidly as possible and hold another summit to announce the outcome as soon as we had an outcome.

Both leaders gave an almost pally press conference at the end of the meeting, leaving the press corps totally confused—how come there was so little to report, if the meeting had gone as well as it seemed? It was noticed that Major didn't stay to lunch, however, and some of the more astute commentators quickly began to realise that something else must have been going on behind the scenes.

We were helped in that meeting by the fact that when John Major came to Dublin, the media was full of the discovery that the British government had in fact been in sustained contact with the IRA for a considerable period of time. There was no recrimination, in public or in private, from us to them about this—we had always assumed it was the case, even though they had never admitted it. Privately, some on our side were angry about the hypocrisy of it all—we had told them about the contacts we had been having, and they had tried to keep us in the dark.

But the absence of recrimination helped our negotiating position. The truth was that the discovery of the IRA contacts more than cancelled out the Emily O'Reilly leak, and our reaction—which was more gracious than theirs had been—put them on the defensive at just the right moment.

There was another negotiating session between the leaders in Brussels a week late—this time a lot more amicable. It was followed by three days of intensive drafting—Seán Ó hUiginn, Noel Dorr, David Donoghue, Martin Mansergh and I worked more or less around the clock. And then it was finished, and the two leaders decided to publish it immediately.

When we arrived in Downing Street on December 15th, a smiling John Major served champagne. Martin Mansergh approached me with a script that he had prepared for Albert at the press conference, saying that it needed some rhetorical flourishes at the end, and would I mind giving a hand? So I sat at the British cabinet table in 10 Downing Street, and wrote a few paragraphs for the Taoiseach on Cabinet Office paper. It was the last time I ever wrote anything for Albert Reynolds, but at least the setting was memorable.

As the agreement was being run-off on the Downing Street photocopier, I managed to grab the first copy, and asked the Prime Minister and the Taoiseach to sign it. Everyone thought this was a great idea, and within a few minutes, Ministers were all busy signing each others' copies. I said to John Major that I felt as if my copy had been devalued, and with a smile he took it back and wrote "The first copy" and the date over his signature. I have it still.

There was a lot of work to be done yet, but the Downing Street Declaration was the first breakthrough. It wouldn't have happened when it did, and it wouldn't have looked as it did, if Albert Reynolds hadn't been prepared to gamble his all, a week or so earlier, on one cut of the deck. It was a great strength—and a terrible weakness.

13

Partnership Tested

"Have you ever heard of King Rat?"

I was talking to one of the truly brave people in Northern Ireland. He's a Catholic priest, Brian Lennon, who worked in Portadown, a town as divided along sectarian lines as any you're likely to find in Europe. He and his colleagues work hard at building and maintaining a sense of community in the town, and they are respected in both communities for their courage and their work.

He had heard that I was willing to meet people who were hostile to the Irish government, and was offering me a real challenge – the opportunity to meet Billy Wright.

Of course I knew Wright's reputation, and his nickname. Although never convicted of murder, he was widely believed, by our security forces as well as by those in Northern Ireland, to have been involved in more than a dozen sectarian killings. He was one of the half-dozen or so most feared people on the island of Ireland, and was also believed to be interested, if not involved, in the incipient drug trade in Northern Ireland.

I couldn't imagine that he was willing to meet a representative of the Irish government, but Brian assured me that he was actually anxious to meet someone from Dublin.

"Mind you," he said, "don't expect an easy ride. He's convinced that people you're meeting already aren't sending a hard enough message down South – and he's already offered me a bet that no-one from down there will have the guts to meet him."

Courage isn't my middle name – so I asked Brian if he thought it would be a safe encounter.

"Ah, I'm sure it'll be okay," came the cheery answer. "And sure if it isn't, I'll be there to give you the last rites!"

To be honest, I didn't see the humour. I don't think I'd have gone, except that the enquiries I made convinced me that Wright was in a volatile state—but that he was also a man with an ego, who wanted to see himself in a leadership role. If he was spurned, he could easily undermine all the efforts then going on to try to secure a decent follow-through to the Downing Street Declaration.

I parked near Brian's house in Portadown, and we drove in his car to a car-park on the outskirts of the town. And then we waited. After an hour, there was no sign of Wright, and Brian went to a public phone to ring him. He came back in a few minutes and explained that Wright was pretending that the appointment was for the following week—the people he wanted to bring with him hadn't turned up. But he had agreed to see us anyway. We were to stay put and he would come and get us.

A few minutes later a large and very sleek red sports car turned into the car park. An arm beckoned from the driver's window that we were to follow. We looked at each other, and I felt my throat go dry.

In another few minutes, we drew up outside a nondescript council house, in one of those estates where everything looks like everything else. Billy Wright got out of his car, and without saying a word, beckoned us to follow him in.

That involved waiting while a number of padlocks and chains were removed, before we were admitted to a tiny hall which seemed to be completely surrounded by a steel cage. And then we were admitted to the sitting room of the tiny house.

What a contrast. It was (I imagine!) like entering the madam's drawing room in a brothel. A purple, fleecy carpet ran wall-to-wall. A modern touch was provided by the biggest stereo system I've ever seen, and white leather furniture completed the bizarre look.

It wasn't until we were in the room that Wright spoke to me. "Won't you sit down, sir?" he said.

I sat, heavily. I had been unnerved by his appearance, and by the man who was with him. Billy Wright had a bullet head, close cropped with small ears, and deep set, piercing eyes. He was dressed in a white singlet, despite the fact that it was a cold day, and military-style trousers. He was accompanied by a short, squat man who, to judge by his appearance, "could'a bin a contender". And to my untutored (and increasingly paranoid) eye, the bodyguard—who never opened his mouth, nor took his eyes off me—was carrying a gun under his jacket.

For ten minutes, Billy Wright spoke at me, intensely, his eyes never blinking. I had to resist the temptation to look at the floor, because I felt it was important to maintain eye contact.

He told me that Dublin needn't think it was fooling anyone. He and his people had seen through the Downing Street Declaration, even if other "so-called" loyalists hadn't. It wasn't peace we were interested in, but a takeover. And he had the men and the resources to see to it that we suffered the next outbreak of violence in the South. It wasn't the Shankill that'd be going up in smoke, but O'Connell Street—and I could tell that to my paymasters. They thought that loyalists didn't have what it took to take the fight to Dublin, but they'd soon find out different.

I didn't know how to react to this tirade. He was the last man on earth I wanted to provoke at that moment, and yet I knew I couldn't let this go unanswered. Eventually, when he paused for breath, I took my tongue from the roof of my mouth and stood up, praying that my trembling knees wouldn't be too visible—or audible.

"I'm sorry, Billy," I said. "I came here to talk on a basis of mutual respect—but I can't listen to these threats."

Instantly he leaped to his feet, and my heart plummeted. But to my amazement, his tune changed utterly.

"I'm sorry, sir," he said, "I wasn't threatening—I was just trying to tell it straight, as I see it."

And from that moment on, while I couldn't say that we got on like a house on fire, it was a much more civilised encounter. What emerged in the end was his bitterness at being excluded from the political leadership of loyalism—an exclusion I could fully understand, although I admit I didn't tell him that. He seemed to believe that only he could be trusted with the future of the union, and that if only people would talk to him, he'd be willing to drive a hard bargain.

In the end, he told me that Dublin was safe for the moment, as far as he was concerned—but if he were to divine any hidden meanings in the negotiations then going on, things could change. With a smile, he said,

"I'll tell you what, sir—I'll give *you* five minutes warning anyway."

Before I left, he suggested that he would be willing to meet again, and next time he would gather some of the real people, so they could see that not everyone from Dublin had two heads, and I could see that loyalists were thinking, reasonable people—but people of strong convictions. I told him I'd come back anytime he wanted to arrange such a meeting—but I never heard from him again.

As we drove away from Billy Wright's strange house, Brian Lennon said cheerily that he thought the meeting had gone very well.

"I'll tell you when my hands stop shaking," I told him.

Not all Anglo-Irish encounters were unpleasant. In February, John Major invited the Taoiseach and his party to a summit in Downing Street to review progress since the Declaration. There had been very little—lots of requests for clarification, and no positive response from the Provisionals. But it was an extraordinary occasion anyway.

It had been arranged for a Saturday morning, and as luck would have it, Ireland were playing England in Twickenham that afternoon. And by an amazing coincidence, the Prime Minister's Office had a bunch of tickets for the match.

The Taoiseach and Tánaiste and their party (including me) flew to London on the government jet, and Frieda came over on an Aer Lingus flight with Kristi Spring. We stayed in the Mayfair Hotel in Piccadilly that night, and the following morning, while the meeting was going on, Kristi and Frieda were given a guided tour of 10 Downing Street. Then we were all put into limousines and swept out to Twickenham, where we were wined and dined under the stand. The Ministers were seated in the Committee Box, and the rest of us were just beside it. To put the icing on the cake, Simon Geoghegan scored a great try for Ireland, and we beat the old enemy on their own ground. Afterwards, we were introduced to Prince Andrew over tea and cucumber sandwiches. All in all, it didn't do Anglo-Irish relations any harm!

I think it might have been slightly wasted on one of our civil servants, who may have had an intellectual aversion to foreign games. Just before kick-off, sitting in one of Twickenham's prize seats, he turned to me and asked,

"Tell me, this is the game with the egg-shaped ball, isn't it?"

In the other world—the world of normal, everyday politics, there were a number of strains under the surface. None of them were unmanageable, but the process of partnership government was suffering occasional stresses.

In the formation of the government, for instance, it had been agreed that the Office of Public Works would be transferred from its traditional bailiwick in the Department of Finance to come under Michael D Higgins' auspices. It made logical sense, and it would have enabled Michael D to end the long-running controversy about a plethora of interpretive centres that were a hangover from Charlie Haughey's time, and were an affront to the environment.

But the OPW didn't want to move, and fought a ferocious rearguard action, in which the Department of Finance played a neutral role—in other words, they supported the OPW. It was immensely frustrating, and profoundly embarrassing for Michael D, who found himself in charge of the policy aspects of the OPW—but unable to change policies with which he disagreed.

Another row had broken out the previous September, between Brendan Howlin and Bertie Ahern. As Minister for Health, Brendan was forced to preside over a nationwide strike by health board dental assistants—even though he supported their cause, and made every effort to try to fix the problem. What stopped him was the Department of Finance's insistence that any concession would blow a hole in national pay strategy. And then, as soon as the strike was underway, Bertie Ahern, as Minister for Finance, made a public offer to intervene. Brendan had taken a very dim view, and the two Ministers had had words.

But rows of that sort are commonplace in any government, and tend to be forgotten. The overall record of the government, after about a year in office, was already very good.

Ministers were performing dramatically well, and an impressive set of reforms was being racked up every day. The legislative track record was breaking records too—the Programme Manager system was doing its job, under the direction of Greg and Donogh Morgan. Taken together with the Downing Street Declaration, 1994 looked like being a year of considerable achievement.

It's an old saying, but true. As soon as things start to look as if they're going right in politics, something will happen to blow you off course.

The first crisis blew up in early March of 1994, and it was one we wouldn't forget in a hurry. It was John Foley who told me that the rumours circulating about a Minister being caught apparently soliciting a homosexual encounter in the Phoenix Park were true—and that they involved one of ours, Emmet Stagg.

Emmet had blossomed in government. As Junior Minister with responsibility for housing, he had fought for a greatly increased financial allocation, and was driving hard to restore public housing levels to what they had been some years previously, prior to the cutbacks that had started in 1987. He was one of the real success stories of the government.

And now, suddenly, the newspapers were carrying broad hints, clearly based on impeccable sources, that a Minister was involved in seedy and possibly illegal practices. Although homosexual activity between consenting adults had been decriminalised within the previous few months, if money had changed hands in any of the transactions that were being spoken about, a crime had been committed.

Everyone, it seemed, knew that Emmet was the Minister involved—and it was only going to be a matter of time before he was named—or worse, arrested and questioned. And we didn't know the truth—what exactly, if anything, had he done?

The stories mainly broke in the Sunday newspapers. When I rang Dick, he had already confirmed from his own sources (I assumed the Department of Justice) that Emmet was involved, and that although the Gardaí had looked into the matter, no charges were in prospect. But what to do about someone who had committed so foolish an indiscretion, even if no crime was involved?

Dick told me that if he believed that Emmet was prepared to make a clean breast of whatever happened, he would support him through the inevitable crisis. But if there was any question of mud being allowed to hang over the government in general, he would have to take the matter in hand—and that would mean only one thing.

I decided to take the bull by the horns, and rang Emmet at home. on Monday morning. He was subdued, and I was blunt.

"Emmet," I said, "these newspaper stories. I gather they're about you."

There was a long silence, and then he said, "yes".

"What are you proposing to do?" I asked him.

Another silence.

"What options do I have?" he asked eventually.

So I told him that I didn't know—that I was ringing on my own behalf, and not Dick's. It was a situation that couldn't be contained—and nobody could be expected to lie on his behalf. I said that I thought if there was an honest admission, he might get a lot more sympathy than he was expecting.

He asked if he could ring me back, and half an hour later that's what he did.

"Look," he said, "what you're asking is going to cause a lot of pain to my wife and family. I'll need time."

"There isn't time, Emmet," I told him. "This story won't go away—you have to deal with it as soon as possible."

"Will you help me?" he asked.

It was my turn to pause. I didn't know what the question meant—would I help him to make a statement, or to make a clean breast of things?

"I'll help you all the way," I told him eventually, "if it's about living with the truth."

"I'll be in Dublin immediately after lunch," he said, "and we'll do it your way."

Almost as soon as he hung up, Tom Butler rang. Tom had taken over as press officer for the party around the time the government had been formed, and had had a baptism of fire at the hands of discontented backbench deputies. But he was gutsy and resourceful, and totally committed to the party's interests. He was ringing to tell me that Jim Kemmy was about to do an interview for the one o'clock news, and had expressed the intention of "outing" the Minister whose identity was being hinted at. I asked Tom to get a message to Jim, asking him not to go ahead with the interview because the person involved was already considering his position.

For reasons I've never understood, Jim ignored the message and did the interview. Although he didn't name Emmet, he made it clear that he knew who he was talking about. He and Emmet had been good friends, and Jim must have known that he was placing Emmet in an impossible position by going public when he did.

Over lunch, I contacted Pat Magner and explained what had happened to date. Pat knew Emmet personally an awful lot better than I did, and I knew I would need his help in dealing with him. Pat came over immediately, and we both met Emmet together at about three o'clock.

When Emmet arrived, he looked about ten years older. He explained that he had already spoken to his family, and that it had been a painful experience for all of them. He had also been in touch with a lawyer, and said that he would like his lawyer to assist in drafting whatever needed to be said. We had no problem with that, and we were joined by Paddy McEntee, the senior counsel, who had been advising Emmet.

Our concern—Pat's and mine—was to ensure that we were told the truth, the whole truth, and nothing but the truth. We were determined not to have a hand in preparing and issuing a statement that we subsequently discovered to be false.

It meant discovering an awful lot about what had happened on the night, about history, about track records. It meant asking unpleasant questions. Emmet, to be fair, never at any stage that day attempted to mislead us or distort what had happened. He was honest and open throughout, and my heart went out to him, because it was clear that he had been carrying an intolerable burden. We were all totally drained by the time we thought we had a statement that told everything necessary.

The hardest part was yet to come. Emmet wanted to let the statement out, and allow it to speak for itself. I believed that it was in Emmet's interests that he go the whole way, and do an interview about his statement. If he hadn't, he'd have been hounded for days until he did one.

So I insisted that he had to face a camera—he would have to do it sooner or later, and it was better to get it over with right now. In fact, I had asked John Foley to let Charlie Bird of RTE know that there might be a statement, and he and his crew had spent several hours waiting downstairs.

Eventually Emmet agreed to do it, and the four of us went downstairs to face the music. Charlie Bird was visibly shocked at Emmet's haggard and drawn appearance. Emmet himself recoiled from the sight of the cameras and lights, and turned to Pat, saying that he couldn't go through with it.

"You can, Emmet," Pat said. "We're here with you."

The interview had barely begun when Emmet broke down. To their eternal credit, Charlie Bird and his crew stopped filming immediately. Pat put his arms around Emmet, and took him out into the corridor. I don't know what he said to him, but when they came back in a few minutes later, Emmet was composed, and did a somewhat halting but coherent interview.

It wasn't over, by any means. But Emmet's courage and honesty at the moment of his greatest trial stood to him. There was as much public sympathy as outrage, and all his government colleagues, publicly at least, stood by him. Privately, there was a good deal of lip-smacking, and remarks were starting to be made about Fianna Fáil being dragged down by the Labour Party.

The Taoiseach made it clear that the government was going to ignore the incident, and that government cohesion would be unaffected. In fact, there was a lot of other stuff going on, which would undermine cohesion quite a bit.

It was approaching Easter, a time of year when normally, proposals for the Finance Bill were in circulation. Generally speaking, the Finance Bill doesn't contain a lot that hasn't already been announced in the budget, although there is scope for the government to introduce new measures if it considers it necessary. Usually, any new measures in the Finance Bill will be there as a reaction to the budget, or to events. Initiatives, if they're planned, will generally be foreshadowed in the budget speech.

But the initiatives planned by the Taoiseach for this year's Finance Bill weren't foreshadowed anywhere, other than in some lobbying documents published by the Institute of Taxation. What he proposed was a set of amendments to the Finance Bill which would have had the effect of significantly relaxing the tax regime for wealthy expatriates. The proposals were circulated to cabinet out of the blue.

Under existing law, Irish expatriates were treated as non-residents provided they lived abroad for most of the year. There was huge tax benefit involved, but also considerable personal sacrifice and discipline. The wealthy people who availed of the regime had to watch their visits home very carefully, and they were very limited in what they could do.

The proposed changes were designed to relax the regime very considerably, and to benefit two groups of people—those who had large regular incomes, and those who were worried about the tax effects on large estates. The net effect of one change would make it much easier to be Irish and rich and mixing your time at home and abroad. The net effect of the other would be to place an upper limit on the amount of tax that would be payable in respect of an estate left on death.

There was no policy reason for the scale of these changes, no public demand for them, and no particular justification—unless you were rich.

It was almost exactly the same situation that Dick had been presented with a year earlier, on the tax amnesty. Then, he had allowed Bertie to fight the battle, and it had been a costly mistake. This time, he made it clear right from the beginning that these changes were unnecessary and unacceptable. In letters to the Taoiseach and the Minister for Finance, he set out his opposition unequivocally.

But the Taoiseach wouldn't take no for an answer. The pressure was maintained, with the Taoiseach insisting that these were rational and necessary tax changes, and his Tánaiste saying no. Senior officials of both the Revenue Commissioners and the Department of Finance met on Good Friday, with the deadline for the Finance Bill rapidly approaching, but no compromise emerged. William Scally and Greg Sparks attended meetings at all hours of the day and night to try to solve the problem, but still nothing emerged.

Eventually, after Easter, the Taoiseach left for a few days in Cyprus, with the matter unresolved. But he made it clear before he left that there would be a cabinet meeting immediately on his return, at which all final decisions on the Finance Bill would be made—including decisions on tax residency changes.

Dick wrote again on the Wednesday after Easter, and the letter was transmitted to the Taoiseach's holiday address. On the Friday after Easter, he asked to see us in Kerry.

William, Greg, John Foley and I met Dick in the Europe Hotel in Killarney at lunchtime. His mood was grim. He told us that Albert Reynolds was determined to have his way in relation to the tax concessions on residency. As far as Dick was concerned, there was no possible justification for the concessions, whose only purpose was to make a small number of rich people richer.

Therefore, he had come to the conclusion that the government would be over on Monday. He met Niamh Bhreathnach that day in Tralee (Niamh was attending one of the teachers' conferences) and told her as much, to prepare her for a catastrophe about to happen.

Then two things happened. First, a long letter arrived for Dick from Albert Reynolds. And secondly, Bertie Ahern arrived in the hotel.

The letter was from Cyprus. It was seven pages long, and hand-written by the Taoiseach in block capitals. Its main purpose was to refute absolutely any suggestion that he was interested in making concessions for the benefit of rich people. His only interest, he said, was in attracting entrepreneurship to Ireland. This struck us as illogical, since the proposed concessions were to be made to entrepreneurs who already made their money in Ireland, and maintained homes here.

When Bertie arrived, it was to try one last time to effect a compromise. I don't know whether Albert had sent him, or whether it was his own initiative, but he and Dick spent an hour together. When Bertie left, Dick told us that he didn't agree with the changes either, but he had been unable to persuade Albert.

We went back to Dublin on the evening train, not knowing what the outcome of this confrontation was going to be. I strongly believed that if Dick backed down, he would inevitably be blamed when public outrage erupted—just as he had been blamed for failing to halt the amnesty. But we were all completely confident that there would be no question this time that something would slip past.

And it didn't. Dick rang me at eleven that night, to tell me that Bertie had been in touch. There would be no vote on the residency issues at Monday's cabinet meeting.

"But," said Dick, "I gather that Albert is pretty pissed off."

14

Triumphs and Disasters

I've always believed that Dick forcing Albert to back down on his proposed residency changes was the beginning of the end. For weeks after that incident, relations were strained between the two men.

It was the right thing to do for a variety of reasons. First and foremost, there was no economic justification for the changes. Secondly, the government could not have survived another tax amnesty controversy. Thirdly, it would have been our integrity that was under question, and not Fianna Fáil's.

In fact, Dick did Albert a huge favour, by ensuring that the controversy didn't erupt. Once the matter was settled, it was over, as far as he was concerned. But I've never been fully convinced that Albert saw it that way.

Around this time the sniping started. It was low-level stuff, mostly Fianna Fáil backbenchers muttering in the Dáil bar about Emmet and Labour Party standards. Deputy Sean Haughey, son of Charlie, brought it to the surface with a speech in which he attacked the Labour Party outright, accusing us of hypocrisy—and there was at least circumstantial evidence that his speech had the approval of the Fianna Fáil press office. Things were getting nasty—and they were to get nastier.

Although the latter half of 1994 was to prove to be more traumatic, in many ways, the stress and strain of the first six months of that year took an enormous toll on everyone involved. Looking back on it now, I often wonder how some didn't collapse under the physical and mental strain of that period. We had had the controversy over Emmet and the stand-off over residency and tax. And throughout all that, we had had the mix of frustration and hope that followed the Downing Street Declaration, with endless requests by Sinn Féin for clarification, and agonisingly slow progress towards peace.

For us, the pressure was caused both by the pace of events and by their size. And side by side with the intellectual and emotional demands of the peace process, an astonishing series of "ordinary" political events unfolded in that period. All of them were critical, and all of them were to leave footprints that no routine tide could wash over.

Dealing with either the peace process or the other events that surrounded us would have been enough for any sane group of people. Living the lives we led during that period often reminded me of the old slogan "you don't have to be mad to work here—but it helps!"

While the Anglo-Irish work was a source of constant preoccupation, the madness started again during the European elections of 1994.

Barry Desmond had resigned from the European Parliament a year before, to take up a position as Ireland's representative on the European Court of Auditors. I had been very glad that Barry had secured that post—there's probably no-one in Irish public life better qualified or suited. But it left the party with a problem.

He had been succeeded as MEP by his substitute in the previous election, Bernie Malone. And it was the unanimous view of the party in Dublin that she would make a weak candidate in the election due in early June, 1994. Without exception, every single one of our Dublin TDs told Dick so when he consulted them. We had to find another candidate— that was their view (although naturally, none were willing to say so publicly). It was Dick who suggested Orla Guerin, the RTE reporter, and I who went to meet her first.

I was enormously impressed. She was bright, articulate, knowledgeable. Obviously, she had a lot of television and radio exposure, and she was a well-known face, despite being young. I reported back enthusiastically that she would make a perfect candidate, and we began exploring the support she would be likely to get in the party if her name were put forward.

Again, the view was unanimous among those to whom we spoke. There was a general consensus that Orla would make a brilliant candidate, and an even better MEP.

But there was a major problem. Although Orla was willing to consider a nomination, it would only be on the basis that she was the only candidate. There clearly was not enough support for the party in Dublin to think seriously about trying to elect two people to the European Parliament. Orla was rightly concerned that a sitting MEP, even if she had never been elected to the position and had fallen into it by accident, would have a lot of advantages over someone coming fresh to the race. There are substantial information funds available to outgoing MEPs, for example, and even though they are not supposed to be used on direct election expenses, they can be used to generate a substantial public profile in the run-up to an election.

We discussed this issue several times, and failed to persuade Orla to run as one of two candidates. In the end, we decided to seek the nomination of only one candidate at the selection convention in Dublin. With one or two exceptions, all the soundings suggested that Orla would win easily.

Among the exceptions were William Scally and Greg Sparks. Although both were supportive of Orla, they knew the Dublin Labour Party very well, and both warned against trying to impose a single-candidate solution on the party. But they were voices crying in the wilderness—our elected TDs were unanimously telling us the opposite.

On the night of the selection convention, in the Riverside Centre in Dublin, Ray Kavanagh had done a detailed tot of all the delegates, and it showed Orla winning by three to one. When the delegates voted, however, it was a different story. They decided to run one candidate, as we requested, by a comfortable enough majority. But the candidate they chose, by a margin of one vote, was Bernie Malone. We had to change tack, and seek the permission of the party to add Orla to the ticket as Bernie's running mate.

And so began one of the most awful campaigns in which I have ever been involved. There was daily tension and disagreement, usually degenerating into shouting matches— about money, about support, about territory. When it came to allocating media time between the two candidates, I had to keep a daily record, to ensure that Orla wouldn't get a second longer on television than Bernie. Because I was regarded as the best person to help candidates prepare for television, I had to divide my time equally between them. That meant spending hours with a candidate who neither liked me nor trusted me, but was determined I shouldn't spend time with her rival.

Every trick in the book was pulled. Bernie fought for Dick's time, then stalked off in a public huff when Orla came too. The impression was steadily created that Bernie had been an outstanding MEP, when in fact she had been there no more than a few months.

The campaign was made even more bitter by scurrilous rumours which started around this time. I've never known how they started or where they came from, but they spread like wildfire. Dick and Orla were having an affair. Orla was pregnant with Dick's baby. Dick was having an affair with Orla's sister.

To this day, there are people who believe all this—who accept it as a matter of gospel fact. Although I never succeeded in tracing the original source of the rumour, I know it was freely discussed at a dinner party in Dublin 4 attended by a Fianna Fáil Minister, who readily confirmed the truth of the rumour. I know it was discussed at a gathering of parents at an exclusive boarding school, miles away from Dublin, in the presence of a senior Fianna Fáil lawyer, who also allowed it to be spread. I know it was discussed at a Labour Party meeting, and confirmed as accurate.

And it was all lies, from start to finish. It was worse than that. It caused immense pain to the people involved—to Dick and Kristi Spring, and to Orla Guerin and her family. Kristi Spring got phone calls at home about it—anonymous and otherwise—and was herself rumoured to be about to leave home. I lost track of the number of apologetic media phone calls I got based on spurious sightings of Kristi in Shannon Airport, and on more than one occasion lost my temper with the reporters making the phone calls.

But in all my time in politics, I've never known a rumour that spread so quickly, or was believed so fervently—even by people who admired Dick. Several times we discussed the rumours, and whether or not it would be possible to confront them head on. We abandoned the effort because it was fundamentally unfair, in principle, to have to try to correct false and vicious rumour-mongering that had caused so much pain.

The only way it could be done would be to expose the victims of the rumours, and their families—who were private and reserved people—to unprecedented public questioning of their private lives. And we knew there would be a "no smoke without fire" effect in some quarters anyway. Most of the newspapers—I think all of them, in fact—put reporters to work on examining these rumours, and none of them was ever able to find anything untoward. Denying rumours that hadn't appeared in print, in those circumstances, would inevitably have given licence to some of the papers to run intensely damaging headlines.

I did feel like calling a press conference myself when, one night shortly after the election, Orla arrived at my house in considerable distress. She had borne all the things that happened to her in that campaign with enormous dignity and grace—proving to my eyes anyway that she would have made an outstanding ambassador for Ireland. But on this particular night she had been at an RTE social function. One of her colleagues, realising that she clearly wasn't pregnant, had passed a remark about Orla having had an abortion. It was too much, and Orla had finally snapped under the strain.

I've always carried a burden of guilt about what happened to Orla Guerin in that campaign—and about the fact that we lost touch almost immediately afterwards. She didn't deserve any of the abuse that she suffered, and it went way beyond the rough and tumble of electoral politics. I don't know whether she would have won without the rumour-mongering, but I am absolutely certain that it was a significant factor in her defeat.

And if Orla didn't deserve it, neither did Dick. I know that that period was one of the most difficult in his life, and he has had to live ever since with the knowledge that people believe untrue assumptions about him. Politicians earn enough opprobrium throughout their careers over the things they do and the mistakes they make—and no politician is perfect in that respect.

But it is cruel and unfair to be attacked over something you've never done, and to have to live with rumour for years afterward. Dick Spring and Orla Guerin never had any relationship except a professional one, based on mutual respect. When politics turns a relationship like that into something underhand, a lot of consciences need to be examined.

Throughout all of this, going back to the start of the year, we were travelling backwards and forwards to London, week after week, gradually building towards a situation where we could be ready for a ceasefire by the IRA. Week after week, quiet work went on in trying to persuade people that the time had come to take the big jump towards peace

In our involvement with the Anglo-Irish process, we were learning, and we were developing new concepts at the same time. The learning was the hard part—because if one wants to be useful in Anglo-Irish relations, you have to have a grasp of language and negotiating techniques, but also of theology, history, philosophy—the sacred texts that are developed in these negotiations are like an intricate wall, capable of standing forever as long as not a single brick is rudely disturbed.

The purpose of the meetings was to begin work on a joint framework to lead to all-party negotiations, and to try to shape their outcome. The work was divided essentially into two parts. Negotiations on political structures were conducted by the liaison group, led by Seán Ó hUiginn. David Donoghue, David Cooney, and myself were the other main members. The British side for these discussion was led by Quentin Thomas, the deputy head of the Northern Ireland Office. Thomas was extremely sharp, quick to spot any weakness or indecision on our side, and very up to the minute on political developments within Ireland. He was also capable of being very funny, and could be very good company.

The other half of the negotiations concerned the constitutional aspects of any possible agreement. For those meetings, the British side was led by Sir John Chilcot, Quintin Thomas's boss—an extremely courteous, hospitable man, who always conveyed the impression of being willing to seek agreement, rather than win the argument. On our side, Seán and myself were joined by Martin Mansergh for that part of the negotiations. We met once a week, the sessions alternating between Dublin and London. Most of the negotiations involved political structures—it wasn't until the middle of the year, after the Corfu summit between Albert Reynolds and John Major, that serious work began to be done on the constitutional aspects of the problem.

Before we got to Corfu, however, we had another domestic crisis to deal with—while the European elections were still at fever-pitch.

Wednesday June 1st 1994 was my birthday, and I was looking forward to a family dinner at home. I never got there. The previous Sunday, a newspaper story had broken about a rich Arab family called Masri. It appeared that two things had happened to this family. First, they had been given a number of Irish passports. And second, they had invested a million pounds in the pet-food firm owned by the Taoiseach's family.

The minute you read a story like that, you know that it's going to shoot straight to the top of the political agenda. And so it proved. John Foley and I spent Sunday afternoon fending off phone calls about the story—about which we knew nothing anyway.

We were both astonished to discover that a scheme existed whereby rich foreigners could buy Irish passports in return for business investments here, and as we enquired into it, it began to appear as if not all of these investments were entirely bona fide. Many of them had the look of risk-free soft loans. On the other hand, many of the investments involved were perfectly legitimate, and more than a few had saved jobs in different parts of the country.

On Monday morning, William Scally, Greg Sparks, John Foley and I met to discuss the issue, and to try to decide what response we should recommend to Dick. John Rogers was in touch with us too, to express a very strong sense of concern about the political implications of the story, and about the ethical implications.

When we contacted Dick, we discovered that he had already asked his Labour Party Ministerial colleagues to set aside an hour the following morning. He intended to raise the matter at the normal Tuesday cabinet meeting, and wanted their views first.

At the meeting first thing on Tuesday morning, all the Labour Ministers were unanimous in the view that this was the most serious thing that had happened since the government was formed. If it were to emerge that the Taoiseach had been peddling Irish passports in return for investment in his own business, his position would be totally untenable.

That was the view Dick took in with him to the cabinet meeting. It was a longer than usual meeting, and described to me afterwards as very frank. The Taoiseach totally denied any impropriety or that he had ever made any representations on behalf of the Masri family.

It was agreed at the meeting that the Minister for Justice, Máire Geoghegan-Quinn (whom Dick liked and trusted) would carry out a full investigation and report back to the cabinet. It had been a different Minister, Pádraig Flynn, who had granted the passports.

It was clear, though, that a semi-private investigation, no matter how well-intentioned, wasn't likely to make the issue go away. There was a huge row in the Dáil that afternoon, with the Taoiseach stoutly maintaining his innocence in the matter, but under fire from all sides.

We met again the following morning (my birthday), and by now it was clear that Dick was going to be under fire from the media and opposition too.

John Foley had told a journalist the previous evening that he felt Dick was satisfied with the explanations given by the Taoiseach, even though no investigation had been carried out. It was the kind of remark any of us could have made, but John was very embarrassed about it, and felt that he had landed Dick in trouble.

After a long discussion, we all agreed that two things would be necessary.

First, Dick would have to investigate the matter himself, and be truly satisfied that nothing improper had been done to facilitate the granting of the passports in question. Secondly, if this scheme was going to continue in existence, we would have to ensure that it was thoroughly reformed to guarantee transparency in future.

We did discuss at some length whether the scheme should be abolished—a course favoured by many of us. In the end, it was decided that abolition of a scheme that had produced considerable investment, and that had both created and saved jobs, wasn't vital. But reform certainly was.

Dick told the Taoiseach that he was going to take the matter in hand himself. When he got his acquiescence, not without some discussion, he asked Máire Geoghegan-Quinn to bring the Secretary of her Department, and the relevant files, to Leinster House.

Tim Dalton, the Secretary of the Department of Justice, is one of those civil servants who can be trusted absolutely. He had served with distinction in the Maryfield secretariat, and was to go on to make a huge contribution to the peace process and Anglo-Irish relations. As fellow Kerrymen, he and Dick Spring had known each other a long time, and his assurances that there was absolutely no question of the Taoiseach making representations to secure the Masri passports was vital to the Tánaiste.

The files said the same thing. There remained, of course, the possibility that the Taoiseach hadn't needed to make representations, because Pádraig Flynn could have known where his interests lay. But how is anyone ever to establish the truth or otherwise of an assumption like that? Such is politics.

Dick was satisfied, in any event, and there was no reason why he should not have been (and no reason has ever emerged since). He told the Taoiseach that a statement was being drafted in which he, Dick, would outline his support, but would also be seeking reform of the overall scheme, to try to ensure that such a controversy couldn't break out in the future.

In fact, while Dick was carrying out his investigation and consulting with the Taoiseach, William Scally, Greg Sparks and Finbarr O'Malley were drafting a set of reform principles, which it was intended would be published as part of the package. I was then put to work on drafting a statement to be issued in Dick's name.

Dick told the Taoiseach that he didn't want this statement to go out without full agreement on its contents between the two of them, and the Taoiseach agreed that it would be appropriate for me to consult Martin Mansergh in the course of drafting. I consulted Martin several times, and we went back and forth to our principals. Several changes were suggested, and agreed between us. Eventually, we had the bones of a statement that reflected the views of both men, and committed both Taoiseach and Tánaiste to a fundamental review of the scheme.

I made a mistake that evening, because as it got later and later my anxiety to have a statement out got in the way of the need to have the statement as strong as possible. I should have incorporated the full set of principles that Dick's three advisers had drawn up into the statement, and secured the agreement of the Taoiseach's office to them.

But rather than face the need for a line-by-line negotiation over them, I summarised them briefly in the statement, and made them look less than the detailed set of reforms that my colleagues had worked out. William and Greg remonstrated with me over it, but I overrode their objections in the interests of meeting the news deadlines. The statement that was issued was strong—but it would have been stronger had we taken the time to incorporate the details of reform.

At one level, it didn't matter very much. The following morning, when the Taoiseach was asked in the Dáil whether Dick's statement of the night before represented government policy, he replied that it didn't. It was an astonishing thing to say, and he shouldn't have got away with it.

But we felt that he hadn't really meant to repudiate the agreement he had made with Dick. We thought he had fallen back on a standard parliamentary procedure, whereby unless policy is announced in the House, it doesn't constitute "promised legislation". When I raised the Taoiseach's remark with Martin Mansergh, he was embarrassed about it, but assured me that the Taoiseach still fully supported the commitment to reform.

His apparent repudiation of that commitment in the Dáil, however, gave an opening to Michael McDowell of the

Progressive Democrats to announce that Dick was "morally brain-dead" for accepting assurances of propriety. The media reaction generally to the incident was to regard Dick as either naive or self-serving in the way he had approached the controversy.

Few, if any, were inclined to accept the argument that in the absence of any evidence whatever of a link between the passports and the investment, there was nothing further that any Tánaiste could do. Had the Taoiseach displayed more of a commitment to reform, instead of being stubborn about it, things might have been easier.

But once again, we had no time to dwell on the issue, however much the media and the opposition wanted to. We were immediately plunged back into the detail of the peace process, this time in the context of an EU summit in Corfu. The delegation sent to Corfu was larger than usual, because battles were going to have to be fought on three fronts. The European Commission was still fighting a rearguard action against our year-old £8 billion agreement, and we would have to fight over the figures again at the summit.

There was also an enormous internal row going on about who would succeed Jacques Delors, and the Irish government would have to take a position that was bound to offend John Major. And we were facing some crunch decisions in relation to our Anglo-Irish negotiations, which would have to be addressed jointly with John Major.

In the end, the delegation was so large that it was decided that the government jet would make two trips. Dick was in Poland with Kristi, accompanying President Robinson on a state visit. Since he had to attend the summit, Joan Burton and her husband Pat were going to fly to Warsaw with the Foreign Affairs part of the delegation to take over from them, and we would then fly on to Corfu.

When we landed in Corfu, the jet went back to Dublin for the second load, with Kristi on board. This was shortly to lead to a major row, when some malicious soul put out the false story that the government jet had been used to fly Kristi Spring home—making it look as if there was a huge waste of public money involved.

John Bruton, who presumably didn't know the full facts, weighed in with a personal attack on Dick, which in turn drew a very sharp rejoinder. Although Dick didn't normally bother with inaccurate stories about him in the papers, he did issue legal proceedings against the *Star*, which had attacked Kristi on the basis of spurious facts. The case was eventually settled with a contribution to charity.

Corfu itself was hot, as hot as I've ever experienced. I discovered how Albert Reynolds maintains his magnificent tan—every spare moment during that summit was spent stretched out on a towel beside the swimming pool in our hotel, or swimming lengths in the pool. Our return home on the Sunday was even delayed in order to enable him to catch a few more rays.

In between the rays, though, it was one of the most intensive meetings I remember, and he and Dick were at their best. Albert saw off all attempts to re-negotiate Ireland's structural funds downwards, and they worked together on the Presidency of the Commission, where the Taoiseach emerged as a pivotal figure in helping a compromise to be struck.

The discussions with John Major were particularly intense, and took place in the British delegation rooms. Privately, the two leaders discussed what they knew about developments within Sinn Féin, and both agreed that matters were rapidly coming to a head in relation to a possible ceasefire.

It was also the first time that the two governments had discussed detailed constitutional matters between them—or at least, perhaps, the first time since 1921. Although the Downing Street Declaration had envisaged change in the constitutional law of both jurisdictions, this was the first detailed discussion of what the possible changes might be.

From John Major's point of view, it was essential, as he put it, that any constitutional change in Ireland would have to demonstrably remove any territorial threat from the people of Northern Ireland. He made it clear that the British had a fixed and strong position in relation to Articles Two and Three of our

Constitution, even though publicly they had always accepted that constitutional change in the Republic was a matter for the people of the Republic.

We began, that day, a negotiation which was to lead to forms of constitutional words being exchanged between the governments. From that moment on, the British government submitted every idea and proposition we put forward to what they called "the Corfu test"—would it represent, as John Major had insisted in Corfu, a clear and demonstrable removal of territorial threat.

The Irish media, who had travelled to Corfu in large numbers and were working in very difficult conditions out there, knew nothing of any of this. Albert Reynolds decided they shouldn't be told, and that led to an embarrassing moment for me.

After the meeting, it would be normal to give a briefing, and the Taoiseach decided he would do it himself. We all trooped down to the gate of the enormous fort in Corfu where the summit was being held, and Albert gave what can only be described as the sparsest briefing ever. We met, we talked, very useful, goodbye now. Anyone could see it was not of much value to the journalists waiting.

Una Claffey of RTE was the one under most pressure, as she had a news deadline coming up. She knew that if I spoke to her, she wouldn't get an awful lot more in terms of substance, but she would be able to flesh out the story with some colour and atmosphere, and perhaps draw more meaningful conclusions about whether progress was being made. As we turned to go back into the castle after Albert's monosyllabic briefing, I heard Una calling out my name.

So did the Taoiseach. Turning to me with a sardonic grin, he said triumphantly, "Una's looking for another leak, Fergus." He clearly hadn't forgotten the Emily O'Reilly leak of the draft Framework Document, and I clearly hadn't established my innocence in his eyes.

It was another conversation with Emily O'Reilly, after we came back from Corfu, that got me into further trouble. By way of trying to repair the damage that had been caused to relationships by the Masri incident and the earlier row about residency requirements, Dick and Albert had agreed that they should put some kind of early-warning system in place, so that both sides would have a way of trying to anticipate major "relationship" problems and iron them out before they hit the streets.

It was agreed that Pat Magner and I would meet on a regular basis with Noel Dempsey and Pat Farrell, the General Secretary of Fianna Fáil. We would meet informally and privately, and report only to our respective leaders.

Shortly after Corfu, I was having a cup of coffee with Emily O'Reilly, who was then working for the *Sunday Business Post*, when she asked me about the imminent publication of the Beef Tribunal report. I admitted that it was obvious that a strong report could put further pressure on the government, which was still recovering from its encounter with the Masris.

It could do more than that, she suggested. A critical report could place intolerable strains on the relationship between Fianna Fáil and Labour. After all, our agreed programme had made it clear that the Beef Tribunal report would have to be faced up to in all its implications. I agreed—strong condemnation, which suggested any kind of dishonesty or improper behaviour on the part of the Taoiseach or anyone else associated with the government, could be terminal.

Anyone could have told Emily that—it was obvious that the Beef Tribunal was a time-bomb ticking away under the government. In fact, I had said so at a meeting of the government Programme Managers. I didn't realise until much later, after the government collapsed, that my remark was interpreted by some of my Fianna Fáil colleagues as a personal threat rather than as an obvious statement of fact.

(When the Tribunal report turned out to be a damp squib, one of the Programme Managers, Danny Carroll from the Department of Agriculture, sent me a present. It was a blank ream of paper, bound between the covers of the report, with an alarm clock taped to it. There was a short note, which simply said "some time-bomb!" I kept the clock, but it never worked.)

Because I was only stating the obvious to Emily O'Reilly, over a casual cup of coffee in the Dáil bar, I was a bit surprised when my remarks made the front page of the following Sunday's paper. Although they weren't attributed to me by name, they could be seen as a threat to the stability of the government by anyone who wanted to see them that way.

So I wasn't too surprised when Pat Farrell raised them at the first meeting of our "early warning" group. He described the remarks as unhelpful "whoever made them". I had a choice between agreeing, and joining in the general condemnation that is always heaped on the head of any anonymous source who says something unpalatable, or coming clean.

So I came clean. I told Pat and Noel that it was I who had spoken to Emily, and even though I regarded the remarks as obvious and true—and still did—I could see that they would regard them as unnecessary. I offered, if it would be helpful, to speak directly to the Taoiseach and explain the background. But I also said that they could take it that the views I had expressed were widely held in Labour. After the Masri affair, I didn't think another instance of Dick rushing to the Taoiseach's defence was likely to arise in a hurry.

Pat Farrell told me that he appreciated the candour, and that he would speak to the Taoiseach. If the Taoiseach wanted to hear from me, he'd let me know. That was the last I heard of the matter—I didn't know, until the Taoiseach claimed it publicly much later, that he was so upset by the story that he had to take action.

In fact, when occasions arose in the following weeks for me to be in the Taoiseach's company, he couldn't have been friendlier.

The Corfu summit had heralded the start of very intense activity, and I was by this stage exhausted. I was very glad when the Dáil rose, and we could all pack into the car and head off to England, where we had arranged a house swap with my brother. I left the phone number with Sally Clarke, in case of emergencies.

At the end of July, I was relaxing in the south of England when the phone rang. It was Sally. The Beef Tribunal report was about to be published, and I was needed at home.

I flew home immediately, and went to the Department of Foreign Affairs. Dick was still in Tralee, and wasn't going to come up until the report was actually delivered, but he briefed me over the phone. The cabinet had discussed the release of the report earlier in the week, and it had been agreed that when it was handed over (to the Minister for Agriculture) no comment would be made by the government until it had been studied. There had been particular concern at the cabinet meeting that premature comment could be damaging to government unity.

My instructions were to go to Government Buildings as soon as the report was available, with Niall Burgess, who was Dick's private secretary. Together we were to take possession of Dick's copy, and once we had it, I was to gather William and Greg and start analysing it.

But there was something mysterious going on. We learned early in the evening that the report had indeed been given over to the Minister for Agriculture, and delivered by his office to the Taoiseach's Department. When Niall enquired, however, he was told that there were no copies available and it would be several hours before the report could be photocopied in enough numbers so that one could be made available to the Tánaiste.

Dick smelled a rat, and made a number of efforts to contact the Taoiseach by phone. Again and again he was told by the Taoiseach's office that Albert wasn't there, and therefore was unable to speak to him. At one stage he was told that Albert had gone home for his tea, but when he rang the Taoiseach's home number, Mrs Reynolds assured him that the Taoiseach was definitely in the office—and had eaten before he left home.

At that stage Dick told Niall and me to go down to Government Buildings to the Taoiseach's office, to try to establish his whereabouts, to get a copy of the report, and to get a message to the Taoiseach to the effect that the Tánaiste wished to speak to him urgently.

When we got there, Niall went off in search of the relevant civil servants, and with some trepidation I went down to the

Taoiseach's office, which is at the end of a long corridor on the first floor. I had often been there before, and was astonished to find, halfway down the corridor, a set of double doors that I had never noticed before—and certainly never saw locked before. They were locked tonight, and my knocking on them produced no result.

At first I went back downstairs, and ascertained from the security people on the front door that the Taoiseach was certainly in his office. I went out into the courtyard, and rang Dick on my mobile phone. From where I stood as I spoke to Dick, I could see the lights in the Taoiseach's room, and his state car, parked beneath the arch under his office. But still Dick was telling me, on the other end of the line, that Albert was not in the building and couldn't be contacted. He was getting angrier and angrier.

I went back upstairs and looked into Seán Duignan's office (Seán's office was halfway down the corridor, outside the locked doors). There was no-one inside, but as I turned to leave the phone rang. I went to the desk and picked it up. It was Dónal Kelly, RTE's Political Editor.

He was surprised to hear my voice.

"What are you doing there at this time of night?" he asked.

"Why not?" was all I could think of to say. "I work here, after all."

"Well, can you tell me when we're going to get the statement that's been promised?"

Before I could answer him, the door opened and Seán Duignan walked in. He blushed deep red when he saw me. I handed him the phone and told him it was Dónal Kelly. If anything, he went a deeper shade of red, and told Dónal that he'd ring him back in a minute.

When he hung up, I asked him what statement had Dónal been referring to. The Taoiseach is putting out a statement, he told me. I asked him was he not aware of a cabinet decision that there'd be no statement until it was an agreed government statement. He shrugged.

"I have my instructions," he said. But he was obviously deeply unhappy.

It wasn't until Seán suggested I calm down that I realised that I too was exhibiting a lot of signs of tension. I was pacing up and down his small office like a caged animal. At one stage I tripped over the phone cable and brought the whole apparatus crashing to the floor. Seán has written since that I was like a figure full of biblical wrath. That wasn't how I felt inside. I was angry, yes, but more tense than that.

I told Seán that my instructions were to get a message to the Taoiseach that his Tánaiste was looking for him, that I knew the Taoiseach was inside. Seán said he would deliver the message personally, but he didn't think I'd be welcome in the Taoiseach's office.

To be honest, that was a relief. The last thing I wanted was to confront the Taoiseach. Before I left, I saw Seán approaching the locked doors, knocking twice, and then a third time after a pause. Rightly or wrongly, I decided that everyone in the building was under instructions to use a code if they wanted to get in those doors.

When I went back downstairs, I met Niall, taking delivery of the very bulky copy of the report. We walked together back to Iveagh House, about a quarter of an hour away, as I wanted to clear my head before I rang Dick.

But when I got him, he was the one who was seething. He had just had a phone call from Jackie Gallagher, a journalist in the *Irish Times*, asking him for his reaction to the Taoiseach's statement that he had been fully vindicated by the Beef Tribunal report. And he still hadn't spoken to the Taoiseach.

"That's it," he said. "Collective responsibility my eye. How can I stay in a government where I'm told that I cannot speak to my Taoiseach about an absolutely crucial matter like this?"

It was my turn to try to get him to calm down. I reminded him about the other bit of business that was rapidly coming to a head—the peace process—and that the inevitable consequence of a crisis in government now would be a long delay, at best, in the ceasefire we were all hoping for.

In the end, the Taoiseach rang the Tánaiste about an hour and a half after my visit to Government Buildings. Very angry words were exchanged in that phone call. Dick told the

Taoiseach that his behaviour—and he blamed him personally for issuing instructions that the Tánaiste was not to be put through to him—had been totally improper.

I've always believed that Dick would have resigned that night, and in normal circumstances should have. Only his inside knowledge of how delicately balanced the peace process was at that stage prevented the ultimate decision—and put Dick once more in a position where he was effectively defending what he felt was the unacceptable behaviour of the Taoiseach.

The next time they met the Taoiseach apologised for the way in which Dick had been misled on July 29th. He said that he felt he had been vilified over the years by the reportage of the Beef Tribunal, and was determined to establish his vindication by the report as he saw it. For his part, Dick served notice that breaches of trust of this kind must never happen again, and told the Taoiseach directly that he would be referring to the need to re-build trust in his Dáil speech on the subject. He would mean every word of it, he said.

There are still a few things I've never understood about that night. First of all, even though the Taoiseach and his legal team had the report a couple of hours before anyone else, it was an amazing achievement that they were able to find so quickly, in the 900 pages of the report, a couple of key sentences, pages apart, on which the Taoiseach was able to base his claim of vindication. It took William Scally, Greg Sparks, John Rogers and myself most of the following day to be able to begin to make head or tail of the report.

Secondly, although the report didn't vindicate Albert Reynolds, it didn't damn him either. He could have waited, and accepted the report as an indictment of public policy, which required *mea culpas* from a lot of people. Trust would have been maintained, at the cost of a little of his pride.

And even if he wasn't prepared to swallow his pride, I've never understood why he refused to take a call from Dick.

If he'd said, "Look Dick, we've been through the report with a fine-tooth comb, and as far as I'm concerned it vindicates me. I've taken enough shit about this in the media, and now I'm going to do my own thing". If he'd approached it that way, they might have had a row, but at least Dick would not have been left with the same sense of personal and political betrayal.

And even in the face of all that, the pace of events still didn't let up. Throughout this entire period, the key issue, in terms of the peace process, was how would the IRA and Sinn Féin respond to the Downing Street Declaration. Throughout the early months of the year, Sinn Féin made endless requests for clarification, and no commitment.

But, as a Sinn Féin Ard Fheis in Letterkenny approached in mid-summer, public expectation grew that they would make a decision that would lead to a ceasefire.

Martin Mansergh's intelligence was better. I attended a meeting in London, with Martin and Seán Ó hUiginn, at which we warned the British government in advance that the vibes from the Ard Fheis would be very negative. Martin asked the British to try to avoid "rebarbative comment" on the outcome (I had to look up the word when we got home—it means offensive), and assured them that a great deal of work was still going on to try to secure a ceasefire.

Although the British reaction was subdued, the aftermath of that Ard Fheis was a difficult and lonely period for everyone involved. For several weeks, it looked from the outside as if all the efforts to secure a ceasefire and Sinn Féin's inclusion in negotiations had failed. The media, by and large, seemed to abandon the peace process. The Taoiseach looked and felt isolated—and he has often claimed since that he was left entirely alone at that moment. In fact he wasn't, because the people who worked for him (including me) were still trying very hard to secure the outcome he wanted.

And we were buoyed up by growing signs which made it clear that the peace process was coming to a head, and the ceasefire was going to happen. All the signs were that it was getting ever closer, and was likely to happen before the end of the month of August.

Because the Taoiseach took a short holiday, he and Dick hadn't really met, from the time of their row over the Beef Tribunal Report until near the end of August, when they were scheduled to meet an American delegation together. It was a crucial delegation, composed of people like Neil O'Dowd, Bill Flynn, former Congressman Bruce Morrison—men who were trusted by the Provos and by the Irish government.

They were on their way to Belfast, to find out from Gerry Adams what the Provos had decided. But they didn't know—nobody fully knew then, just a few days before the ceasefire—whether it would be permanent or temporary.

It was crucial that they get the right message, and that they transmit it. And the situation was complicated by the fact that Dick wasn't sure that he trusted Albert enough on some of the issues, and insisted on a half-hour meeting with him (alone) before the American delegation arrived.

Whatever happened at that meeting, it certainly made Albert very sharp—and crystal clear.

"Permanent," he snapped at his distinguished American visitors. "No pussy-footing. I haven't devoted two years of my life to this in order to be insulted with a temporary ceasefire. And another thing—I want their announcement to be written in language that an eleven-year old can understand. No messing—there's to be no messing."

It was easy to see that the Americans were taken aback by his firmness. Whatever issue they raised with him, the answer was the same—a single-syllable barked reply. On one issue in particular, he was especially succinct—in a way that he never quite managed to be when the British subsequently, and foolishly, made it an issue of principle. He was asked about the retention of weapons by the Provos.

"What do they need weapons for?" he asked.

"They don't of course—but they could argue that a minimal amount must be kept for defensive purposes," he was told.

"Look," he said, "they're either at war or they're in politics. If they're in politics they don't need guns. Full stop."

Two nights after this exchange, I found myself in the unusual position of keeping Albert company, in his office, at two in the morning. Despite the tension of the previous few weeks, he was friendly, and kept insisting that I have tea, while he grappled with the latest problem. We weren't going to get a ceasefire unless the Provos could get their former Chief of Staff, Joe Cahill, into the United States to talk to their American supporters.

And no-one would make a decision on a visa. Despite a positive recommendation from the American Ambassador, Jean Kennedy Smith, and her staff in Dublin, the US State Department, whose right it was to issue or refuse visas, was not prepared to take the risk. The only one who could over-rule them was the President himself. And he had left Washington for his holidays in Martha's Vineyard. Albert had already spent a good deal of the evening in negotiation—personally—with Under-Secretaries and Deputy Secretaries in Washington, to little avail. Now he was on the phone to Nancy Soderberg, the Irish expert on the National Security Council, and a key player.

"Lookit, Nancy," he said to her. "You get to him—tell him the ceasefire's in his hands. If he does this thing, it means peace—and you have my absolute guarantee on that. If he doesn't, we're going nowhere."

He wouldn't let her go until she had promised that if she failed, she'd get him a number so that he could ring the President himself. Two hours later, she rang back. Albert took the call, and gave his widest grin.

"He's going to do it. Cahill gets his visa, and we get a ceasefire!"

It was hard to believe. He had pulled off the impossible, and of all people, I was the one who shared the moment with him. We shook hands, and I congratulated him—genuinely. For just one moment, we were like co-conspirators for peace.

But moments, by definition, don't last long.

The IRA ceasefire was declared on August 31st, 1994. The Beef Tribunal report was debated in the Dáil the following day, September 1st.

Dick had a difficult task in that debate. All of the events surrounding the publication of the report were in the public domain by then—the fact that Albert had had the report delivered to him four hours before it was given to Dick, and had broken a government agreement by using selective quotes from the report to claim "total vindication" for himself.

Those of us who had read the report without Albert's keen eye for vindication believed that Judge Liam Hamilton could have been harder, but that he had still made trenchant criticisms of the failure of public policy that had to be referred to in the debate.

In addition, Dick felt he had no choice but to refer to the breach of trust that surrounded the publication, and especially Albert's handling of the situation. He knew too, going in, that he would be criticised himself for letting Albert off the hook.

So he had the quandary of addressing the breach of trust, and still not de-stabilising the government—and with it, the infant ceasefire. It was one of those no-win situations where you know that no speech is going to persuade everyone. It was difficult to write, and difficult to make, and it took most of the night for those of us involved in the drafting.

Within minutes of the speech being delivered, and without any rest, we left for the United States, where Dick had been asked to brief President Clinton on the implications of the ceasefire.

We flew to Amsterdam on the government jet, and from there to Washington on a KLM flight. En route we were told that the President was sending a plane to meet us and bring us to Martha's Vineyard where he was still on holidays.

I had visions of Air Force One, but as it turned out, we travelled on Air Force 36 (or thereabouts), a clapped out Lear jet which hit the runway in Martha's Vineyard with a terrible bump. My life was further complicated by the fact that I hadn't been told that it was the President's wish that everyone would dress casually, since he was on holidays, so I travelled in my best (wool) suit. It's what you do when you're going to meet the President of the U.S., I thought, but it wasn't exactly the thing for still sweltering Martha's Vineyard!

It was an important meeting, and important to break the ice. Although we had met the President several times before in Washington, it was made clear to us that Dick was the only visitor for whom the President was willing to break his holidays, and it was vital to establish the right level of rapport. As it happened, the President's opening remark, when we all settled in the sitting room of the old colonial house in which he was staying, provided the perfect opportunity. He had only recently taken up golf, and was finding it a frustrating experience.

Within minutes, John Foley (the best eight-handicap golfer I've ever seen), was helping the most powerful politician in the world to address problems in his grip and take-away, while diplomats from both sides sat frozen in their seats.

When we were leaving, the President shook everyone's hand. John was overheard by the world's media saying, "Don't forget, Mr President, keep it a little looser". The first question Dick was asked at his subsequent press conference in Edgartown was to explain the deep meaning behind the remark!

Although we had already been up for most of two nights, we still had to travel to New York, where Dick addressed a meeting of about 200 Irish-American community leaders (including some who had been most instrumental in brokering the ceasefire with Sinn Féin). After he had answered their questions for nearly two hours, we made a mad dash to Kennedy Airport, just in time to catch the Aer Lingus flight home. Again, travel through the night affected both my temper and my (by now) very rumpled wool suit.

Twenty-four hours later, still disoriented from the two-day trip to the United States, we set off for Berlin, to brief Klaus Kinkel, the German Foreign Minister, about the ceasefire, and to begin the process of finding a European source of funding to support it.

While we were in Berlin, the famous handshake between Gerry Adams, John Hume, and Albert Reynolds took place on the steps of Government Buildings. I've always regretted ever since that Dick wasn't there too, as his absence was used by "people close to Albert" to suggest that Dick's support for the process was less than total.

On the way home from Berlin on the government jet, Niall Burgess gave Dick the agenda for the government meeting of the following day. One of the items on it concerned the appointment of a Chief Justice. There was a memorandum with the Agenda from Máire Geoghegan-Quinn, making it clear that she would be proposing to government that Liam Hamilton, then President of the High Court and author of the Beef Tribunal report, should be appointed Chief Justice, and that decisions would be expected on the same day on who should succeed Judge Hamilton as President of the High Court (although no successor was named in the documentation).

This had been put on the government agenda without any reference to Dick. Given the previous breach of trust, he was astonished to read all this, and angry.

It was clear that there was more trouble ahead.

15

Partnership Shattered

The next three months—September, October, and November of 1994—were the most productive of what I fondly refer to as my political career. And the most miserable.

On some days of each week, I was part of an intensely talented and committed team that negotiated the Joint Framework Document, led by politicians at the top of their abilities. On other days, I grappled with a crisis that threatened to destroy the careers and personalities of a host of individuals, and left scars on all who were involved.

I ended up as one of the minor heroes of one process, and one of the major scapegoats of the other.

The negotiations on the Joint Framework Document were intense and unremitting. Each week, we would go to the Northern Ireland Office, at the end of the Mall in London, or they would come to Iveagh House. Each week we would battle over words and phrases, every shred of language being submitted to endless parsing and analysing. We had arguments about the difference between "equity" and "equality", about whether there should be a comma in the phrase "selfish strategic or economic interest" (after the word selfish). From an earlier position of being somewhat scornful of an emphasis on language, I came to appreciate the importance of every nuance, and the danger of tampering with what we called "terms of art".

Above all I came to appreciate the brilliance of the people I was dealing with. Seán Ó hUiginn and Martin Mansergh were among the principal architects and designers of the peace process. It would not have started, and the British would not have negotiated their way through it, without the involvement of these two men.

Others played a major role throughout that time too—in ways that have never been recognised. David Donoghue (and before him Declan O'Donovan) kept a steady flow of information and insight coming from within Northern Ireland. David Cooney, whom I had first met when he played a key role in helping to negotiate the £8 billion in Brussels, proved to be an outstanding and tough generator of new ideas and approaches. Rory Montgomery, Ray Basset, Philip McDonagh and a number of others all contributed ideas and language at times when they were sorely needed, and became masters of their own individual parts of the process.

It would be impossible too to overstate the role played by our Ambassadors abroad. Ted Barrington in London, and Dermot Gallagher in Washington, were both superb negotiators, and incredibly effective generators of access. Through months of difficult negotiations, the Irish government was a player in a process that involved three Governments— one small and insignificant, and two of the largest and best-resourced in the world, with centuries of tradition and muscle behind them. And we more than held our own—thanks to the creativity, resourcefulness, and talent of a small number of people.

The bottom line for me was that I knew I could go anywhere in the company of people like this, and be proud of a good day's work at the end of it. And little by little an agreement of huge breadth and scope began to take place.

As far as Dick Spring was concerned, this was also a time when his talent and energy was stretched to the limit. The concepts that were being discussed at "official" level could not be developed without very considerable political involvement. He was immersed in the Joint Framework Document negotiations from the beginning, together with Sir Patrick Mayhew, and they put hours of intensive work into it, even while other major political crises were developing and unfolding. I've never seen Dick better than during those hard negotiations, especially at all the more critical moments when nerve needed to be held.

And on several occasions during that period, our work was reviewed at the highest level, in summit meetings involving Albert Reynolds and John Major.

One of these took place during the month of October, in Chequers. Apart from the opportunity it gave me to see the place, it was the first experience we had of the British obsession with decommissioning arms. Most of that meeting was taken up with a discussion of the subject, and there was no doubt in our minds that the British Prime Minister attached great importance to it.

The meeting ended with an agreement to establish a small group of officials from both governments, headed by Sir John Chilcot and Tim Dalton, Secretary of our Department of Justice. The Dalton/Chilcot Group, as it came to be called, went on to play a key role in the wider development of the peace process. But later assertions that the Fianna Fáil and Labour government never got involved in decommissioning were essentially untrue. It was an issue from the beginning, and we always knew it was going to be a difficult one to resolve.

Despite the intensity of the work, there were lighter moments too. After one long meeting in London, Sir John Chilcot announced that he was going to take us to his club—the Traveller's Club in Pall Mall. We took port and cheese, after a hearty lunch, in the room where Scott planned his ill-fated journey to the South Pole.

Excusing himself to go to the loo at the end of the meal, Seán Ó hUiginn said, with exquisite timing, "I'm going outside, gentlemen. I may be gone for a while!"

On another occasion, Seán Duignan and I found ourselves surplus to requirements at a meeting in Downing Street. We were ensconced in the Prime Minister's Library, while the meeting turned into dinner in the Cabinet Room nearby. As time passed, and we got hungrier and hungrier, it began to seem that we had been completely forgotten.

Eventually the door opened, and a lady looked in and said, "Oh there you are, I've brought you some refreshments". And she brought in a great silver tray, on which were two mugs of weak tea and a single plate, with Marietta biscuits and potato crisps on it. We both expressed the hope that they were doing better in the Cabinet Room.

The fascinating thing about that library is that it is stuffed from floor to ceiling with first editions, all signed by the authors and by the Prime Minister who received them. High up on one shelf I came across a novella, whose name I can't remember now, by Somerset Maugham. It was a first edition, signed by Maugham and by Winston Churchill.

To Seán's horror, I speculated about how good it would look on my own bookcase at home. In the end, however, visions of clanging bells and John Major clapping his arm on my shoulder as I tried to smuggle it out of the building persuaded me that I should leave it where it was.

I did steal one thing from Lancaster House, where we had a number of meetings. Lancaster House was built by the Grand old Duke of York, and there were several references in our discussions to whether it was a suitable venue for the work we were doing. But after a long dinner there one night, I pocketed a book of matches that were adorned with the Royal crest.

It was a philanthropic gesture—at the next meeting between Sinn Féin and the Irish government I took pleasure in presenting them to Rita O'Hare, Sinn Féin's press officer, who is like myself an inveterate smoker.

On the constitutional side of the discussions, Seán Ó hUiginn, Martin Mansergh, and I became, I think, a great team. Seán was a tough and hard negotiator, brilliant in his assessment of how far things could be taken. Martin was erudite, and constantly amazed the British side with his analytical approach to the context of our negotiations. I had a good eye for language and for the moment to seize a compromise, and I've always been reasonably good at lateral thinking in negotiation—if a problem can't be solved one way, there are always different ways to go around it.

On one occasion, Quentin Thomas, on the other side of the table, speculated about whether or not the Taoiseach was entirely serious about making an agreement that would enshrine the principle of consent in the Irish Constitution. Before Martin could respond, I gave a spirited account of the risks that Albert Reynolds had taken, and the lengths that he was prepared to go to in search of an honourable compromise. Afterwards, Martin thanked me for leaping to Albert's defence, and agreed that it had been all the more effective coming from me rather than from the Taoiseach's own man. Over the following weeks, I was to reflect several times on the irony of that!

Our constitutional negotiations built up to a point where we were, on both sides, ready to sign off on an agreement that we could recommend to political masters. The meeting at which agreement was due to be made took place on November 11th, in Government Buildings. It ought to have been a quietly triumphant meeting. I missed it, however, because it happened at exactly the moment when the Fianna Fáil and Labour partnership was finally, and irrevocably, shattered.

To trace the story of that shattering, it's necessary to go back to the moment on the government jet when Dick was shown the agenda for the cabinet meeting of September 7th.

He told me then, on the government jet, that he had strong ideas about the appointment of a Chief Justice, and how such an appointment could be used to modernise and reform the courts. It was for that reason that he wanted to keep Hamilton, whom he regarded as an excellent manager of the busiest court, where he was, and why he wanted to push the case of Donal Barrington, then serving a term in Europe, because he thought he would be a forward-looking and progressive Chief Justice.

He also told me, for the first time, that Harry Whelehan had recently come to him and expressed an interest in the Presidency of the High Court, should Liam Hamilton be appointed to the top job. Dick had been surprised by that approach, because he understood that Harry Whelehan had taken to learning French because he had some interest in an appointment to one of the European institutions. I asked him had he given Harry any satisfaction, and his reply was "you must be joking!"

He never saw Harry Whelehan, who had no judicial experience but did have a controversial and conservative track record, as a possible vehicle for reform. He had discussed the matter briefly with Albert Reynolds some time before. They had, in fact, discussed the possibility that Donal Barrington should be the Chief Justice, and that Liam Hamilton should stay where he was. In his capacity as Attorney General, Harry had done some research for them on the point, and had established that Barrington was technically disqualified because of his absence in Europe.

And now suddenly, Dick was being confronted with a proposed government decision—which looked for all the world to him like a ready-up. Even though no name was mentioned, the very fact that no other name had been discussed with him led Dick to believe that Harry's was the only name that would be put forward.

I remember telling him that it couldn't be true. This was all happening only days after Dick's Dáil speech about breaches of trust, there was no doubt that Albert would want to resolve the matter amicably. You can't be right all the time!

I had had very little contact with Harry Whelehan. Up to that moment, the only time I can ever remember speaking to him was at some function, where I was introduced to him and we exchanged pleasantries about the fact that we had sometimes been mistaken for each other. I remember remarking that I didn't know whether that was to his disadvantage or mine.

I have a layman's view of his record, particularly in relation to the X case, in which I profoundly disagreed with his actions. Also as a layman, I totally disagreed with the stance he took, and the advice I presume he gave, in relation to the issue of cabinet confidentiality, particularly as it affected the Beef Tribunal. But other than that, my impression was of a nice man, who went around with a slightly innocent air.

The following day, after a brief discussion between Dick and Albert, the proposed appointment was withdrawn from the government agenda. The two men had several conversations about the matter over the next couple of days, and it seemed to be going well.

At the end of the week, I accompanied Dick to a meeting of the British-Irish Association in Oxford. Just before going into dinner, we met John Rogers, who was also attending the conference.

If Dick had discussed his ideas about legal and judicial reform with anyone, it would have been with John, who if anything would have had stronger views than Dick about the future of the courts.

John was keen to know if any progress had been made. Dick told us that Albert had now agreed that Harry wasn't suitable for the job, and that he had told Harry so.

"How did Harry take it?" I asked.

"Badly, apparently," Dick replied. "But Albert is still working on him."

I had to go back to Dublin that night. The following day, Albert and Dick had another conversation, and Albert said that Harry was pressurising him to change his mind. Dick, however, was happy that Albert was going to stand firm. Dick had to go to Japan and China on government business, and the matter was going to be discussed again when he returned.

But lo and behold, in the miraculous way that sometimes happens in politics, as soon as Dick was out of the country stories began to appear, on television and in the newspapers, to the effect that the government would be appointing Judge Hamilton as Chief Justice at its next meeting, together with Harry as President of the High Court. According to the leaks, either Eoghan Fitzsimons or the former Fianna Fáil TD Henry Abbott would succeed Harry Whelehan as Attorney General

The stories were authoritative. Una Claffey is one of the most thorough and responsible journalists in Ireland, and when she is reporting something like that, you know it has been very well-sourced.

Obviously, whoever was the source had waited until Dick had left the country. I asked Seán Duignan if he knew anything about the source of the stories, but hand on heart, he told me that he had nothing to do with them. I had no reason to disbelieve him.

But I couldn't contact Dick, because of his schedule. John Rogers and I were in Dick's office in Iveagh House the night before the government meeting, wondering what we could do in his absence, when he rang through. We brought him up to date — including the fact that the offending item had been reinstated on the agenda for the following morning. He was furious, and told us to make sure that the other Labour Ministers were fully briefed before the cabinet meeting.

When we met the Labour Ministers the following morning, they all found the thought of another potential row, so soon after the Beef Tribunal one, very unwelcome. Mervyn Taylor just couldn't believe it.

"There must be some misunderstanding," he said, "Albert would never push through appointments like these without total agreement."

Halfway through the meeting, Dick rang, from a public coinbox in Narita Airport in Tokyo. He and Ruairi Quinn had a short discussion — interrupted by Dick running out of yen. Before he was cut off, he and Ruairi agreed that the Labour Ministers would seek to prevent the appointment.

The cabinet meeting was delayed for three hours, while Ruairi and Brendan Howlin negotiated with Albert on behalf of the Labour Ministers. Eventually, after much toing and froing, it was agreed that the appointment of Liam Hamilton would go ahead, but that decisions regarding his successor would he held over until they were agreed between Albert and Dick in the first instance.

Those of us who were involved in the matter on the Labour side thought that this was a satisfactory outcome, and that now Albert would be willing to compromise. We all had the view that an unworthy attempt to make an important government decision by sleight of hand had been seen off.

Later that afternoon I met Joe Joyce of the *Sunday Tribune* casually, and he asked me about the appointments. I told him, truthfully, that the appointment of Judge Hamilton had gone ahead, but that an attempt to fill the vacancy he left behind had led to a row, and the delay of the start of the government meeting. I also told him that the matter had now been resolved, and that Taoiseach and Tánaiste would be discussing the matter further when Dick came back from the Far East.

The following morning, I went to Sweden on party business, as part of a delegation that was observing the Swedish elections. On the Saturday evening, I found myself in the main square in Gothenburg, in the middle of a fantastic fireworks display, and decided to ring home to try to share the experience with Frieda. Between the explosions, Frieda told me that Una Claffey was frantically looking for me. I rang her, and she asked me to confirm the truth or otherwise of a story about the controversy by Ken Whelan in the *Irish Press*. I told her I knew nothing about the story, and she read me bits and pieces from it. I confirmed its general accuracy, subject to some minor details that I can't remember now.

In summary, I've always believed that the whole matter would never have become controversial in the first instance had it not been for the attempt to slip it through the cabinet when Dick was out of the country, and had it not been for the efforts to promote Harry Whelehan through the media in advance of any decision being made.

I didn't set out to publicise the matter—the controversy which erupted was entirely of Fianna Fáil's own making.

But in the ensuing weeks, the controversy continued. And the more public it became, the more determined Albert seemed to be to have his way. Matters became farcical when their conflicting schedules meant that Dick and Albert were unable to be in Ireland at the same time for a couple of weeks on end. It became a news story when they spoke to one another on the phone.

Needless to say, all of this was causing amazement among our party back-benchers, who knew little of the background, and especially the way in which relationships had deteriorated throughout the previous six months.

Some of the Labour Ministers too evidently thought things were getting out of hand. Dick gathered his Ministers and advisers in Iveagh House early in October to discuss the issue. There was a lot of worry on all sides, and an obvious desire for agreement. It was a contentious and difficult meeting with everyone feeling the tension of a government under acute pressure.

The following day the *Irish Times* reported that Labour Ministers had rounded on advisers at a private meeting the previous night, and had made it clear that they thought we were pursuing a private agenda to wreck the government. That thought hadn't been expressed at our meeting, but obviously someone thought it appropriate to tell the *Irish Times* that it had. It was the first chink in our armour.

In the end, on the second Sunday in October, eight Labour TDs went on RTE to say that in their view, the appointment of Harry Whelehan shouldn't be cause for breaking up the government. It sounded very much as if they were telling their leader to get sense.

Certainly Albert, listening to the programme with Noel Dempsey, thought that Dick was now sufficiently isolated, and he immediately suggested a meeting to take place later that night.

Dick felt totally let down, and beaten. The meeting was scheduled for Baldonnel airport, because Albert was arriving in Baldonnel from one function and Dick was leaving there for another. (Albert's counsel in a subsequent libel action was later to describe this meeting as reminding him of a scene in *Casablanca*!)

Before he went to Baldonnel, Dick resigned himself to the notion that he would have to swallow his reservations about Harry's appointment in the interests of restoring some cohesion to government. He made an agreement with Albert that once certain necessary court reforms had been published and adopted by government for subsequent legislation, he would allow the judicial appointments to be brought back to the cabinet table.

He didn't however agree, at that meeting, that they would go ahead automatically—but there's no doubt in my mind that at that stage he believed the matter was over, and he was going to have to eat humble pie over Harry.

Out of the blue, a fortnight later, the *Sunday Independent* carried a story by Veronica Guerin about Father Brendan Smyth. Originally mentioned on UTV, but largely unnoticed, it transpired that an extradition warrant for Smyth, a priest accused of sexual offences against children, had lain unattended in Harry Whelehan's office for seven months.

Suddenly Dick's position made a lot more sense. How could it have happened? And how could anyone be seriously considering the promotion of an Attorney General who had allowed it to happen? Dick decided that, no matter what it cost, and notwithstanding his earlier decision to back away, he simply could not allow Harry to be promoted to the second most senior judicial post in the land unless and until he was satisfied that there was proper accountability for the handling of the Smyth case.

He asked Albert to seek a report on the matter from Harry. Albert readily agreed. What they got was a short note written by Matt Russell, the senior civil servant in the Attorney's office—who was also the man who had handled the file.

It said, in effect, that there was no big deal about the delay, and was completely self-exculpatory. Both Taoiseach and Tánaiste considered it totally inadequate, and a further report was requested.

This report was made available to Dick on November 10th. But it was accompanied by a demand from Albert that Harry's appointment couldn't be delayed any longer, and he scheduled a decision for a government meeting the day the report was delivered. As it happened, that meeting was totally taken up with discussion of the murder, by the IRA, of a postal worker in Newry—the first breach of the IRA ceasefire.

But Albert insisted that there be a special meeting the following day—Friday November 11th—to make the decision.

Dick's Ministerial colleagues, and some of his advisers, met in his Iveagh House office after the November 10th meeting. This was a much more cohesive session. Everyone agreed that Harry's explanation for the delay in extraditing the paedophile priest was totally inadequate, and indeed seemed to exonerate his office from any blame.

Dick sent his Ministerial driver off with a hand-written note to Albert, saying that he and his colleagues regarded the explanations as totally inadequate. In the circumstances, he wrote, Labour Ministers could not support Harry's promotion unless and until a satisfactory explanation had been offered, by Harry personally or by Albert in the Dáil.

Back came a note from Albert saying that he regarded a government meeting as the only appropriate place for Harry to offer his explanations.

Dick wrote again—one last effort—saying that the least the Labour Ministers expected was that Albert would answer questions in the Dáil before final consideration of any appointment being made.

He knew full well that if Harry was made a member of the judiciary before offering public accountability for an apparently grievous lapse (to put it at its kindest) his new-found status as a judge could render it impossible to question him afterwards.

A number of things happened on the Friday afternoon. First, we got the results of two by-elections in Cork. Both had gone badly for the government, but were desperately disappointing for us. Gerry O'Sullivan, whose death had caused one by-election, had been an outstanding and popular Labour TD, and a successful Junior Minister. We had every confidence that his daughter Lisa would do well in the by-election in Cork North Central, but instead we had been hammered—through no fault of Lisa's. And in Cork South Central, where Toddy O'Sullivan was an equally popular TD, we had been badly beaten too. I have no doubt that such a dire outcome, and the message in it about Labour's popularity, wouldn't have escaped Albert's attention.

I was also scheduled that day to attend an afternoon meeting with Martin Mansergh and Seán Ó hUiginn. It was the meeting at which we hoped finally to reach agreement on the language in the Joint Framework Document dealing with constitutional issues.

I didn't go, because I wanted to be present when the cabinet meeting was over. I learned afterwards that a note had been sent into the meeting to say that half the cabinet had resigned, causing consternation on both the British and Irish sides— neither of them was sure for a moment which cabinet was referred to!

I'll never forget the grim atmosphere in Dick's Leinster House office when he and the other Labour Ministers returned. William Scally, Greg Sparks and I were waiting for them. Ruairi Quinn explained that there had been total dissatisfaction at the meeting with Harry's explanations. Brian Cowen in particular had objected to Albert's intention to publish the report, and had argued that it should be shredded instead, because he felt it fell far short of an adequate explanation.

Notwithstanding that, when the discussion on Harry's report was complete, Albert had immediately proposed Harry's promotion to the Presidency of the High Court. Every Fianna Fáil Minister had agreed, and the Labour Ministers had left in silence.

As Ruairi was recounting the events in the cabinet room, Dick leaned against the edge of his desk, his head down. When Ruairi had finished, Dick was the next to speak.

"Look," he said, "this is my row. I'm not going back in there, because I couldn't work with Albert again. But if it would help …"

It was Niamh Bhreathnach who anticipated his thought.

"Forget it Dick," she said. "We didn't walk out after you— we walked out with you."

That ended any discussion of that topic.

Instead, they agreed that a special meeting of the parliamentary party would be called for the following Sunday (November 13th), and I was told to go off and start work on a background note that Dick could use at that meeting. Before I left, the phone rang. It was Albert.

The conversation was brief and stilted. Dick said that he'd be consulting his parliamentary party, and that the situation was now grave. Then he hung up, and looked at us.

"Do you know where he is?" he said in amazement. "He's already up in Aras an Uachtaráin. The appointment is made!"

The die was cast, or so it seemed. Once the appointments were announced publicly, it would have to become clear that Labour Ministers had not participated in Harry's promotion.

Indeed, the following day's papers were already reporting as the main story that having dissented from the decision, Dick was now going to resign from government, and that the government would inevitably fall.

Things began to move very fast. At the private parliamentary party meeting in Jury's Hotel on the Sunday, Dick set out his ground.

In his speech, which was never published, he told them that we had

> reached a difficult moment in the life of the party—a moment when we must confront fundamental issues of public accountability. We must seek to balance those issues against the continuing needs of a peace process that is delicately balanced, and the risk of introducing temporary uncertainty into the economic management of our country.
>
> What we cannot afford, I believe, is the luxury of allowing electoral considerations, whatever they might be, to make our decisions for us. Whenever we face the electorate, whether that be sooner or later, we must seek to do so in the knowledge that we have tried to do what is right.

And he went on to say that the government had been a good and successful one. It had undertaken a number of major challenges, and had made a huge difference to the economic future of the country. It had begun, in a way that no previous government ever had, the process of building a durable peace on the island. It had already established a formidable reforming and legislative record, based on the most comprehensive government programme in the history of the state. It had made tremendous strides in undoing the damage that had been done to essential social services in Ireland by previous administrations.

Both the mistakes and the achievements were in most cases the result of collective cabinet responsibility, he said.

> As a member of that cabinet, I must accept responsibility for mistakes if I want to claim credit for achievement. However, last Friday collective cabinet responsibility

broke down. The ethos of partnership, which has informed most of the achievements of this government, was abandoned.

And then he went on to outline in detail the events leading up to the government decision on Harry Whelehan. He concluded his speech this way:

> There is one final decision to be made. We have declined to share in the moral decision to make this appointment until it went hand in hand with accountability. We remain, as members of the government, collectively responsible in the constitutional sense. We must decide whether that is the right and proper position to be in, having regard to our commitment to the people we serve.
>
> I believe I have to say that ultimately, the decision is mine to make. I hope that members of the PLP will accept that.
>
> Before I make that decision, I want to hear the views of all members of the PLP. I undertake to consider those views carefully, and to take them into full account. I must also take into account the wide range of outstanding and critically important matters still awaiting the government's attention.
>
> I understand that on Tuesday next, the Taoiseach intends to address all these matters in the Dáil. No final decision is possible, I believe, until we hear what is said then. In the meantime, no Labour Minister will attend the government meeting scheduled for Tuesday morning.
>
> At the end of the day, when all other questions have been dealt with, one remains. We have allowed a child abuser to remain at large in our community, when we had it in our power to ensure that he was given up to justice. Is no-one to explain why? Is no-one to take responsibility? Is no-one to account to the people of this country for so grievous a lapse?

> Government owes no higher duty to its people than to strive might and main to protect their children. We have a duty, as representatives of the people, to ensure that there is full accountability to them in respect of any failure to protect them. We must, and we will, do that duty.

That speech and others have sometimes been interpreted as the Labour Party's way of saying that other people are soft on paedophilia. It was nothing of the kind—it would be an absurdity for us to suggest such a thing. The speech was about trust, and about accountability, nothing more than that.

When Dick had finished, speaker after speaker affirmed total support for Dick's position. It was unanimously agreed that it was impossible to approve Harry's appointment until a satisfactory explanation had been received as to his delay in processing the extradition warrant for the paedophile priest.

When he saw the television pictures of this meeting, and Dick's press conference afterwards, Albert finally seemed to get the message that we were serious. He made several efforts to persuade Dick by phone that it was all a terrible misunderstanding.

So did other Fianna Fáil Ministers—on the Saturday night, for instance, Ruairi Quinn and Brendan Howlin met Michael Smith and Máire Geoghegan-Quinn, with Dick's approval. They reported to Dick afterwards that there was nothing that Fianna Fáil weren't prepared to do—except, of course, that they had done something that couldn't be undone, in proceeding with the appointment and rendering Harry immune from any questioning.

The general feeling was that Albert would have to make a remarkable speech in the Dáil on Tuesday. In the event, he fell between two stools. His speech basically said that Dick Spring was a lovely man, but there was no reason whatsoever not to promote Harry Whelehan. It wasn't a speech that was going to change anything.

That night Dick was scheduled to present the "People of the Year" Awards in the Burlington Hotel, and his wife Kristi had travelled up from Kerry to accompany him. I argued that it should be called off, because he was under immense strain, and I just didn't see how a live TV appearance was going to work. But he refused, and in fact, he was totally relaxed on TV, like a man without a care in the world.

About half-eleven that night, as I was getting into bed, the phone rang. It was Pat Magner, the oldest friend I have in politics, and someone whose instincts are almost never wrong.

"Listen," he said, "Dempsey is putting pressure on us to talk. They're saying they can do a deal."

"Forget it," I said. "What's done can't be undone."

He pressed me as to whether I was sure—"others think a deal might be possible," he said. I said I was sure, and that all I wanted to do was go to bed.

To this day, I'm sorry I didn't get back into my clothes. I should have realised the kind of pressure that would be exerted through the night, by people who are past masters at cobbling things together. The fact that Dick hadn't resigned already— that he was waiting until it was his turn to speak in the Dáil— was clearly being interpreted as willingness, even at that late hour, to do a deal.

But I didn't get up—and maybe if I had, a deal would have been done anyway. Fianna Fáil were desperate enough to agree to any form of words—the problem was that this was a situation beyond words.

We made a bad mistake in talking to them that night, because for the first time, the solidarity that existed between us as a group broke down. It took a long time to re-build that solidarity, and to get over the feeling that we had let each other down when our backs were to the wall. I still find the memories of that night, and what it led to, among the most painful in my political life.

The following morning William, Greg, John Rogers, John Foley, Sally Clarke and I met Dick at 8.00 am. We all believed, I think, that this was the last time we would see the inside of the Department of Foreign Affairs. After some desultory discussion, he left at about nine to attend a meeting of his Labour Ministerial colleagues.

There would be another debate in the Dáil that afternoon, and Dick would be announcing his resignation then.

I went to my own office in Government Buildings to begin drafting Dick's resignation speech. Some time close to 10.30 am, just before the Dáil convened, I was asked to go up to Dick's Leinster House office. Most of the Labour Ministers and Ministers of State were there, getting ready to go down to the Dáil.

There's a small toilet and shower just off the Tánaiste's Dáil office. It was originally built for Jack Lynch, before the Taoiseach of the day moved across to the new Government Buildings. Dick took me in there, as the only private corner of the room, and told me that a new case had been discovered. The Duggan case—as it has come to be known—showed that Harry's report on the Smyth case had been misleading. It was clear that all those present felt that this new discovery changed everything, and that it would now be possible to clear the matter up to our satisfaction.

Albert would crawl, and we would be seen to have been right all along about Harry.

To be more specific, Albert was now prepared to attack in the Dáil the judge whose appointment he had rammed through the previous Friday, and defended the previous day. Dick showed me a piece of paper which contained some sentences that Albert proposed to use in his Dáil speech—sentences that Brendan Howlin and Pat Magner had negotiated through the night, mainly with Noel Dempsey and Charlie McCreevy on behalf of Fianna Fáil.

At one stage too they had discussed the issues with Dick's brother Dónal, and he seemed, I gathered, to support the compromise. (I learned later that Dónal's involvement had been fairly minimal, and that he had never believed Fianna Fáil would accept a form of words that would involve Albert doing a complete u-turn.)

It was the consensus of senior Labour Party people present that the government should be preserved, because the peace process was still in its infancy.

Dick told me, standing in that little toilet, that for all these reasons he had signed an undertaking to lead the party back into government, and had dated it 10.22 am that morning.

I knew from his face that he was unhappy about the decision he had taken, and when he asked me how I felt about it, I thought I was going to be sick.

"He can't do it." I said. "Albert can't say these things about the President of the High Court."

"But he's going to," Dick told me. "He believed all Harry's reasons for the delay, and now he feels let down."

I could hardly speak. I stammered out something about Albert demeaning his own office, and the office of the Presidency of the High Court, if he followed this approach, and I did not see how he could do this and still be supported.

All the time I could see that Dick was in agony over the decision he'd made. You don't work for someone for fifteen years without knowing at least a little bit of what's going on inside, and I think that Dick had decided that he had to do what was in everyone's interest except his own. Dick left the bathroom before me, because the bell that summons TDs to the Dáil was already ringing. I think I almost staggered down the corridor. On the way I met Niamh Bhreathnach, herself hurrying to the chamber.

"What do you think?" she said. But I found myself unable to speak.

Ten minutes later I was sitting on a park bench in Stephens Green. I'm not sure what was going through my mind. I knew that Dick's decision to lead his team back into government was not one he had taken easily, or for the sake of hanging on to office himself. But I couldn't, for the first time in all the years I had worked with him, support his decision.

It was not that I felt sympathy for Harry Whelehan—I didn't—but rather that I could not see how the damage that was about to be done to important institutions could be undone. The Office of the Taoiseach, the Office of Attorney General, the second highest judicial post in the land—all were about to be dragged through the mud. Nothing like that had ever happened in my memory — it reminded me of the book *The Final Days* about Richard Nixon.

What was more, I felt certain that Dick would, in the end, bear the brunt of criticism. The government would be discredited by the attack on a sitting judge that was proposed — and it would immediately be presented as Albert only doing it because Dick had forced him to.

I had a scrap of paper in my pocket, and I scribbled an incoherent resignation on it. When I stood up, I discovered to my astonishment that my eyes were blurred with tears. I must have looked a sight — red-eyed, scribbling on bits of paper, unsure where to go next.

There was nothing for it but to go and give Dick my scrap of paper. But when I got back to his office, he was briefing his colleagues about a startling new development.

He had just discovered, following a conversation he had had with the new Attorney General, Eoghan Fitzsimons, that Albert had known about the new case since the previous Monday. This new case, which Ministers believed strongly undermined Harry's defence of his position, had therefore been raised with Albert *before* he had gone into the Dáil and unreservedly defended Harry and his promotion!

Brendan Howlin in particular was shocked. He told us that he had heard about the Duggan case for the first time a short time before Dick had signed the agreement to go back into government. He believed from what Charlie McCreevy and Noel Dempsey had told him that the Duggan case represented entirely new and significant information.

But how had Dick found out about it?

There had been a lot of commotion in the Dáil chamber at half-ten. Albert had come in to seek an adjournment of an hour, because the speech he had agreed to give had not yet been fully typed. When the Opposition had seen the Labour Ministers take their places, they guessed that the government was still together, and started baying for blood.

In the midst of the commotion, Michael Bell, our TD from Louth and chairman of the parliamentary party, slipped Dick a note. It contained a name and phone number.

"I think you should ring this number," Michael said. "He knows something about the Brendan Smyth case."

After the adjournment, Dick had walked through the Dáil corridor, feeling the note in his pocket. He's not an impulsive man normally, but he went to his office and rang the number.

The person at the other end told him there was another case, involving a monk. Dick knew that, but how did the stranger know? Because, he was told, he had met Angela Phelan, a well-known gossip columnist, who was friendly with the Reynolds family. She had told him that she had been in Albert's house on Monday night. Albert had been incandescent with rage about the mess that Harry had made.

Albert had talked about how Harry had hung him out to dry when there might have been another precedent for dealing with the Smyth case. Eoghan Fitzsimons, the new Attorney General, had raised it with Albert on Monday afternoon.

Dick was utterly bemused. How could this be true? Albert had defended Harry in the Dáil on Tuesday, after all.

And if it was true, how could the information be of any use? It was totally third-hand, and he wasn't in a position to reveal the name of the person he had rung to anyone.

Dick told William Scally and Greg Sparks what he had discovered. But how to check it?

"There's one person who can confirm that for you," William said. "The Attorney General."

"I can hardly ask him in the circumstances," Dick objected.

"You're still the Tánaiste," William reminded him.

And the Attorney confirmed that he had raised the issue of the Duggan case with Albert on the Monday. As Dick subsequently said in his Dáil speech, Albert had some information which should have been conveyed to the Dáil on Tuesday.

Dick and his colleagues all agreed unanimously that this new information changed everything—they couldn't support Albert now. Dick hurriedly scribbled out some notes on what he wanted to say to Albert, and he and some of the other Ministers went off to see him.

There's always been confusion about what exactly happened at that meeting. I know that when our Ministers came back, Ruairi was extremely rueful because he felt he had blurted out the phrase "we've come for a head" without thinking. He knew immediately that it was a stupid thing to say—we all knew that whatever decision Fianna Fáil wanted to make, it had to be their own. Putting us in the position of head-hunters made us look cheap.

In the Dáil that afternoon, Dick made a speech that we had worked on for the rest of the morning, setting out in detail all of the events that had led up to that moment, and sparing nothing—including the fact that he had been prepared to go back into government that morning. There was a hush in the packed chamber as he spoke. The suspense in the speech built as he came to the moment where he had found out the whole story, and told the Taoiseach he could no longer vote confidence in him.

I always called that speech the "however" speech, after the moment when Dick announced that he couldn't support the Taoiseach. In terms of the importance of the occasion and the audience it reached it was one of the most dramatic speeches I drafted over my time in politics.

There was one final thing to be done. The Labour Ministers had still not resigned from government, and William pointed out that if Albert rushed to the Park to dissolve the Dáil, they would be technically locked in as government Ministers throughout an ensuing election—constitutionally, Ministers who resign after the dissolution of the Dáil are still caretaker Ministers. Each of them wrote a quick letter of resignation, and they were delivered by hand to the Taoiseach's office.

I sat in the public gallery the following morning, watching Albert Reynolds announce his resignation as Fianna Fáil leader, and telling the Dáil that he did not intend to seek an election unless a new government could not be formed. He would remain as caretaker Taoiseach until the Dáil elected a successor.

It was a graceful and dignified exit, as Charles Haughey's had been before him. The most memorable line was his reference to the peace process, and his rueful "you get over the big hurdles, it's the little ones that trip you up".

The more I thought about it, the more I came to believe that Albert Reynolds was a complex man, difficult to understand. I've had a number of opportunities to observe the love and respect his family have for him, and I admire that about him. I've also had plenty of reasons to be grateful for the opportunities he gave me to work on Anglo-Irish relations, and for his openness to ideas and suggestions in that area.

But when I discussed the fall of that government with Martin Mansergh, a few days after it happened, he told me that "the Taoiseach was engaged in a power play that went hideously wrong—what he wanted, he had to have, and that was the end of the matter".

And I'll never understand why Albert was so determined to secure the appointment of Harry Whelehan. In particular, I'll never know why that appointment became more urgent after the discovery of the Brendan Smyth case, rather than less.

In the end, my conclusion is that conspiracy theories should be ruled out. In my opinion, Albert felt he had been bested in relation to residency tax changes, made beholden in relation to the Masri affair, and abandoned in relation to the publication of the Beef Tribunal report. In my opinion he was wrong on all counts, but that didn't matter. He decided that the battle over Harry Whelehan was one he had to win.

Albert Reynolds had the potential to be truly great. A lot of the criticism levelled against him was unfair—especially in relation to his style and use of language. And I was one of the people who levelled those criticisms. But other criticisms are valid—that he couldn't take no for an answer, that sometimes his pride clouded his judgement.

In the end, I believe that Albert Reynolds suffered from an inferiority complex. He led us to a great achievement, in the form of an IRA ceasefire, and he presided over the greatest economic recovery in Ireland's history. His government, in a short space of time, introduced more far-reaching legislative reform than any other government.

But it wasn't enough. His bottom line was respect, and he never felt he got enough. His endless quest for vindication about the events of that period, and his inability to accept some responsibility for the events that brought down his government, are proof enough for me that Albert Reynolds needed not just to be right, but to be seen to be right.

In the weeks leading up to the fall of that government, I came to realise that Albert Reynolds saw me as a malevolent influence, determined to wreck his government. In the weeks after the fall, I soon enough found out that he, and other members of his government, saw me as a convenient scapegoat for the fall.

My own feeling about what happened was—and is—that none of it was necessary, and all of it was sad. And I feel that a good government was ended by one man's stubborn refusal to accept that he couldn't win every argument. And that man wasn't me. It wasn't Dick Spring, who sought to maintain a partnership that he believed was good for the country. In my honest opinion, the man who brought down that government was Albert Reynolds, and no-one else.

16

A New Marriage

The government in exile met in my house a few days after the fall. At least that's what it felt like. There was nowhere else to meet where we could be assured of privacy. Dick had gone down to Kerry immediately after resigning as a Minister to test the political temperature at home, and had rung on Saturday to say that the signs were very reassuring. Other Ministers— Brendan in Wexford, Michael D in Galway—had encountered the same reaction. There was a universal reaction that they had done the right thing in resigning from government.

But what to do next? Public opinion was divided, and the ex-Ministers—and the rest of us—were confused. Opinion polls published over the weekend showed that the party's public support had soared in the immediate aftermath of the crisis. But the public generally didn't seem to want an election, and the preferred option seemed to be a re-formation of the outgoing government, this time with Bertie Ahern leading it.

When we gathered, it quickly became clear that that was what most of the key Labour people wanted too. Dick listened to the discussion, over tea and whiskey, as we tried to explore all the options.

I started the evening opposed to any negotiations with Fianna Fáil. As I listened to the arguments, my conviction wavered. This was a government that had been interrupted in mid-stream. There was a huge amount of work on hand, and most of it had already been agreed in principle with Fianna Fáil. And there were two issues, bigger than all the rest, that might not be possible to complete without Fianna Fáil's active participation and support. They were the divorce referendum and the Joint Framework Documents.

I knew from my own work that the Framework Documents were virtually ready—(in fact, as it transpired, there was to be a lot of tense negotiation before the Documents were completed).

And I knew too that there was a little work to be done, but not that much, in preparing the ground for a divorce referendum. Mervyn Taylor, Richard Humphreys, and Anne Kinsella had formed a brilliant team in the Department of Equality and Law Reform, and had already piloted through a range of reforming legislation. They were ready for the big one, and now they were out of position.

All our ex-Ministers were there, together with John Rogers, John Foley, William Scally, Greg Sparks, and Pat Magner. There was some tension—the events of the previous few days had generated some friction between us that had not fully dissipated. But we tried to concentrate on the issue, and in the end, the question boiled down to this: could we deliver on the programme to which we were committed without Fianna Fáil?

By the end of the evening, we were virtually unanimous— we had to try to put it back together. I was doubtful, and so was William Scally—both of us put forward the proposition that we should consider an election. But I don't think our hearts were in it. The opinion polls that had been published that morning showed an overwhelming majority of people against an election, and it was difficult to argue with that.

We both agreed that of the other alternatives, a re-formed Fianna Fáil and Labour government was most likely to succeed in the major tasks that lay ahead.

The one dissident, that night, was John Rogers. He argued strongly that you just never knew where you stood with Fianna Fáil. Even though Bertie Ahern was likely to be a different proposition from Albert Reynolds, we still didn't know who was involved in the events that led to the fall of the government, and particularly in the crucial events of the last weekend. Until we knew, John argued, there was every likelihood that a new government would be suffused with suspicion. He was a lone voice, but a prophetic one, as it turned out.

No final decision was made that night, because a meeting of party members had been hastily arranged for the Riverside Centre in Dublin on the Monday night, and Dick wanted to test the temperature there too. Several hundred members turned up, and the mood was overwhelmingly supportive.

And so we drifted into a fortnight of rather desultory negotiation with Bertie Ahern. After Albert Reynolds had resigned as leader of Fianna Fáil (although he remained as Taoiseach), there had been a short and intense campaign between Bertie and Máire Geoghegan-Quinn for the leadership, which Bertie had won easily. Máire Geoghegan-Quinn had resigned from government during the heat of the crisis a few days previously—and had tried to made it clear that she had done so to try and save the government, by taking the rap herself for the Smyth affair. In fact, in the middle of the crisis, she had come to Dick in considerable distress and asked him if her resignation might not save the day. He had told her that she would be foolish to blame herself for the stubbornness of others, and had urged her not to resign. But she'd gone ahead and done it anyway—and it did her no good in the subsequent contest with Bertie.

As a result of Bertie's election, there were some differences—for example, Mary O'Rourke and Ray Burke, who had been dumped by Albert Reynolds, were now back in favour and playing a leading role in the negotiations. Finbarr O'Malley, Richard Humphreys and I had devised a set of 36 points which we called a "Charter for Renewal", and all of these were put on the table for negotiation—all of them were accepted with alacrity by Fianna Fáil.

Although this time, it was former Ministers negotiating with Ministers, we ignored civil service advice, as we had in the previous negotiations, and put forward our own ideas. Martin Mansergh and I were deputed to write some new paragraphs about Northern Ireland—in fact, Martin wrote them, and I didn't disagree with a word in them.

Essentially, the programme was always going to be non-contentious, with the possible exception of one item. That was referred to direct negotiations between Dick and Bertie.

That item was how to deal with the whole Attorney General/Father Brendan Smyth saga. Dick indicated to Bertie, right from the beginning, that it would be necessary to have the fullest possible disclosure about what happened and why.

We knew, or thought we knew, some of the story. After the appointment of Harry Whelehan had been concluded, and the remaining Fianna Fáil government had had second thoughts, Ministers had agreed to send Eoghan Fitzsimons to Harry on the following Monday night to plead with him to postpone his swearing-in, on the grounds that a collapse of the government had the potential to destabilise the peace process. When that didn't work, Albert Reynolds had gone into the Dáil on Tuesday to defend Harry's appointment.

And then other Fianna Fáil Ministers discovered on Tuesday what Albert had known on Monday—that there had been a legal precedent for the Smyth case, and that the grounds for delay in that case had turned out to be spurious. They had used the new discovery to negotiate with us on the Tuesday night. But they had also sent Eoghan Fitzsimons out to Harry Whelehan again, this time to tell him about the new discovery, and to warn him that his position might not be tenable if it were revealed on the Wednesday. Again they had been rebuffed by Harry.

But if none of the reasons that had been advanced for delay in the Smyth case were valid, what was the real reason? It had been implied in the Dáil that there had been Church interference, but there seemed to be no substance to that. We wanted to try to get to the bottom of it—to establish once and for all why Harry Whelehan, and more particularly Matt Russell, who had been in charge of the file, had seemed to sit on it for so long.

Dick and Bertie agreed on this point—in fact, Bertie seemed more curious even than Dick about the whole background to the affair. They got on well together in their direct negotiations. Of the two, Dick had been under the more pressure, but Bertie, throughout that week or so, seemed tired and weary, and even somewhat downhearted.

He told Dick at one point in their discussions that he had come to the belief that his phone was being tapped during the leadership election. Dick didn't know whether he was being paranoid.

One of the other issues was what to do about Ray Burke. Several of the Fianna Fáil Ministers said privately to their Labour counterparts that if we had a problem with Ray Burke, it could be resolved. They seemed to be dropping hints that they wouldn't mind us objecting to his inclusion in the cabinet.

It was puzzling. We knew that Ray Burke wouldn't have been popular—in fact, he was hated—by many of the Fianna Fáil people who had been in the ascendancy under Albert Reynolds. But was there more to it than that? Burke had always been surrounded by rumours, but there weren't any more going around at the time than usual.

Dick had always taken the view, in all previous negotiations on government formation, that he didn't welcome advice about who should be included in his cabinet team. As a result, he didn't believe in offering advice either. You made your own choices, and you lived with the consequences. So he never, as far as I know, expressed any view to Bertie Ahern about whether or not Ray Burke should be in whatever cabinet they formed together.

Apart from little niggly things, everything seemed to be going well. As the date for the resumption of the Dáil drew nearer, everything seemed to be in place. On the Sunday before the resumption, John Bruton gave what seemed to us like an agitated interview on the radio news, calling on Dick, even at that late stage, not to go into government again with Fianna Fáil, and sharply criticising the behaviour of Fianna Fáil and everyone associated with it. It seemed like sore losing.

The following morning, the heavens fell in. On the way into work, I bought an *Irish Times*, and there on the front page was a story by Geraldine Kennedy that was to wreck the formation of the government. In it, Geraldine reported that what we had all believed up to that point was wrong. Instead of asking Harry Whelehan to step aside on the Monday night to protect the peace process, Eoghan Fitzsimons had instead told him that the government was aware of the legal precedent in the Duggan case that night. On the following night, he had asked him to consider the risk to the peace process if he continued with his appointment.

The implication was clear. We had believed until that moment that only Albert Reynolds knew about the Duggan case on the Monday, and therefore what happened on the Tuesday was down to him alone. Now, if this story were true, it seemed that other members of the government knew about the Duggan case on the Monday, and were to some degree complicit in what happened in the Dáil on the Tuesday.

When I arrived in Leinster House, I went straight to Dick's office. He was sitting at his desk already, and looked at me with what I can only describe as a sardonic grin.

"We're never going to be out of trouble with these guys, are we?" he said.

We discussed it, and agreed that this placed a huge cloud over the negotiations. If we concluded them in the face of this new evidence, it would make a mockery of the stand that Dick had taken, and believed in.

He wanted accountability for the Smyth debacle, and he couldn't enter into a relationship with people who he believed had played ducks and drakes with relevant information, using it as a tactical weapon in whatever way suited them. Albert Reynolds had been accused in the Dáil of withholding critical information and had forfeited the confidence of the Labour Ministers as a result—how could others who had been just as involved succeed him?

Dick drafted a short note to Bertie, letting him know that he regarded the negotiations as being suspended until this issue was clarified, and seeking a report from the Attorney General on the matter. And then we sat back to wait.

It turned into a very long day. Sometime in the morning, I met Geraldine Kennedy in Leinster House. We stood and chatted in one of the corridors, and within minutes I knew that her sources were impeccable and her story was true. She didn't tell me her sources, but I knew from her demeanour that this was one story that had clearly come from a very good source indeed. Geraldine had herself believed, and reported, that the sequence of events was the one we all believed, and was horrified to discover that the truth was the opposite of her own earlier story.

Later, after the suspension of the talks hit the lunchtime news, I got a call from a very agitated Vincent Browne. He spent an hour on the phone, for reasons I've never understood, trying to convince me that there was nothing new in Geraldine Kennedy's story, that Máire Geoghegan-Quinn had said it all in the Dáil debate on the crisis a couple of weeks earlier.

I remembered the speech—it was the one in which she had sought to take the blame for the whole fiasco—and we argued the toss backwards and forwards. Afterwards, I went and got hold of Máire Geoghegan-Quinn's speech, and read it again. She had indeed dropped heavily coded hints of prior knowledge of the Duggan case, but in a way that couldn't possibly have made sense until you knew the true position.

While we were waiting, extraordinary things were happening in Fianna Fáil. Albert Reynolds, who was still Taoiseach, had gone to Budapest on a European Union mission. When he heard that we had requested a report from the Attorney General on Geraldine Kennedy's story, he issued instructions that no report was to be given to us until he had had first sight of it. That was his right, of course, as acting Taoiseach, but all it was going to do was to sour the atmosphere further.

What it meant was that as Labour ex-Ministers waited around until late in the evening, the acting Tánaiste and leader of Fianna Fáil spent hours trying to chase his former leader, now the acting Taoiseach, around Europe, to persuade him to part with a factual account of the final days of the previous government.

Meanwhile, Ruairi Quinn, who was horrified at the thought that a new government couldn't be formed in the atmosphere that had now been generated, had to represent the party on RTE's "Question & Answers". He found himself being grilled by the audience about how, in the light of Geraldine's story, any trust at all could exist between the two parties. As he said himself when he came back into Leinster House, it was the first time in a long political career that he had found himself completely out of answers.

In the end, after something like eleven hours, the government jet took off from Budapest, with Albert Reynolds and the Attorney General's report on board. He had still not given permission for it to be released to us, and it was now impossible to make contact with him, and wouldn't be possible again until the jet landed. But Bertie, who knew the report confirmed Geraldine's story in essence, decided that the game was up, and handed it over to us anyway.

One reading was enough for Dick to decide that we could no longer do business with many, if not all, of the Fianna Fáil Ministers, and he cancelled the negotiations there and then, with the reluctant, but unanimous, support of his Ministers.

Immediately, we were plunged into negotiations with Fine Gael and DL. They could perhaps have been forgiven for deciding to screw us into the ground, but it didn't work out that way. That was partly because John Rogers and Dermot Gleeson, who had emerged as a close adviser to John Bruton, got on very well together. Dermot and John were both senior counsels, and used to hand-to-hand negotiations. In this case, Dick wanted it fully understood that he wasn't prepared to allow any of the Ministers or Junior Ministers who resigned from government with him to be left out in the cold. Dermot got the message.

The trouble was that not all of Dick's colleagues understood the same point. Just as the negotiations, which were otherwise largely untroubled, were coming to an end, I was approached by Pat Rabbitte of Democratic Left. He told me that he had been given to understand, early on in the negotiations, that there would be two seats at the cabinet table for DL. And he had been given to understand it by one of Dick's closest Ministerial colleagues, who had pretty well offered up one of the six positions we held.

Pat was asking me to intervene with Dick, who appeared to be very stubborn about this necessary concession. I told Pat that

I'd be happy to intervene, if he—Pat—would tell me which of Dick's colleagues he felt should be shafted.

The concession had been made without any authority from Dick, who was furious when he heard about it. But it resulted in the compromise whereby Pat became a kind of "super" Junior Minister, with a seat at the cabinet table, and went on to become an outstanding member of that government.

In every substantial respect, the programme of government we agreed was the same as the one we had negotiated with Fianna Fáil—which in turn was broadly the same as the one we had negotiated with Democratic Left in the immediate aftermath of the 1992 election.

It remained a good and ambitious government programme, in my view the most radical and comprehensive ever implemented by any party in government. If we could make no other claim after our period in government, we would be able to claim, I believed, that we had fundamentally altered the way governments are put together and their programmes implemented. There was a lot of talk about politics moving to the centre, and all politics being the same. But I believed that we had created a new centre—and it was left of centre, and that we had dragged other parties to it.

My fondest hope, at the start of John Bruton's government, was that I would be able to fade back into obscurity. There had been a spate of stories, all fuelled by Fianna Fáil, during the crisis that had brought down the previous government, and all designed to paint me as a sinister, Rasputin-like figure who held an unhealthy sway over Dick Spring. John Rogers and I had been portrayed as the people who had conspired to bring down the previous government, and phrases like "unelected advisers" began to come into vogue.

We could laugh about the stories, but they were having a number of effects. First of all, they helped to fuel resentment among some members of the Parliamentary Labour Party— people like Róisín Shortall and Pat Upton—who felt that their influence on decisions was being minimised. That created unnecessary and unhelpful tensions within the party, of which I was the unwilling focus.

Secondly, the credence given to the idea of unelected advisers helped to give some credibility to the otherwise absurd notion that Fianna Fáil had been innocent bystanders in the fall of the government.

My hopes for a quieter life, back behind the scenes, were dashed as soon as the Dáil Committee that had been set up to enquire into the circumstances surrounding the fall of the government began its work.

Because of the rather odd way the Committee structured its work, they took a procession of Fianna Fáil witnesses, all of them alleging or insinuating that the government had been fatally undermined by the Machiavellian machinations of unelected advisers—or one of them in particular. We had to sit on the sidelines, waiting for our turn to give evidence, while this went on for several days.

To make matters worse, there was an interval of a weekend between the two sets of witnesses, and the Sunday newspapers were able to have a field-day with the unelected advisers and their reputations. On "Questions & Answers" on Monday night, Bertie Ahern repeated his belief that my role had been decisive, and Anthony Coughlan, a Trinity lecturer to whom I've never spoken in my life, alleged that our well-known Fine Gael backgrounds had led John Rogers and myself to believe that the previous government had to be destroyed, because of the line it was pursuing on the peace process!

Among the allegations that were in constant currency throughout this period were the assertions that I had made the secret phone call that undid the "10.22 agreement", and that I had planted the Geraldine Kennedy story that had brought the Bertie Ahern/Dick Spring negotiations to a halt. In a very funny piece that he wrote for the *Sunday Times*, Eoghan Harris repeated this latter libel as if it were a matter of gospel fact—but he deprived me of a cause of action by declaring that not only was I responsible for scuttling the negotiations, but I was a national hero for doing so!

What really rattled me was the evidence of Martin Mansergh. I had come to regard Martin as a friend—he had clearly come to regard me as a traitor. In the discussions between John Bruton and Dick Spring on the formation of their government, I had urged Dick to recommend to John Bruton that Martin be approached, on a non-partisan basis, to be asked if he would continue to act as an adviser to the government on Northern Ireland matters. Martin had declined the offer, although he knew, I think, that it had been made in good faith.

And now, in his evidence to the Dáil Committee, he appeared to be part of the group that was trying to make the case that I had an interest in undermining the Reynolds government. Various casual remarks I had made, and my non-attendance at one meeting, were stretched and misconstrued to suggest that my motivation was always partisan and usually mischievous. I was surprised and hurt by the tone of Martin's evidence, because I had expected better from him, if not from any of the others.

On the Labour side of the evidence, we had agreed that it would be better if each of us who had to make a statement prepared it separately. Although all the signs pointed to a high degree of co-ordination among the Fianna Fáil witnesses, we wanted to avoid any such accusation being levelled against us. William Scally took on the role of being the only person who saw all of our individual statements before they were sent to the Committee.

He refused to allow Dick to see mine or me to see Dick's, and I had to take William's word for it that there was no major conflict of evidence between any of the Labour witnesses. After fifteen years of always having had an input of some kind into every major statement issued by the Labour Party, I found it hard to work alone—I don't think I would have been able to take instruction on the matter from anyone except William.

My instinct, when I read Martin's evidence, was to lash back at him. After talking it over with William, I decided instead simply to express my surprise and hurt at what he had to say. After I had given my evidence, on a day that was much more tense than I had expected it to be, I met Martin on my way out of the Committee Room. He immediately came over to me, and in the hearing of a number of members of the Committee, apologised for some of the harsher conclusions he had drawn in his own evidence.

It was a relief to all of us when the Committee came to its inevitable conclusion. It was a highly partisan operation from start to finish, and in the end was unable to agree on any findings whatever. Naturally, that didn't stop Fianna Fáil and its former leader from claiming total vindication!

A good performance in front of the Committee was important for me, because I was aware that I was being looked at askance by some of the new members of the government. My relationship with the new Taoiseach, John Bruton, for instance, had never been good—if I had been labelled as a wrecker in the first weeks of his government, it would hardly have inspired a great deal of confidence in him.

As it was, I viewed John Bruton with some trepidation. All of us who had worked for the 1983-1987 government had strong memories of someone who could best be described as an intellectual bully—certainly not someone who could pull together a set of strong personalities into a coherent team.

I was wrong—or else he had changed quite a bit. Within days of becoming Taoiseach, he had reconstituted the cabinet sub-committee on Northern Ireland, and invited a number of officials (including me) to attend every meeting. At the first meeting, he made it plain that he would rely on the expertise of those who had spent many years negotiating with the British government, and that he wanted people to be able to speak freely at every meeting.

From that moment, until I resigned eighteen months later, I found John Bruton open, honest, and always willing to listen. Status didn't matter at meetings with him—if you had an opinion, he wanted to hear it.

That's not to say that everything ran smoothly all the time on the Anglo-Irish front. John Bruton saw the process in which we were involved—the process he had inherited—as "buying into a Sinn Féin agenda", and every instinct in his body rebelled against it. He had a deep pride in, almost a visceral commitment to, the role that Fine Gael had played in the foundation of the state, and he was offended by Sinn Féin's basically dismissive attitude to "Dublin" (which was their name for the Irish government).

But he listened, and listened especially to Nora Owen and Proinsias De Rossa. Nora Owen, in all our discussions on Northern Ireland, was a rock of common sense. Whenever John Bruton was finding something particularly unpalatable, she and Dermot Gleeson would take a hand in persuading him that sometimes increments of progress could only be achieved by swallowing hard.

On the other hand, I sometimes thought that John Bruton looked to Proinsias De Rossa as a sort of conscience. Proinsias' dislike of Sinn Féin was visceral, and palpable—it made meetings between the government and a Sinn Féin delegation sparky and uncomfortable affairs. But he recognised the value of tough negotiation, and was clear-sighted about the objective of the exercise.

That made him pragmatic, and his advice was always carefully listened to. It was never necessary for him to spell out his dislike of Sinn Féin—but I grew to admire the way in which he could give an objective view, often implicitly supporting their objectives, as being necessary for peace and progress, while hating everything they stood for.

The change of tone that inevitably resulted from the change of personalities and perspectives made a very substantial difference to Dick. Over the previous two years, he had frequently found himself in the position of urging caution on Albert Reynolds, and of putting forward a Unionist perspective in government discussions. Now, in the interests of identical policy objectives, he was the one who frequently urged the harder line, trying to push his new colleagues on.

The result was that Dick's image underwent a transformation, from being the pro-unionist Foreign Minister in Albert's government to being the greenest member of John Bruton's. There was no public utterance that anyone could point to, or no basic change in his position—it was essentially the backdrop that changed, and not him. But that's how public images are formed a lot of the time.

The priority, though, was to get the work done. We had concluded 95% of the Joint Framework Documents prior to the fall of the government, and there was every possibility now of getting them published. Only two things had to happen. The British government had to be persuaded, and the Irish government had to be persuaded. No big deal.

For several days in January, immediately after the formation of the government, the Joint Framework Documents were hotly debated by the government. Those who had been involved before were effectively introducing the newer members of the government to a range of concepts, including new constitutional formulae, that they had never seen before. It was hardly surprising that an incoming government would want to take ownership of such a fundamental document, and we were put through our paces by the Taoiseach and the new Minister for Social Welfare.

The new Taoiseach had also decided that he wanted to bring his own personnel into the negotiations. Specifically, our negotiating team was expanded to include Paddy Teahon, the Secretary of the Department of the Taoiseach, and Tim Dalton, the Secretary of the Department of Justice (who had already had extensive involvement on the issue of decommissioning with senior British officials).

These changes introduced a degree of tension into the arrangements, it has to be said. For a long time, the pattern of negotiations on the Irish side had been that they were handled, on a day-to-day basis, by the Foreign Minister, who reported regularly to the government. In situations where summitry was called for, the Taoiseach's office got involved, but did not normally run any oversight on the work of the Anglo-Irish division of the Department of Foreign Affairs.

It wasn't the intention of the Taoiseach to introduce such oversight now, but it looked a bit that way. There were occasional sparks as a result on our side of the table about who was doing what and with whom.

But it didn't interfere with strong negotiation on the Framework Documents. These were finalised at a very long, and very difficult meeting, in the Department of Foreign Affairs, on the Saturday before they were published. The meeting took place against the worst possible background. Someone at the heart of the British cabinet had taken all the paragraphs from the Documents that were most unpalatable to Unionists, and had leaked them to the *Times* newspaper, where they were given a further spin by a well-known anti-Irish commentator. As a result, the Unionists were already gearing up to reject the Documents sight unseen.

Sir Patrick Mayhew made no secret of his belief that it was one of his own closest colleagues, Viscount Cranbourne (a shadowy figure to us, but a member of the British cabinet sub-Committee on Northern Ireland) who had leaked the documents. He was willing to recommend going ahead with publication anyway, but was absolutely insistent that he had to be able to tell his Prime Minister, hand on heart, that the final phraseology we agreed on would pass the "Corfu test"—that it would be clear to unionist opinion that the Irish government was totally committed to removing any sense of territorial threat from our Constitution.

And he wanted the language of the Document, as it referred to North/South bodies, softened to appear less like a Southern intrusion into the internal affairs of Northern Ireland.

We didn't have any intrinsic problem with negotiating more palatable language. Our main problem was that we were in possession of a unique document. Because of the circumstances in which it had been negotiated, the Joint Frameworks had the capacity to attract the support of not just the government, but also of Fianna Fáil, who were now the main opposition party. For the first time in history, the Irish government was about to publish a commitment to recognise the legitimacy of a new dispensation in Northern Ireland, and none of the nationalist parties—including Sinn Féin—were in a position to denounce it.

Unless, of course, we agreed to significant changes in the document that would enable Fianna Fáil to say they had never had sight of them.

This dilemma preoccupied us for most of that Saturday, and made us dig our heels in about the language of the document. I've never seen Sir Patrick as agitated as he was that day. Clearly, the leak of the Documents had put him under intense pressure. At one point he virtually shouted at Dick that he wasn't prepared to leave, or to sign up to anything, unless he got the changes he wanted.

Eventually we adjourned the meeting, and Dick, Seán Ó hUiginn and I went into Dick's office. We put together a new form of words that was as close as we could get to reconciling our concerns with Sir Patrick's, and Dick went off to have a quiet chat with him. When he came back, it was with a thumbs-up sign.

The Joint Frameworks Document was published just outside Belfast at the end of February. The night before, a joint briefing meeting was held in Hillsborough. It had two main purposes— to celebrate a considerable achievement, and to allow the new Taoiseach and the Prime Minister to get to know each other better.

Over dinner, where I saw John Major in his most relaxed mood ever—although he too clearly felt a deep sense of betrayal by the leak of the Frameworks—a good deal of work was done in preparing for the question and answer session that would follow publication the following morning. Although the Prime Minister's speech for the occasion was ready, he was looking for suggestions about some closing language. Seán Ó hUiginn—the world's best speech-writer when literary allusions are called for—and I co-operated on a few paragraphs, so I was able to add John Major's name to my CV as someone I had written for!

After dinner, I found myself closeted in a corner of the ballroom of Hillsborough Castle with Sir Patrick Mayhew. We discovered a shared love of West Cork, and he told me of his family connections with Castletownsend. He also introduced me to port, a drink I had never had before. Each glass seemed more pleasant than the previous one—until I tried to stand up when the bottle was empty.

I think that night was probably the only time in my life that I was shown to my bedroom by a Knight of the Realm—and assisted when my legs proved unwilling to follow my orders. The following day, I could only marvel at the high good humour that Sir Patrick displayed, as he joked with the assembled media. I have never experienced such pain. A port hangover, I discovered, makes you blind, and it makes the same noises in your head as one of those hammers that they use to dig up the roads.

However, I have to record the compliment that Sir Patrick paid me, just before we left, as he was saying goodbye to Dick: "Excellent fellow, that Finlay—puts together a perfectly grammatical sentence, no matter what condition he's in!"

But in addition to discovering the agony of a port hangover in that moment of history, I also discovered the cure. Sheer terror will do it every time.

I haven't mentioned before the downside of being adviser and Programme Manager to a Foreign Minister. As the holder of that title, I was the envy of my colleagues, the only one of them, apart from John Foley, guaranteed a lot of international travel. And the only one with a deep-seated and life-long fear of flying.

It's like back pain, in the sense that everyone else, unless they share the condition, thinks it's funny. One who sympathised was Noel Dorr, who was himself, as Secretary of the Department of Foreign Affairs, the most travelled public servant in Ireland. And his fear of flying was worse than mine, so that every journey he undertook, far from being a perk of the job, was an act of genuine courage and patriotism.

Every sufferer has some fear around which it is based— usually irrational, but none the less gripping for that. In Noel's case, he was convinced that any sudden movement that he made on take-off would throw the plane completely out of kilter. At the end of the runway, as the plane began to accelerate for take-off, he would freeze completely in whatever position he was in, and remain completely immobile until the plane levelled off.

I, on the other hand, believe that I am going to die falling backwards out of the sky—and it's going to be undignified and messy. Whenever the nose of the plane is pointing upwards, I have to have something above me to hold on to, and if there's nothing there, I am in a paroxysm of fear.

I've tried everything to get rid of it, from valium to too much whiskey, but it's always there. And in any event, too much of any "medication" on the journey somewhat dilutes your effectiveness when you arrive!

The matter is complicated by the government jet. Yes, it's comfortable, especially for eight to ten people. And it's state of the art, with all sorts of super-duper technology to keep it safe. But it's a military aircraft, and they fly at higher altitudes than commercial aircraft. And military flyers, skilled as they are, always seem to be in a hurry to get up to the required height. And down again—they don't descend, they dive.

To be fair, the Air Corps pilots, when they discovered my little problem, couldn't have been more helpful. They suggested on several occasions that I might fly in the cockpit, and on one or two journeys, when there was room, I did. Flying into Dublin that way at night, especially from the west, is breathtaking, and very reassuring.

But when you're not welcome in the cockpit—when they're too busy to worry about you—it heightens the certainty that something bad is going to happen. And one of the worst flights of them all was the flight back from Belfast on the day the Joint Frameworks were launched. It was forty minutes of gut-wrenching horror, caused by an electrical storm that was positioned all the way between the two cities. As we bucketed around the sky, unable even to raise a glass because the contents were slopping around too much, everyone was green. I was promising God that I'd never touch port again.

The Joint Framework Documents were among Dick Spring's greatest achievements. He managed the negotiations personally, frequently leading them in intense sessions, and coping with a traumatic change of government at the climax of the negotiations. They were a framework, in every sense of the word, for everything that has happened since—the Good Friday Agreement would not have been possible without the agenda they created.

And the British government that was persuaded to agree with them was already entering its death throes, and entirely dependent on Unionist goodwill. Especially in that context, Sir Patrick Mayhew's courage in the face of unionist hostility has never been appreciated enough.

The magnitude of Dick's achievement in the Joint Frameworks has never been recognised, partly because two Taoisigh have added them to their own list of achievements. But as an exercise in team-leading, persuading, and negotiating—especially given the forces that were ranged against success—I doubt if it will ever be bettered.

The other reason, perhaps, why the Joint Frameworks were not seen as a huge achievement was because almost immediately, Dick was embroiled in controversy over them. Or rather, over some remarks that President Robinson made about them, in the course of an official visit to Japan, when she expressed sympathy with Unionist difficulties in coming to terms with them.

It was already beginning to seem as if Dick was destined to cross swords with President Robinson at every opportunity. There had been the famous row over the handshake with Gerry Adams, and then in 1994 Dick and Mary had been at loggerheads again. That time it was over whether President Robinson was entitled to accept an invitation to chair a philanthropic think-tank to enquire into the future of the United Nations. Dick's Department of Foreign Affairs had advised the government that they saw no objection to her accepting the invitation, despite policy difficulties it could cause. But the government as a whole had decided otherwise, and had refused permission.

President Robinson was so angry at the government decision that she had sought independent legal advice, before ultimately backing down. She had also implied strongly, in correspondence with Albert Reynolds, that she believed Dick had leaked some of the details of the row. He in turn had been furious at this innuendo, and had written a sharp letter to the President.

So when the next row broke out, immediately after the Framework Documents, it looked like the makings of a feud. But it was nothing of the kind. In fact, there was no row at all, despite newspaper headlines that made it look as if Dick was having a go.

It happened at a "pol. corrs lunch" in Iveagh House, hosted by Dick as an off-the-record occasion. President Robinson had just returned from a somewhat controversial trip to South America, where she had met the former dictator of Chile, General Pinochet, and had failed to meet a number of key members of the Irish community.

About twenty or so political correspondents attended the lunch. Most political correspondents would attend several such lunches a year, hosted by Taoiseach, Tánaiste, or other Ministers or party leaders. The format almost never changes—after lunch, a question and answer session, the journalists free to ask any question they like, about any aspect of policy or current events that interest them. Sometimes they get answers, on or off the record, sometimes they find it a bit frustrating.

This was, I thought, an unusually good question and answer session. It was free-flowing and fairly wide-ranging, covering issues like the peace process and Irish neutrality. The answers were very forthcoming and open—and all on the record.

There were a number of questions about the President's recent visit to South America. This was the only point at which Dick demurred, saying that there was a well-established tradition about not dealing with the office of the President in this kind of setting. It was suggested *to him*, by the journalists present, that if he wished to say something about the trip off the record, they would be interested in hearing it.

He then took the opportunity to say a number of things about the trip. First, he said that the President had been unfairly treated by the media in respect of the trip. He mentioned some of the people that the President was alleged to have spurned in South America, and pointed out that she had in fact spent time with them, and had affirmed the work they do in a very positive way. He listed some of the factual inaccuracies in the reporting, and told the journalists that Irish missionaries, among others, had advised against the President visiting some of the poorer areas. He said that the only two people in the Irish party who had spoken to former President Pinochet were the journalists covering the trip.

Finally, he was asked about the remarks the President made in Japan about the Framework Document, and made what Stephen Collins, who was then writing for the *Sunday Press* subsequently described as "mildly critical" comments.

That's what happened at the lunch—all that happened, at an otherwise very convivial occasion. Later that afternoon, I was telephoned by Dónal Kelly of RTE. He told me that there was some debate among his colleagues about whether the information imparted at the lunch on an "off the record basis" was for background purposes only—in other words, was it not to be used; or was it capable of being used without attribution to the Tánaiste? I told Dónal that it was clearly only for their information, and not to be used. He confirmed that that was his own view, and said he would pass it on to his colleagues.

In summary: a question and answer session that lasted about half an hour. Wide-ranging questions, and open and full answers, all on the record. Less than five minutes off the record, and all but one sentence of that strongly supportive of the President. And what happens next?

Someone rang Aras an Uachtaráin, and told Bride Rosney that a senior politician has been attacking the President "off the record". Bride Rosney did what I would have done in the circumstances. She refused to comment on off the record remarks, but offered to come out swinging if the politician cared to identify himself.

And suddenly we had a story, along the lines of "President throws down gauntlet to politician". Twenty four hours later, because in the words of Chris Glennon of the *Irish Independent*, "it's a quiet weekend for news", he decided to "out" the politician concerned. And then we got a further week or so of columnists and pundits fulminating about the cheek of the Tánaiste for attacking the President.

Naturally, with one or two honourable exceptions—Una Claffey, Geraldine Kennedy, and Gerry Barry of RTE among them—not one of the journalists present at the lunch stood up and said, "hold on—this wasn't the way it happened. This just isn't the whole story."

I was infuriated by the whole episode. It was a classic example of controversy for its own sake. The story worked for the people who ran it because it fitted into a thesis that Dick Spring was somehow jealous of Mary Robinson.

For example, Conor Cruise O'Brien wrote a learned and erudite piece revealing that he knew the real reason behind Dick Spring's spite. The real reason was a new set of protocol guidelines issued by Aras an Uachtaráin for Ministers. Dick Spring—he of the over-bearing ego—regarded them as an insult to his own status, because he would be overshadowed by the President on public occasions.

That only problem was that the guidelines weren't issued by Aras an Uachtaráin at all, who had very little input into them, but by the government secretariat, for the guidance of new Ministers. They consisted of writing down protocols that had been operated for years, and they had the full approval of both Taoiseach and Tánaiste in advance of being issued.

To cap it all, Independent Newspapers, which had broken the story in the first place, then went out and conducted an opinion poll about whether Dick Spring was right to attack the President. If I had been polled, I would have said that Dick Spring was wrong to attack the President. But I knew he didn't—and so did some of the people who commissioned the poll.

That episode was particularly damaging for two reasons. First, it broke right across the national conference of the party, which was being held in Limerick. It was a good conference, and we had a lot of achievement in government to celebrate, but it was totally over-shadowed by an entirely spurious controversy.

Second, it was a kind of watershed in Dick's relations with the media. He had always had a somewhat prickly and testy relationship with media people, never sure which of them he could trust to give him a fair shake. From the earliest days I worked with him, he had an attitude about the media. From the time of that episode on, there was a deeper mistrust, and frequent hostility. He just couldn't understand how so many had been prepared to get on a bandwagon that bore so little relationship to the facts.

But the controversy that started next was much more fundamentally damaging—its repercussions were still being felt long afterwards. It began when Sir Patrick Mayhew made a speech in Washington in which he called on Sinn Féin and the IRA to demonstrate their goodwill towards the peace process, and instanced a number of tests that might be applied as a measure of goodwill. The third test he mentioned—Washington Three, as it became known—was the decommissioning of weapons.

Although ways and means of achieving decommissioning had been discussed between the governments since the previous October, we had explained to the British government, again and again, that public demands for it would be seen as tantamount to demanding surrender. An undefeated IRA had committed itself to peace, to secure the entry of Sinn Féin to a negotiating process. Demanding decommissioning as a pre-condition of entry could only have disastrous consequences.

The nearest that the British came to understanding this point was to include it, in Sir Patrick's Washington speech, as a test rather than as an issue of principle. Disastrously, the test became elevated to a principle within days. The Taoiseach, when he was asked about it during St Patrick's Day celebrations in the White House, unwisely demanded concrete steps towards decommissioning. Dick, harried in Dáil Eireann by Michael McDowell, was forced to admit that decommissioning meant handing over weapons.

The British seized on statements like these, and suddenly decommissioning became the primary obstacle to Sinn Féin's entry into talks with the other parties in Northern Ireland. It was an entirely hypocritical stance, because Ministers, and Unionist leaders, argued that Sinn Féin could come in once a token had been offered. In other words, they couldn't negotiate with 100% of their arms intact—but 99% would be okay.

Within weeks the whole issue had generated an impasse in relations between the governments, and threatened to derail the entire process. With an Anglo-Irish summit looming in June, it was clear that unless there was a breakthrough of some sort, we were facing disaster.

Shortly before the summit, I sat down late one night and drafted a letter, which I urged Dick to send to John Bruton the following day. He read it carefully, and made a number of amendments, before sending it out to be typed on his own letterhead.

It proposed the establishment of an International Body on Decommissioning, which would address the issue at the level of principle, and which would be composed of people likely to be trusted by all sides—chaired by an American, because no-one else would be acceptable to Sinn Féin, with a Canadian and a Scandinavian to provide balance.

The Taoiseach agreed to put the proposition to John Major at the summit at the end of June, although none of us had a great deal of confidence that Major would accept it. He was bound to see it as an attempt to buy time on the issue, and perhaps even to side-step it altogether, and he seemed to be stuck on achieving a hand-over of arms.

But to our surprise, John Major did accept the idea of an International Body—essentially because if he hadn't, the summit would have been billed as a total impasse.

But between June and December, from the time the International Body was proposed to the moment it was set up, we had endless haggling over terms of reference and especially over personnel. The British government was implacably opposed to George Mitchell chairing the Body, and it wasn't until it was made clear to them that their rejection of him was a personal snub to President Clinton—who was due to visit Ireland at the end of the year—that they relented. In the interim, relations between the two Governments sank to their lowest ebb.

I was among those consulted about a planned summit in September. I was asked specifically by the Taoiseach, along with other officials, to comment on a letter from John Major which outlined proposals for a summit that included putting further public pressure on Sinn Féin to begin decommissioning, and a very hard line on their entry into all-party negotiations.

This, in part, is what I wrote.

> The letter in my view needs a blunt response, and quickly. I believe you may have to consider communicating a view that you would prefer to hold no Summit rather than a Summit that would destabilise the peace process ...
>
> If I may explain why I feel so strongly.
>
> We have tried, at recent meetings with the British, to convey the view that the stability of the peace process is delicate, and may even be in a dangerous condition. We have not done so for the sake of gaining advantage, but because we believe it to be the case. At such discussions, the British have always dismissed our concern, and have effectively portrayed themselves as totally convinced that the war is over, and that the Provos have nowhere to go.
>
> Nobody knows which analysis is correct—we do know, and have said so, that if the British are wrong, it will be too late to do anything about it the day we discover it.
>
> It is possible that <u>both</u> our analysis and the British is wrong in some degree. I have already passed on to the Tánaiste information which has come into my possession, from a person I know reasonably well, who claims to be close to members of the IRA Army Council. This information would not constitute hard intelligence, in my view, but does represent a possible "third scenario". I make no claims as to its accuracy, though I do believe in its plausibility, and would argue that it could be treated as a working hypothesis. It is this.
>
> The IRA Army Council has never held a Convention to declare the ceasefire permanent. Until they do, Adams cannot use the word permanent. But a decision to make it permanent requires a two-third majority, and Adams, although confident of a simple majority, does not know if he can bank on two-thirds. And he would want even more than that in order to avoid a split.

That means that a rump on the Army Council which has never given its consent holds a disproportionate influence. They have been pressing for a Convention, or at least a full "review" meeting, and will not brook any talk of de-commissioning. Their attitude to Adams is "you promised us round-table talks, with no strings attached—when are you going to deliver?".

This group is not agitating for an immediate resumption of violence. They are pressing for a harder political line, in the form of a three-month or six-month deadline. Adams knows that any such ultimatum would immediately mean the end of negotiations—in other words, violence might as well resume immediately, since no-one will touch Sinn Fein in the face of such a threat.

He is continually trying to head it off, by persuading and cajoling the recalcitrants not to push him into a review. Some believe that if his hand is forced, he will side with the hard-liners rather than allow a split. So far, he has persuaded them not to call the relevant meeting, but he is seen in some quarters as running out of time.

As I say, I have no way of knowing if this is an entirely accurate picture. But if it is, or if any sort of similar situation exists within the IRA, the important point is this:

it means that the issue of decommissioning is not some "macho" test between Sinn Fein and the British, but rather a test of wills between different elements of the IRA. In any such test, we have to help Adams to win.

That in turn means two things. It means that, unpalatable as it may seem, there is at this point an identity of interest between the Irish government—and all who want to develop the peace—and Gerry Adams (that identity of interest has existed, of course, since the day of the ceasefire).

It also means that progress towards all-party, inclusive political dialogue must be the first priority, as that is the only way that Adams can win through.

In other words, the exercise we are engaged in now cannot be about putting pressure on Sinn Fein to give the Unionists the sense of victory they seem to want, and that the British seem to want to give them. It must be about easing pressure on all those who need to talk.

The British don't seem to understand any of this (and their lack of understanding is bolstered by the belief that violence is no longer an option for the IRA anyway). In addition, they can never seem to shake off their need to always come back for another slice when they are negotiating.

They seek always, almost as a reflex, to divide and conquer, either by setting up a myriad of relationships on the other side, so that they can pick and choose who they deal with, or else by continually confusing the issues.

Mr Major's letter (seeks) to co-opt the US Administration to a one-sided view of decommissioning … We did not put forward the International Commission solely as a way of overcoming Sinn Fein's difficulties with the handing over of weapons. We put it forward as a way of bridging the gap between two irreconcilable positions—Sinn Fein's and the British government's.

There is no doubt whatever that if Sinn Fein were to see the Commission as a way of leaning on them to achieve British objectives, they would reject it outright. And there is equally no doubt that if the American government were to see the Commission as anything other than a way of facilitating progress on the decommissioning issue, hand-in-hand with significant progress towards the start of dialogue, they would be mad to have anything to do with it.

In other words, the main purpose of the Commission is to help both sides to begin to deal with de-commissioning in ways that remove it as a pre-condition, after a period of time and voluntary co-operation.

Rather than recognise that, Mr Major's letter seems to see the Commission as a cunning trap for the Provos, designed to make them subject to intolerable pressure to meet the pre-condition. The trick is not to let them into the secret until it's too late.

This is mad—but in addition, it serves no interest of the Irish government, and it could fatally undermine the peace by proving the point of the hard men.

The Irish government's paramount interest is to see the peace preserved and developed—and it is ironic that while there may be no political "up-side" in working towards that end, the "down-side" of being associated with failure would be catastrophic in political terms.

Having regard to all of the above, I strongly believe that the wisest and only course for us now is to demonstrate—to the British as well as to Sinn Fein—that our policy is both coherent and consistent, in its development and in its execution. We must demand the strongest possible profile for the political element of the package, and we cannot allow ourselves to be trapped into being co-opted, along with the US, as a stick with which to beat Sinn Fein. The step-by-step approach that we have been following, designed as it is to slowly draw everyone into dialogue, without asking anyone to compromise their ideology before they get to the table, remains the only viable way forward.

You will recognise, I know, that I do not put forward these views as a friend or ally of Sinn Fein—far from it!—but rather because I believe absolutely that the peace was won by accepting the principles of parity of esteem and inclusiveness, and can only be lost by losing sight of them."

In the end, and after a great deal of heart-searching, John Bruton took the courageous and correct decision to cancel a summit with John Major—the first time in my involvement in politics that anything like that had ever happened. It was a difficult decision, but it made the British government begin to see the dangers in their stubborn approach.

We had to hope that progress would be made before it was too late. And in the meantime, I had another job to do—and more trouble to get into.

17

Divorce and Breakdown

Over the years, I've developed a sort of philosophy about campaigning. The campaign that is taken seriously is the one that's clearly serious—organised and prepared, determined to be relevant, always central to the action, impossible to ignore. The campaigners have to believe in the message, and understand it. There has to be conviction, and commitment has to be sustained. When you're absolutely convinced you've won, give it one last shot anyway—and then another one, because no campaign is over until the results are counted.

All these things are vital. Forget any of them, and a campaign will founder. Until it was almost too late, I forgot all of them in the campaign to change the Constitution on divorce.

From the moment he had been appointed Minister for Equality and Law Reform, Mervyn Taylor knew that the key measurement of his success would be the outcome of the divorce referendum, whenever it happened. He prepared diligently, as only Mervyn could. Over the first three years of his Ministry, he put together a phenomenal body of legislation, completely modernising the law on marriage, separation, children and property.

His aim was simple. He wanted to arrive at the point in relation to divorce where it would all boil down to one net question—should we allow people the right to re-marry, if they have become trapped in a dead marriage?

The changes he put through achieved that. Helped by incredibly talented and hard-working people, like Paul Mulhern and Anne Kinsella, and by his brilliant legal adviser Richard Humphreys, Mervyn affected a quiet and thorough revolution in family law.

When the time came to embark on the referendum necessary to complete the revolution, he enlisted my help. Together we commissioned research and sought advice from all the best brains in the business. The advice was unanimous, and coincided with my own view. This was an argument best fought out in reasonable terms among reasonable people. The way to win was to avoid stirring up memories of the past, and above all to keep reminding people that there was, after all, only one issue to be addressed.

Divorce and separation were already practical realities in Ireland. People divided property, arranged the care and custody of children and dependents, and went their separate ways every day of the week. Thousands of people lived in long-term, stable and happy second and third relationships. But they could never get married again.

It was a simple message, and true. It was bound to be the basis for an effective, low-key, reasonable campaign. Except for the thing we all forgot.

It's easier to make people afraid than it is to make them hope. It's easier to appeal to that fear rather than to encourage generosity. And Ireland possesses some of the most skilled and experienced practitioners of the politics of fear there are.

Our understated campaign was a gift to them. The opinion polls encouraged our complacency, giving us a clear and unassailable lead before we started. In the course of the campaign, our hands were further tied by the so-called McKenna judgement, which forbade the spending of public money in pursuit of government policy.

At the start of the campaign, we advertised publicly for an advertising agency, and six companies tendered. One of them, Quinn McDonnell Pattison, was head and shoulders above the others in terms of the creative work they had prepared. Another, McConnells, offered strong strategic insights in the course of their presentation. All of us who had viewed the different presentations wanted to work with both agencies, but the two agencies found it impossible to agree a way of working together.

We recommended QMP, and I got into trouble subsequently because I told Conor Quinn, the head of the agency, that he was likely to get the contract on merit—but that he should prepare for flak, because he happened to be Ruairi Quinn's brother. When this emerged (after the campaign was over) I was accused of manipulating the appointment of QMP as an act of political favouritism.

It wasn't true, but I've always thought the worst feature of the whole episode was that, because of our fear of the McKenna case, we decided not even to use the brilliant campaign they had developed. Instead they were employed to place boring advertisements throughout the campaign, until finally the McKenna judgement put a stop even to them.

Sooner or later, people are going to realise that there is something deeply undemocratic about a government being unable to promote its own legitimate policies, and being forced to pay for the promotion of policies to which it is opposed—and which, by definition, it cannot see as being in the public interest. No real public interest, and no democratic value, is ever going to be served by the crazy McKenna judgment. Instead, the judgement paves the way for absurdities, like tax revenue being spent to encourage people to vote against the Peace Agreement. How much longer will it be until some powerful vested interest realises that the democratic system has been rendered impotent by the McKenna judgement, and uses private and secret money to start manipulating the law of the land?

Some elements of the pro-divorce campaign, however, worked very well. Mervyn gathered a small group of people around him—principally Kathleen O'Meara and a small number of highly skilled civil servants—and together they plotted a systematic journey around Ireland, that brought Mervyn to every local radio station and virtually every newspaper office. Over the weeks of the campaign, he put in dozens of hours on chat shows and phone-ins, patiently explaining the changes that were being proposed, and answering questions from the public in every county in Ireland.

He also never shied away from any confrontation with the opponents of divorce. One of the big mistakes that had been made in the 1986 referendum on the same subject was to give William Binchy, the principal spokesman for the anti-divorce lobby, the virtual freedom of the airwaves. There was no one pro-divorce spokesperson back then, no one person as knowledgeable as Binchy. But this time, everywhere Binchy went, Mervyn offered to debate him, and inch by inch he whittled away at Binchy's arguments.

If we had put together a better campaign behind Mervyn, we would have won easily. And it wasn't because his government colleagues were unwilling. We simply misunderstood the mood. The various voluntary groups who worked on the campaign were totally frustrated by what they regarded as political party inactivity, and there were lots of rows and tensions at every meeting. In the end, some of them went their own way, and the individual contributions that some made to debate contributed more of a spark than the government campaign in its early stages.

The McKenna judgement, and the opinion polls which came out around the same time—and which showed support for change tumbling—finally galvanised the political parties. Over the space of a weekend, we put together posters, leaflets, and bodies, and finally got an "in-your-face" campaign going.

In the end, the fear of defeat did more than all the strategic analysis had. The Taoiseach did a brilliant interview on radio on the last Sunday of the campaign, and undoubtedly swung some undecided voters our way. And we were helped by some of the final anti-divorce posters, which were so far over the top that they offended the moderate opinion we had been trying unsuccessfully to attract.

I still remember feeling that the outcome—the closest result in a referendum in the history of the state—was an anti-climax. We had won, but only by snatching a victory at the end. It was a scrambled goal in extra time on a particularly muddy afternoon. If the weather hadn't intervened, ironically—with rain in the west and sunshine in Dublin—the result could well have gone the other way.

To me, the lesson was simple. If you believe in something, go for it. We almost blew the divorce referendum through a mistaken analysis of what was necessary. I was determined that that wouldn't happen ever again.

But as I was to find out later, life isn't as simple as that either.

For now, even if I felt like celebrating, there wasn't time. By the end of 1995, and throughout the first couple of months of 1996, Anglo-Irish relations and the peace process were in deep trouble.

President Clinton was coming to Ireland in December, and as the time for his visit grew closer, it looked more and more as if he would be coming to a disaster. There seemed to be no way we could persuade the British to relax the decommissioning issue, or even to sideline it, in order to enable progress to be made toward the start of negotiations. As pressure built up, the British seemed to grow more obdurate by the day. The Taoiseach and the Tánaiste were under immense pressure to reconvene the summit that had been cancelled, but to their everlasting credit, they refused to do so until there was something concrete to discuss.

Those who have criticised John Bruton's role in the peace process since then seem to me to have forgotten how hard he struggled to hold on to peace. In so far as things were in his control, there was no stone left unturned, no effort left unmade, to keep the process alive. The failure in the end was not his.

Both the British government and Sinn Féin have always had one thing in common, though they may not care to admit it. They have both always seen Northern Ireland as a struggle with two main protagonists—themselves. Both the British and Sinn Féin fought for the support of the Irish government primarily as an act of strategy, because our support was critical to victory.

And victory has always been at the heart of that struggle. Even though both sides know, instinctively, that victory isn't possible, every step of the peace process was dogged by the desire of one side to score a point off the other.

There's an element of simplification in that, of course, because there are issues that complicate the aims and objectives of the two protagonists.

But the result is that the hardest place to be is trying to steer a middle course between both. And as the battle for hearts and minds intensified over the eighteen months of the first IRA ceasefire, the role of the Irish government—no matter what its composition—was always going to be impossible. Once either of the two protagonists decided to take unilateral action, there was nothing any Irish government could do to stop them.

But by keeping pressure on the British, through refusing to hold a summit until it would have worthwhile results, and by keeping equal pressure on Sinn Féin, John Bruton did everything one man could do to keep the process going.

Eventually, however, just at the point where the Irish government would have had to advise President Clinton to stay away, the British government relented. At a hastily-convened summit, they finally agreed to the composition and setting up of the International Body we had agreed in principle nearly six months earlier. Their reluctance to agree, naturally, made it easier for Sinn Féin to buy into the International Body—something that probably wouldn't have happened had the British proposed it in the first place! And George Mitchell, John de Chastelaine, and Harry Holkeri were to go on to have a profound influence.

But everyone knew the ceasefire was running out of time. We were no closer to getting a starting-date for talks, no closer to securing the entry of all the parties. John Major was increasingly hamstrung by the parliamentary arithmetic. A deadline emerged—the end of February 1996. If we hadn't made progress by then, the Provos were certainly going to re-assess the ceasefire.

The International Body reported at the end of January in 1996, a model of clarity and simplicity. They had done exactly what we thought they could, and should, do—they had addressed the issue of decommissioning at the level of principle, and recognised that it was an issue which defined victory or defeat for the protagonists.

Then, in perhaps the biggest own-goal of the entire peace process, John Major said "thanks, but no thanks". In a speech to the House of Commons, he ignored virtually the entire report, except for one tiny paragraph which suggested that elections to a new assembly might have merit. Instead of seizing on the report as a basis for finally getting negotiations going, he drove a wedge of solid mahogany into the peace process.

I watched his speech with some of my colleagues, in a state of disbelief. I thought, and said aloud, that's it. That's the end of the peace process.

But we had to keep going. There were times in the process when the British, we believed, would talk more frankly to the Americans than they would to us. This was one of those times. We needed the help of the Americans now, and over the next week or so, the phone lines between Dublin and Washington—and, we believed, between Washington and London—burned up.

It seemed to be paying off. At a meeting with President Clinton and Anthony Lake (the National Security Council chief) in Washington, Dick learned that the Americans had good reason to believe that before the end of February we would have an agreement with the British on a firm starting date for talks, and a mechanism for Sinn Féin's entry.

We left Washington in a mood of celebration—we knew we were on the verge of the next breakthrough. In the plane on the way home, we discovered it was too late. The Provos' patience had run out. That was February 9th, 1996—the day the ceasefire ended.

Of course we got a firm date two weeks after the end of the ceasefire. And of course, everyone believed that we only got it because the Provos had used muscle. I've always believed the opposite.

I've always believed, and always will, that if the Provos had waited until the end of February before ending the ceasefire, they'd have had a firm date for the start of all-party negotiations—and they'd have had it in a way that would have made it impossible for John Major to avoid sharing the table with them at the opening of those negotiations.

But as it was, once Sinn Féin had put themselves outside the pale yet again, the search for mechanisms of inclusion became endlessly complicated. It often seemed to me that we were operating in a kind of Kafkaesque dance, where the British and the Irish governments were ostensibly seeking the same objective, but in reality diametrically opposed ones. We were trying to include, they were trying to exclude. We were trying to make peace among undefeated enemies, they were still in love with the notion of victory.

No doubt, and with total sincerity, the British would see it the other way around—them trying to bring all the parties together on a basis that would threaten no-one, us interested in appeasing one side only. That's how impenetrable the whole process became.

For me, it culminated in a bizarre set of meetings, in which I became a member of the first Irish delegation to break off negotiations with the British government since, I suppose, 1921. Not that anyone noticed at the time, but it happened like this.

I travelled to London with Dick in early June 1996. He was staying for several days, those of us who were with him were only going to dinner. That was the plan, anyway—Dick was accompanying President Robinson on a state visit to the United Kingdom, and was going over a day early, with his negotiating team, for a meeting with Sir Patrick Mayhew about the procedural rules for the all-party talks—which were scheduled to start on June 10th.

We were bogged down on one primary issue—the issue of "sufficient consensus". All-party talks, involving the bitterest of enemies, couldn't begin until there was some measure of agreement on how agreement could be recorded.

Simple majorities wouldn't be enough—that would only allow the Unionists to push through anything they wanted. Blocking mechanisms, on the other hand, could end up acting as Provo vetoes. "Consensus", in the ordinary meaning of the term, would never be achieved. So it was vital to come up with a set of rules that would allow progress to be made, but without anyone's vital interests being trampled on.

Paddy Teahon, Tim Dalton, Sean Ó hUiginn, David Cooney and Rory, all travelled. It was a high-powered team, reflecting the importance of reaching a quick—and right—decision on the issue.

The arrangement was that we would meet with Sir Patrick Mayhew and his team for dinner that night, and deal with the issue once and for all. It shouldn't take more than a couple of hours.

It didn't work out that way. Sir Patrick Mayhew was not his usual ebullient self, and it quickly became clear that he had no instructions to make any significant concessions. We came to believe that they had already committed themselves to David Trimble—if the Unionists turned up at the negotiations, the rules would be written in a way that would give them an in-built majority. As usual, the politics of Anglo-Irish relations were simple enough, even if the language was always highly technical and elusive.

It took a great deal of urging by Dick to eventually persuade Sir Patrick that if we didn't have an agreement on this matter before the talks started, they would run into the sand almost immediately. And there was going to be no way that we would be agreeing to a set of rules that favoured one side of the talks process over the other.

By one in the morning, we had a formula that balanced the need for progress with the need for minority protection. It took about three hours longer than we thought, and meant that those of us who had only travelled over for the meeting would now have to stay overnight. Dick Spring was whisked off to a suite in the Dorchester Hotel—paid for by the British government, as that was also where President Robinson would stay, and we went to find rooms elsewhere.

Because of the lateness of the hour, it was agreed that we would go the following morning to the Northern Ireland Office near Trafalgar Square, to tie up some loose ends. There was to be no need for Ministers, as only minor matters were outstanding. When we got there, we were met by Quentin Thomas with an apology.

"I'm sorry," he said, "but last night's agreement is no longer operative."

Sir Patrick had failed to persuade John Major to accept the formula he and his officials had worked out with us. Instead, Major had written his own formula, and it was this that was now being given to us by Thomas, as a final offer.

We had no authority to refuse a paper from the British Prime Minister, but neither could we renege on an agreement made by our own Tánaiste. And we had no-one to consult—the official visit by President Robinson was now underway, and Dick was in Buckingham Palace with her.

It was Seán Ó hUiginn who made the decision for us.

"In that event, Quentin," he said, "these negotiations are over. We will report their failure to our political masters, and no doubt they will decide the political consequences."

Thomas asked, "Do I take it therefore that you are refusing to even consider the Prime Minister's proposal?"

"Yes," Seán said. And we left.

It is not a comfortable feeling to represent the Irish government in an official capacity, and to have to report to your government that you have spurned a written proposal, sight unseen, from the British Prime Minister. It's slightly more uncomfortable when you have done so in a June heat-wave, in the same clothes you wore to dinner the night before.

We went to the Dorchester, as Dick was expected back there. When we reported what had happened, he gave us two bits of advice. First, as far as he was concerned, he had made an agreement, and we had behaved absolutely correctly in spurning the attempt to change it. And second, those of us who needed fresh underwear and shirts were encouraged to go and buy some straight away.

I don't know how many days after that we spent in the Dorchester Hotel—I think it was two, but it seemed like a week. Our instructions were to wait, while Dick Spring took every opportunity that the state visit threw up to get across the message that there would be no change in the Irish position— save that when we got home, we would have to make it clear that the Prime Minister had reneged on an agreement made by his Secretary of State.

We coined the phrase "Free the Dorchester Six" to describe our immobility. We looked longingly at the mini-bar in Dick Spring's suite, and at its extraordinary price list—all the time unaware that its contents had been supplied by the British government!

And then, two or three days before talks were due to begin, John Major decided to honour the agreement made between Dick Spring and Sir Patrick Mayhew. Not a dot or comma was changed. And we went home.

18

Back to Square One

I came home to a change. If the previous year had been tough for the government and for Ministers, it had been even tougher for the party. In March, Ruairi Quinn and Eithne FitzGerald had had to apologise to Dáil Eireann for a fund-raising lunch. The impression had been given, in the correspondence sent out, that people willing to pay £100 for lunch would be able to bend the ear of the Minister for Finance as he prepared his Finance Bill.

There was no corruption involved—nobody who knew Eithne FitzGerald would believe for a minute that she could be involved in anything that smacked of political favours. But the letter had been allowed to go out, and it looked on the surface like a venal attempt to sell favours for money. Certainly that was how it looked to Fianna Fáil, who professed themselves shocked at the event.

Later, Michael D Higgins became embroiled in controversy over a fund-raising race night which raised £1,200 for his constituency, because one of the supporters of the occasion was a person he had appointed as chairman of the Independent Radio and Television Commission. Everyone in Dáil Eireann knew that Niall Stokes and Michael D had been close friends for years, but that didn't stop the opposition braying that Niall was now in an untenable position.

Although the controversies were minor in themselves, they should never have happened. We were now, inevitably, in the run-up to an election, and the last thing we needed was issues that seemed almost designed like bullets aimed unerringly at our own feet.

What we had was a management problem. Nobody was carrying weight between the party and the government, and they were functioning as two totally separate entities. Those of us who were working for the government were going flat out, and nobody was working full-time at preparation for the election.

I suggested the remedy myself, albeit with a slightly heavy heart. The result was my resignation from the Department of Foreign Affairs, just as the all-party talks were getting under way. I moved full-time to Ely Place, the Labour headquarters.

My brief was to help prepare the party for the general election, which would have to be held inside a year or so. My first step was to commission research, to see, as scientifically as possible, how we stood with the electorate.

Just how big a challenge we faced was quickly revealed. In focus group after focus group, people were sending us the same message. Ever since 1992, and the formation of the Reynolds/Spring Government, the electorate had harboured a grudge. A year out from the election, I quickly discovered that we were in for a good hammering.

It didn't matter that the achievements of the party in government were real and substantial—and it didn't matter that the choices we had faced in 1992 were immensely difficult. The political folklore—set in cement—said that we had campaigned against Albert in 1992, and then leapt into bed with him. In fact, by the middle of 1996 it seemed to a great many people that we had been plotting to form a government with Albert all along.

The other message from the research was this: the policies you pursue, and the achievements you create, are less important than the way you go about them. Our Ministers were widely seen as among the best for years, for example—but they were also seen as technocratic, distant, arrogant. There was no sense of them being on anyone's side—just an impression of a group of people doing competent jobs.

Overall, the big message was trust. Or rather, the lack of it. One big thing outweighed all the other things that had been achieved—we had promised change, and kept Albert Reynolds in office. And then we had compounded the impression by forming a government with Fianna Fáil's enemies in 1994.

Clearly, we would get into bed with anyone, anytime, anywhere.

There was, at least in my view, a huge gap between fact and legend. But not in the perception of people who had voted for us in 1992, a significant proportion of whom were telling our pollsters they would never vote for us again.

Side by side with what we were finding, the published opinion polls were saying that the overall approval rating of the government was continually going up throughout that period, but the support for each of its individual components was sliding steadily at the same time.

There was a fundamental dilemma in all of this. The electorate—our electorate, at least—approved of a Labour Party that was sharp, aggressive, and independent. That was the way they wanted us to campaign. But any relationship with Fianna Fáil that wasn't mandated beforehand would be seen as a betrayal by the same people that wanted us to be independent of other parties.

It was a no-win situation. If we campaigned as an independent party—especially at the end of a successful period of government—we would be inviting the suggestion that we were preparing to go back in with Fianna Fáil. If we campaigned as part of the outgoing government, we would be sacrificing the independence that our voters wanted us to rediscover.

It was around this time that my old friend, Albert Reynolds, popped up to distract me from the task in hand.

In July I had a phone call from a London solicitor, Katherine Rimell, who explained that she represented the *Sunday Times*, and that the paper was being sued by Albert over a piece concerning the fall of his government in 1994. I hadn't seen the piece—it hadn't been published in Ireland—and she faxed it to me.

As soon as I read it, I realised—even though my name wasn't used—that it was largely based on comments I had made to Alan Ruddock, the Irish editor and the author of the piece. I hadn't said anything to him that I didn't believe to be true, and now he was being sued. I didn't know Alan Ruddock well, but in all my dealings with him, I'd found him to be straight.

It didn't seem right to me that a piece he had written, which was essentially truthful, even if the language was snide in places, should be the subject of a libel action. Katherine Rimell had explained to me that because the case was taking place in a foreign jurisdiction, I couldn't be compelled to give evidence.

And I knew that without my consent, Alan Ruddock couldn't, and wouldn't, reveal his sources.

In some ways, that made the dilemma worse. How do you turn your back on something you've said yourself, and allow someone else to hang for it, just because your name isn't going to be mentioned?

I thought about it for a long time. I knew that none of the other probable witnesses from Ireland were likely to be interested in taking part in the case. And there wasn't any reason why they should be, since they hadn't contributed to the story in the first place.

In the end, I wrote to Katherine Rimell, telling her that I would, reluctantly, give evidence for the *Sunday Times*. In my letter, I told her that:

> ... I disagree, most of the time and strongly, with your client's editorial line. I also believe that your client has taken a position in relation to Northern Ireland which is usually damaging to the process there. Furthermore, I have deep and continuing admiration for the position adopted by Mr Reynolds in relation to Northern Ireland, and for the way in which he conducted negotiations with the British Government and others in respect of that intractable problem. Although there were aspects of his tenure of office with which I disagreed, I strongly object to the term "gombeen" which the article in question used to belittle him.
>
> The bottom line, however, is that the article (despite some immaterial inaccuracies which I have already pointed out, and despite its occasionally sneering tone) is essentially true, in my opinion. As an occasional participant in the events covered by the article, and

having carefully considered the papers you sent me, I believe I would have no choice but to give evidence to that effect if asked, and to stand over that evidence to the best of my ability.

Several months went by, and I heard no more. Gradually I began to harbour the hope that the case might be settled.

But it wasn't to be, and as the date for the hearing of the action grew closer, I began to be aware of pressure within the Labour Party to have nothing to do with it. Several of our Ministers rang me to ask me was I sure I wanted to be involved (I told them all, truthfully, that I didn't!), and there were a couple of newspaper pieces along the lines of how awful it would be if people were travelling from Ireland to give evidence in a British court against an Irish statesman.

Eventually, Dick himself told me that people were ringing him about it, and that it was widely seen as wrong that I would be willing to give evidence for the *Sunday Times*. I spoke to all of my closest colleagues—William, Greg, John Foley, Sally— and all were doubtful, but personally supportive.

After a sleepless night, I wrote to Dick—I think the first time I ever wrote to him in fifteen years. Among other things, my letter said:

> I have come to regard the issue as an issue of principle, and I can't shake off that conviction. To be more precise, I would regard it as a totally dishonourable act, having agreed to appear, if I were now to withdraw.
>
> Although I was approached first by the Sunday Times, I was also asked to appear, in writing, by Mr. Reynolds' lawyers. I agreed to appear for the Sunday Times, primarily because the story in question was written by Alan Ruddock based primarily on briefing given by me. The briefing was truthful, and so is the story, and Alan Ruddock does not deserve to be sued over it.
>
> On the basis of principle, therefore, and also for reasons of practicality, I do not see how I can withdraw.

I am very concerned, however, at any suggestion that my appearance could damage the Labour Party. You know me well enough, I know, to understand that I would never willingly risk damage to the Party. I think that can be avoided by a simple and sober recitation of the truth as I know it.

But I am willing to take any additional step you might consider necessary, up to and including resignation from my position, to make it totally clear that my appearance in the witness box has nothing whatever to do with any vendetta by the Party against Mr. Reynolds, but is simply in the interests of the truth, in so far as that is possible.

Dick rang me when he got my letter, and told me simply that there was one person whose support I didn't need to worry about—him.

But in what turned out to be one of the most frustrating experiences of my life in the end, the *Sunday Times'* lawyers never called me as a witness. They asked me to travel over, and to sit in the body of the court, but the night before I was due to appear, they told me they had decided not to call me. The other side—Albert Reynolds' lawyers—had withdrawn a number of witnesses, and they had also objected to a large body of the evidence I proposed to give, which was contained in a witness statement to which they had had access. My appearance could not go ahead without a lot of legal argument about what I could say, and they had decided it just wasn't necessary.

I was relieved at the time, and flew home immediately, feeling that I had made the honourable effort. It wasn't until I was in a taxi on the way home from Dublin Airport that I heard Joe Duffy on RTE radio reporting that I had given all the appearance of someone who couldn't wait to be out of the court room, and that the word "chicken" was being bandied about me all over the High Court.

I was furious, especially as I had explained all the circumstances to Joe Duffy myself before leaving the court, and tried to find a public phone in order to ring Myles Dungan, the programme presenter, and try to put my side of the story. We were badly stuck in traffic, and the taxi driver had to put up with my fulminations for ten minutes before we found a kiosk.

When I got inside, I discovered that I only had one unit left on a phone card, and had to explain to Myles Dungan on air that I could be cut off at any minute. As I did so, I saw my taxi driver running up the road to a local supermarket.

Seconds later, he came tearing down again, pulled open the door of the kiosk, and handed me a new phone card. Although not a Labour man, as he told me later, he was no supporter of Albert Reynolds either!

Worse was to come later, when Albert Reynolds' lawyer, in summing up for the jury, concentrated most of his fire on me. Implying that I had been afraid to be cross-examined, he referred to me as a snake in the grass, a creature who skulked in the darkness and fashioned the dagger that Dick Spring had plunged into Albert's back! All of this was carried prominently in every Irish newspaper, and on RTE.

It was highly theatrical, and very hurtful at the time. Because legal privilege applied to everything said in the courts, I had no possible redress. I could only reflect in the end that someone who was prepared to go to such lengths to protect his own character, as he saw it, was so cavalier about the character of another.

I did have the satisfaction ultimately of being able to send a cheque for £2,500 to the Special Olympics arising from the way in which RTE had reported my appearance, around the same time that Albert was being awarded a penny in damages.

My troubles paled into insignificance beside the plight of a number of women who contracted Hepatitis C from infected blood transfusions. Although the infected transfusions had begun to be used in the 1970s, they only came to light in the early 1990s, when Brendan Howlin was Minister for Health. Despite political criticism that was made of Brendan later, I have always believed that he acted decisively and honourably when the discovery was made, in making it fully public and in trying to ensure counselling and support for the women involved.

The women were angry, and entitled to be. The neglect that had been involved in the transmission of this disease had been on a criminal scale, and they were determined, rightly, to ensure that it was fully exposed. The official reaction, on the other hand, was always motivated by concern for an on-going and secure supply of safe blood for necessary transfusions. The "system" felt that the women ought basically to be happy with financial compensation, but that nothing should be done which would jeopardise the credibility of the Blood Bank. A wide range of measures was taken to ensure that the Blood Bank was properly managed for the future, but there was always a reluctance to open up the past to too much examination.

This was underpinned, in my observation, by ignorance of just how devastating Hepatitis C could be. Although people knew it was a serious condition, I don't believe that many of the civil servants and politicians who dealt with the crisis realised fully that it would cause death.

That changed with the death of Brigid McCole, a middle-aged woman from Donegal. The mother of a large family, she had refused to accept compensation, and had pressed on with a legal action against the state, because she was determined to get at the truth of what had happened to her.

In the course of 1996 I discovered that the Blood Transfusion Service Board had made a lodgement in the case, without notifying the government in advance of their intentions. A lodgement means a sum of money is handed into court as a prospective settlement in a civil action. The plaintiff in an action is always advised about the amount of the lodgement, although the court itself is not told. If the plaintiff then refuses to accept the lodgement, but is awarded less by the court than the amount lodged, the plaintiff will then be liable for the costs of the case.

In other words, a lodgement is a fairly routine legal device, used to exert pressure on plaintiffs to settle their cases out of court. The difficulty in this case arose from the fact that Michael Noonan, the Minister for Health, was on the Dáil record as saying that he was happy to let the case run in the High Court, and that the court case would be a suitable vehicle for getting at the truth of what had happened to Hepatitis C victims. The two positions were incompatible—you couldn't want a case to run, and be exerting pressure at the same time to have it settled.

Michael Noonan is, and always has been in my experience, a principled and honourable politician. I had no doubt that this lodgement, which wasn't compatible with his public statements, had to have been done without his knowledge. I brought what I knew about the matter to Dick's attention, and he brought it to the cabinet. A long discussion took place around the government table, but by then it was too late to withdraw the lodgement.

Later, I wrote a personal letter to Michael Noonan, suggesting that a judicial tribunal should be established to finally get at the truth. He replied that he had already come to that conclusion himself, and had forwarded papers to government proposing the establishment of a tribunal. William Scally and I were to spend several days negotiating on Dick's behalf over the terms of reference, with the Department of Health and the Attorney General's office, in order to try to get as much transparency as possible.

To this day, I believe that the most painful lesson to be learned from the Hepatitis C scandal is the lesson that policy makers must always have a facility to reflect, and that their choices should be based on more open and critical analysis. The dilemma in the Hepatitis C case concerned a clash between public policy and the public interest—between protection of a legitimate vested interest, on the one hand, and the nebulous concept called the full truth, on the other. Without an ingrained commitment to transparency throughout the system, at every level—from cabinet to higher executive officer—the vested interest will always win.

The Hepatitis C crisis wasn't the only one that bedevilled the government in its last year. In June, the crime reporter Veronica Guerin was murdered, and the IRA also murdered a Garda, Jerry McCabe, in Limerick. Both murders opened a floodgate of anger about crime, especially organised crime, and made crime into a huge political issue. Veronica Guerin had been a fearless reporter, often exposing the dark underbelly of a new and growing Irish mafia, and her death was particularly shocking. It led to a spate of legislation—and also to the impression that the government had been "soft" on crime until these particularly vicious killings had woken them up. Like most political impressions, it wasn't based on reality, but it added to the pressure the government was under.

That pressure was compounded in due course by the discovery that Michael Lowry, a Fine Gael Minister, had been in receipt of large amounts of money, in highly dubious circumstances, from the supermarket tycoon Ben Dunne.

Michael Lowry was a strange, intense man. He had been involved in earlier controversies, claiming that he had been placed under surveillance by shadowy figures, apparently because of some determination on his part to clean up the semi-state sector and rid it of political corruption (his best efforts failed to find any).

While I was still working for the government, I had been stopped in a corridor by Michael Lowry, who told me that one of the reasons he had been certain of the surveillance was that no-one—not even his wife—knew where he was living in Dublin! I had reported this conversation to Dick, together with the observation that I thought there was something odd about him.

Lowry's inevitable resignation from government over the scandal of the money he had received from Ben Dunne was to have, in the end, unforeseen consequences. It was subsequently discovered that Ben Dunne had given even larger amounts of money to Charles J Haughey, and this was to lead in turn to the spectacle of Charlie confessing to venality and greed in front of a judicial tribunal.

In all the years I worked in politics, there was no more stylish and dominant figure than Charles J Haughey. Even at the height of the battles between Dick and him—battles about fundamental issues of public accountability—it was impossible not to have a sneaking admiration for his arrogance, his mastery of the Dáil, and his incredible self-belief. I can still remember thinking, as he made his pathetic admissions in the end about how he was beholden to the money and vanity of rich men, that even his style was an illusion. He left public office with his grandeur intact, and his legion of admirers were prepared to defend him to the death. But he even betrayed them in the end, because he was such easy prey for anyone with a fat purse.

None of these crises, of course, were helping us to get organised for the election that was looming. Pat Magner and I formed a team, and we drove around the country trying to assess the readiness of the branches and constituencies. Everywhere we found good spirit and morale, but a depressing lack of organisation. We determined to try to put that right, by preparing and supplying as much of the material as they would need ourselves.

And we also warned, everywhere we went, that we were in for a hell of a battle. I had fully briefed the national committees of the party about what I was finding out through research, and no-one was under any illusions about how tough it was going to be.

There were some encouraging signs too though. In the run up to every election, we run a business appeal. This normally consists of writing to the top hundred or so businesses in the country appealing for money. We always specify that cheques must be made out to the Labour Party, and anything that doesn't come in that way is automatically sent back. The totals are always put into the party accounts, which are published in conjunction with national conference.

It's never been a task I enjoyed—especially as I've always believed that politics in a democracy should be funded to reasonable levels by the exchequer, but if you don't do it, you simply can't compete in an election campaign with the bigger parties.

At different times, such appeals have different levels of success. But in 1996 we had the most successful one ever, with some unsolicited contributions made out to the party as well. Several contributors referred in letters to their admiration of Dick's work in the peace process. Obviously business was well disposed towards the party—and probably expected us to be still in government after the election!

By the turn of the year, we were almost ready for an election, at least in the mechanical sense. Candidates had been selected, posters and leaflets had been organised, material had been prepared for distribution showing that we had developed a phenomenal track record in government. And it was all real— we were able to demonstrate that not only had we kept more than 90% of the promises that had been made in the two programmes for government we had negotiated, but we had kept a huge proportion of the promises in our original manifesto. By any objective standard, we had delivered the change we promised—in spades.

But there were two strategic issues to be addressed. When would the election be? And how would we approach the issue of credibility in relation to the one promise we were seen to have broken—the relationship with Fianna Fáil?

There has been a lot of confusion about the first issue ever since that election. It's been widely believed that John Bruton wanted to wait until November of 1997, and that he was pushed into an earlier election by the other two parties, and especially by Labour. That wasn't the case, in my understanding.

In fact, early in 1997, Pat and I were asked to meet with strategists from the other two parties. What Fine Gael put to us at that meeting was the notion that we would go early, catch Fianna Fáil on the hop, and force them to cancel their Ard Fheis, which was due immediately after Easter.

That was the only proposition, to the best of my knowledge, that was discussed between the three parties. In the end, it was ruled out, by agreement, because it was felt that we needed to have a party conference, specifically to address the issue of credibility. We knew—everybody knew—that we were likely to be the weak link in the rainbow chain. If anyone was going to lose seats in large numbers, it was going to be us. And it was essential, if that was to be avoided, that we be given a chance to address the credibility issue four-square.

On several occasions after that, I was asked about the possibility of delaying the election until the end of the year. Each time, I gave the same advice. If the party leaders wanted to hold on, they would have to make it unequivocally clear, in the most direct possible language, that they were going to complete their programme, and wouldn't be going to the country until well after the summer. If they didn't agree on a very full statement, the momentum towards an election that always takes hold in Dáil Eireann would take care of the matter for them.

In the end, that's what happened. They never discussed November in the kind of depth necessary to develop an unshakeable rationale for waiting. They drifted instead, until it was too late to halt the momentum for an election in June.

The other issue, the one of credibility, was more difficult for us. We strongly believed that if we failed to give a categoric reassurance that we would not countenance government with Fianna Fáil after the election, we would be dogged by the subject throughout any campaign.

And all the questions would be based on the implicit assumption that we were preparing the ground for a repeat of 1992. There was no room for shilly-shallying on the subject. But unfortunately, our research also told us that we would be better off, in electoral terms, as an independent voice. We had always believed in, and I had always advocated, campaigning independently, putting up alternatives, all the time seeking to be relevant. That was going to be impossible in a supportive role as part of a government seeking re-election.

Although it was an agonising decision, with no right way to turn, the decision was in the end made for us by the mind-set of the Ministers. Ministers was what they had become, each in charge of a Department, each believing that their Departmental issues were in some way fundamental Labour issues. Some of them were—but many of them were the kind of issues that come up in any manager's experience.

Of all of them, only Dick was able, by the end, to separate his party role from his Ministerial role. If we had tried to campaign as an independent party, we would have looked ludicrously like a collection of Ministers and Junior Ministers who weren't sure what party they belonged to.

I don't mean that as criticism—not one of them ever let the party down in government—but by the end of it, they had been so fully absorbed into the processes of government that it was impossible to escape its clutches.

This translated itself into the way in which their Programme Managers operated as well. Near the start of the campaign, I attended a meeting of Programme Managers to try to secure some progress on some minor outstanding issues. As soon as I raised them, there was instant bickering, of the kind that civil servants protecting their corner are capable of. All of them had lost sight of the priority that was now staring us in the face.

I was amused, after the election, when some of our former Ministers told the party that it had been a mistake to campaign as part of the government. Those of us who had worked with them, and had admired their achievements in government, knew full well that they would have been unable to stop thinking and behaving as Ministers for a minute, if the decision had been to strike an independent position.

The decision, to campaign as part of the government, was also fully in accordance with Dick's own instincts. He was proud of the work the government had done, feeling that there was a good record, and nothing to be ashamed of. He was also instinctively loyal to the two colleagues he had worked closely with for the previous two years, John Bruton and Proinsias De Rossa. And he had come to believe, rightly or wrongly, that government with Fianna Fáil was just unmanageable. There were too many dark corners.

So, after making our decision, and spelling it out clearly at the Limerick conference, we embarked on a campaign that was all about our 1992 voters taking revenge on us. We had known for a year it was going to happen, and we had known that there was little we could do about it. Every now and again, something happens that gets stuck in political folklore, and is never forgotten. The ill-starred relationship between Dick Spring and Albert Reynolds was one of those things.

The funny thing was, the campaign itself was one of the best I've ever worked on. William Scally had prepared a comprehensive manifesto, and we gathered together in head office a fantastic team of young people.

Tom Butler ran the campaign press office magnificently, and the logistics of the campaign worked like a dream. Rónan O'Brien and Tom Duke got a campaign website going on the Internet, and altogether we put together an operation that was as quick and responsive as any I've ever been involved in.

Not only that, but the feedback on the ground was fantastic. All over the country, the message was the same—candidates were doing well, people were friendly on the doorsteps, all our canvassers were encountering high levels of recognition for the work we had done and the people we had in the field. Dick got a warm and friendly reception everywhere he went—not as frenetic as in 1992, but nobody had expected that.

As a result, my media briefings got more and more upbeat. I began to believe that maybe we could turn it around after all. Every time the little voice in my head reminded me about the scientific work I had done, and the doom-laden warnings I had issued to the party, another voice told me to be quiet.

But the science was right, and the feedback on the ground was wrong—or else we misread it. On the night of the count, seat after seat tumbled. Good people, deputies who had worked hard and never did a dishonourable thing, all lost their seats.

Eithne FitzGerald, who had effected a revolution in the conduct of politics through her ethics legislation; Joan Burton, who had been the best Minister for the developing world we had ever had; John Mulvihill, who had been stalwart in his defence of Irish Steel, and unfailingly loyal throughout a massive crisis; Brian Fitzgerald, a rock of decency and good sense, who had played a quiet and important role in relation to Northern Ireland; Toddy O'Sullivan, whose 1981 campaign was the first I ever worked on. All of them, and many more, fell.

Above all, perhaps, Niamh Bhreathnach. I am absolutely confident that history will record Niamh as one of the two or three best Ministers for Education the country has ever seen. She was swept from her job in a tide of indifference, in a constituency where she had made a profound difference to thousands of families.

It was hard to bear. I woke up the morning after the election thinking that when I had joined the party, we had sixteen deputies. Now, after the hardest and best work I could do for fifteen years, we had seventeen. Some track record!

We all, I think, felt the same. Everyone had worked their guts out, and there are times when it's hard to forgive democracy for the way it works. But when I thought about it, I couldn't feel totally responsible for the election outcome. It was waiting to happen for four years, and I had warned the party about it well in advance.

But I was tired and dispirited, and couldn't face the task of starting all over again. So I went to Dick, as soon as the Fianna Fáil/PD government had been formed, and told him I wanted to leave.

We talked about it for a long time. He was tired too, but the new government looked anything but stable. There was every possibility that the tables could be turned, and sooner than we thought. And besides, there was one more fight to be fought.

Mary Robinson had announced that she didn't intend to contest a second term, and Dick had told the party at its national conference that we would be putting up a candidate. Now we had to find one, and mount a credible campaign. So I agreed to stay on, at least until that was done.

Before Pat Magner suggested that we should go to see Adi Roche, I knew of her, and the work that she had done in Chernobyl, only vaguely. After four hours in her company, I was bowled over by her grace, courage, and honesty. On the way back to Dublin, I said to Pat that I believed Adi Roche could light a spark of idealism throughout Ireland, if she was give the chance to do so.

But she was never going to be given the chance. I suppose I'm too close to it still, but I don't know what happened—or rather, why it happened.

The Labour Party, dispirited and disillusioned with itself, still licking its wounds, expected her to sweep to victory, and when it turned into a struggle instead, walked away from her. Those who were prepared to fight for her, as hard as was going to be necessary, could be counted on the fingers of one hand.

The other parties supporting her campaign, with one or two exceptions, went through the motions. Liz McManus, for instance, the Democratic Left TD for Wicklow, worked night and day on Adi's campaign, and put in a better performance than virtually anybody else.

Others were more of a nuisance than a help. The Green Party wanted to be associated with Adi, but were prepared to make no more than a nominal contribution, and caused endless trouble with daft proposals for her campaign and daft ideas about structure and management. Patricia McKenna MEP found it impossible to hide her disdain for the Labour Party and all its works at every meeting we had.

The media, which knew Adi and everything she stood for, and respected her enormously, nevertheless felt the need to be "professional" in its dealings with her. That meant treating her in a way that no-one without experience of party politics could possibly be prepared for.

I know it was a shock to Adi when the media hounded her, in the first week of her campaign, to defend herself against the transparently vindictive remarks of embittered former employees and colleagues. But it was deeply traumatic to see newspapers digging up a twenty-five year old story about her brother, as the only bit of dirt that could be thrown at her.

Throughout a difficult campaign, her courage and resilience, even in the face of the appalling media snobbery that mocked her reaction to music (it was somehow unpresidential to show that she was enjoying it), were an inspiration to everyone who worked with her. I discovered that Adi's husband Seán has an ever worse fear of flying than I have, but he still got into a tiny helicopter to accompany her from Clonmel to Dublin on a particularly windy day. When I saw him getting off the helicopter, his face green and his legs unsteady, I took an executive decision and ordered him to be driven back down the country. He protested, but I think we'll be friends for life as a result!

The only thing that Adi was afraid of, I discovered, was Mary McAleese in her persona of "constitutional lawyer". As a seasoned environmental campaigner, Adi liked nothing better than to be put into a roomful of nuclear physicists and told to eat them for breakfast.

But she developed a fear of the mystique of constitutional law—an arcane but essentially worthless science—that I could never break through. By the end of the campaign, she knew a lot more about the Constitution than most people, but never developed the confidence to demonstrate it.

As the campaign wore on, we became more and more isolated. Those of us—Tom Butler, Marie McHale, Angie Mulroy, myself, and others—who worked in the campaign office were working around the clock, and visibly getting nowhere. Labour volunteers and workers were supplemented on a full-time basis by Mags Murphy of DL and Edel Hacket of the Greens, both of whom are, I hope, very proud of the fantastic commitment they gave. Adi herself, supported by a small group of party activists, including Pat Magner and Anne Byrne, and some family and friends, and with the indefatigable Seán at her side, covered thousands of miles without complaint.

All to no avail. The campaign developed into a sort of referendum on whether it was all right to be a Northern nationalist, an issue which centred on Mary McAleese and made her the centre of attention throughout.

It also helped her to get away without any serious examination of the profoundly illiberal views she had expressed throughout the 1980s, a blessing for which I'm sure she will always be grateful.

At the end, the only thing left to Adi was her integrity and her dignity. I had promised her before the campaign began that we wouldn't ask her to compromise her views or her values—something I've never done anyway—and I'm proud of the fact that she came through the campaign with her values intact.

And she had dignity by the bucketful. On the last day of the election, she came to the campaign headquarters to thank the people who had worked there. It was the only time she broke down. And she broke down when she told us that she hoped she hadn't let any of us down.

Nothing could be further from the truth. I will always be proud of Adi Roche, proud of who and what she is, and the contribution she can and will make. In our tired and dispirited way, we let her down.

I still carry an Adi Roche sticker on my car. It reminds me that there has to be room in politics, despite all the cynicism, despite all the games and machinations, despite all the venality and grubbiness, for the sort of idealism that Adi will always represent.

19

Looking Back

Polling day in the Presidential election was on a Thursday. I had worked around the clock for the previous three weeks, and on the day before polling, when I knew the only issue was how to deal with defeat in a dignified way, I went down to Tralee to see Dick, and to tell him I would be resigning on the day of the count.

I didn't have to say anything. He knew already. We had lunch in the Tralee golf club, and reminisced about good times and bad. Neither of us was explicit, but by the end of the day I knew his mind was made up too. And I discovered something that surprised me. There was no pain, no wrench, in his decision to go. The bottom line was that he had done everything he could, and now it would be someone else's turn. He was already looking forward to spending more time with his family.

It has always been my conviction that Dick became leader of the party, and stuck with it through thick and thin, more from a sense of duty than of ambition. Dick revered his parents, and especially his mother. Her death, shortly after the general election, had severed the last link with a tradition stretching back more than half a century—and I think had ended the feeling that he had a duty beyond his family and his town.

I thought there would be some sort of wrench for me, after all the years. But I surprised myself too. I've loved the job I had for most of the time I was in it, and I loved leaving it. I'll explain why in a minute.

Since then, I've had a chance to reflect on some of the things I've learned over fifteen years.

I've learned that good politics is about being serious. A politician or a party that is serious about its values, that understands them at some level even if it can't articulate them, will always make an impact.

I am, or have been, a person who works in practical politics, interested in results, and committed to a democratic process. I've always believed myself to be socialist, and the values of community, of economic and social freedom, of solidarity, and of equality mean a lot to me. The right of the state to intervene in the creation and the distribution of wealth have always been axiomatic for me.

Above all, perhaps, the value of democracy has been central to whatever political philosophy I have.

But I always feel that I have to qualify any reference to my political philosophy by mentioning that I don't like to be asked to articulate it in too much detail. Like most of us, I suspect, my philosophy is more in my heart than my head—I know what I'm for and what I'm against, and I'm not always sure why.

A couple of years ago, I got myself into trouble for saying that all-party talks in Northern Ireland wouldn't be worth a penny candle if Sinn Féin weren't fully involved. It was an interesting exercise in labelling, because from that moment on I was identified by some at least as a Provo fellow-traveller.

But I've never regarded myself as a nationalist, even though being Irish, and living and working in Ireland, is the only thing I want to be and do.

I've never seen myself as a republican, but I value enormously the idea of a republic. As the father of a person with a disability, *and* as a believer in the notion of a republic, I've always believed that the greatest weakness in our Constitution is the lack of any meaningful reference to equality, other than in the context of the administration of justice.

But political philosophy without organisation and strategy is sterile—just as strategy without philosophy is bankrupt. What makes them both work is the kind of coherence, unity, and discipline that comes from being serious. That's what I've learned, and tried to apply.

I've also learned that politics, in the end, is about people. Decent, honest people, in the main, struggling to do the right thing, often afraid to admit when they've got it wrong. The greatest politicians I've worked with and observed are those that never stopped learning —including from their mistakes. And the best had their foibles, just as the most venal had their redeeming features too.

If there's a thing that troubles me now about politics, it's the relationship between politics and the media. I worry, as every citizen should, about a politics that's too cozy with some sections of the media. But I worry too about a media that in some cases has become puffed up, overbearing in its self-importance, and out of touch sometimes with ordinary human imperfection.

We have become very unforgiving, and that will do us damage if it goes too far. Accountable democracy is, to some extent, like the water that flows from our kitchen taps —we don't know how dependent we are on it until the moment it's turned off. And the cynicism that a certain kind of never-ending superior commentary brings in its train is polluting the water, just as much as the greed and vanity of a few politicians has.

I've learned a lot about leadership too in the last fifteen years. The kind of leadership that allows everybody to be the owner of an idea; the kind of leadership that doesn't back away from a challenge that's probably too big for sensible people to take on; the kind of leadership that is willing to enable people to participate fully, rather than issuing commands.

Some leaders have instinctive qualities, some learned—all have the gift of listening, and hearing as well (and they are different gifts).

Above all, I think I've learned about teamwork. In the end of the day, the main reason I stayed with a job that had more than its fair share of ups and downs was the people I worked closest with.

A great many people who contributed to the development of the Labour Party had much lower profiles than I've had —but made a contribution that I find hard to measure. People like John Rogers, William Scally, Pat Magner, Greg Sparks, Finbarr

O'Malley and John Foley made a formidable team —and are a remarkable combination of wisdom, foresight and strength. They all have one thing in common —a sharp social conscience, the kind of integrity that acts as a prod.

Sally Clarke, Ita McAuliffe, Marie McHale, Marion Boushell, Anne Byrne, Sinéad Bruton, Denise Rogers, Tom Butler —they have the same conscience, the same integrity, and nobody knows the hours of work and effort that they put in, and their dedication to one over-riding cause.

I've been lucky, in the last fifteen years, to have been able to count all of them, and many more, as friends and colleagues.

And the glue that bound us together was Dick Spring.

He has one major fault, and I suppose I share it. He's always been unwilling to articulate the sense of vision and commitment that's in his gut.

His Kerry reticence, and his increasing dislike of the new and harsher form of journalism, prevented him from ever being seen as the man we knew him to be. Throughout his political career, he coped with physical pain, and also with untrue and vicious rumours about himself, and he coped with both with grace and style.

In my view—yes, I know I'm biased—he is simply the outstanding leader of his generation. And nothing became him more than the realisation that it was time for change.

The manner of his resignation from office was in sharp contrast to the departure of so many others —and ought to nail forever the lie that he cared about the trappings of office. Many who negotiated with Dick over the years believed that canard —and found out, to their cost, that someone who cares more about the things he believes in than he does about the mercs and perks side of the job is a hard man to beat at the negotiating table.

Above all, I think he taught me about character. Character isn't the same as courage—and courage is an over-rated thing in a politician anyway. Character enables a politician to stand by the things he believes in when it's necessary—but also to keep his options open. It enables him to look outwards, without losing touch with his own. It enables him to know that values are what matter at the end of the day, above anything else. It enables him to keep going, and to know when it's time to stop.

Part of the legacy that Dick left the Labour Party is character. It may be the hardest part to live up to. But there are good people there, well capable of meeting any challenge. They need no advice from me, and the only advice I want to offer anyway is contained in the words character and values. Change everything else, but don't change them.

The last fifteen years have seen enormous change. And being part of it has been exciting, painful, fun, and challenging. For me, there have been ups and downs, and I wouldn't have missed any of them for the world. I was bitter when the general election and the Presidential election were over, for all the reasons that I hope I've made clear. And I was glad to leave, to clear my head.

But when your head clears, the bitterness disappears. You remember the ups more than the downs, the ladders more than the snakes. And you come to realise that whether you hit a ladder or a snake, you chose to play the game, and you rolled the dice yourself.

In the end, the only thing that matters is: was it worth it? My answer is, yes it was. I think I can honestly say that between us all, for fifteen years, we made a hell of a difference.

Index

Abbott, Henry, 248
abortion, 5, 13–14, 33, 81, 89, 116–17
'X' case, 115–17
Adams, Gerry, 111–12, 191–6, 237, 240, 284, 290
Administrative Council, 50, 53, 56, 84, 114
Agriculture, Department of, 73–4, 232
Ahern, Bertie, 113, 148, 170–3, 209–10, 215, 216, 275
government negotiations, 1995, 266–73
Air Corps, 283
Ancram, Michael, 190
Andrew, Prince, 209
"angel paper," 190
Anglo-Irish Agreement, 1985, 31–2, 83, 111, 181, 198
Anglo-Irish relations, 208–9, 218, 227–9, 264. see also peace process
decommissioning issue, 288–9, 293, 299–305
Dublin Summit crisis, 201–3
Joint Framework Document, 222–3, 242–6
peace process, 185–204
Arnold, Bruce, 107
artificial insemination, 29
Arts and Culture, Department of, 155, 156, 162
Atlantic Resources, 26–7
Attley, Billy, 44, 46, 47
Attorney General, 29–30, 66–7, 150, 151, 260

Ball, Jonathan, 180, 183
banks
and Goodman, 75–6
Merchant Banking collapse, 77–9
Barrington, Donal, 246
Barrington, Ted, 243
Barrington's Hospital, Limerick, 60
Barry, Gerry, 286
Barry, Peter, 31–2
Basset, Ray, 243
Beef Tribunal, 76, 99, 108–9, 118–22, 139–41, 153, 238–9, 249, 264
documents to FF, 149–51
report published, 232–6
Spring's evidence, 147–8
Begley, Thomas, 195
Bell, Michael, 13, 261–2
Bergin, Emmet, 57
Bermingham, Joe, 40, 41–3
Bhamjee, Moosajee, 126, 128
Bhreathnach, Niamh, 56, 57, 162, 168–9, 215, 254, 260, 320
Binchy, William, 33, 297–8
Bird, Charlie, 213
Blood Transfusion Service Board, 312–14
Boland, John, 11, 16, 25, 28, 69
Bord Gáis, 16
Boushell, Marion, 52, 124, 328
Brennan, Seamus, 118–19
Briscoe, Ben, 129–30, 132
Brooke, Peter, 111, 181
Brosnan, Joe, 178
Browne, Bernard, 160

Browne, Dr Nöel, 84
Browne, Vincent, 272
Bruton, John, 17, 22–3, 25, 34, 98, 102, 270, 277, 298, 317, 319
  government negotiations, 1992, 130, 131–5, 143
  government negotiations, 1994, 273–4
  heads Rainbow Coalition, 1994-97, 278–319
  leads FG, 96, 125, 127
  peace process, 278–84, 288–9, 293, 299–300
  and Spring, 148, 228
Bruton, Sinead, 120, 123–4, 126, 328
Buckley, Frank, 57–8
Burgess, Niall, 187, 232, 234, 240
Burke, Ray, 118–19, 268, 270
Burke, Tim, 52
Burton, Joan, 162, 227, 320
Butler, Sir Robin, 111, 112–13
Butler, Tom, 212, 319, 323, 328
Byrne, Anne, 52, 68, 323, 328
Byrne, Eric, 129–30
Byrne, Gay, 117
Byrne, Jackie, 124

cabinet confidentiality, 118–19, 120
cabinet meetings, 197–8
  1982-87, 15–17, 23, 27–8
Cahill, Bernie, 101, 102, 103–4
Cahill, Joe, 238
Carroll, Danny, 230
Carroll, John, 43
Carysfort deal, 100–1
Casey, Bishop Eamonn, 120
Celtic Helicopters, 102
Chief Justice, appointment of, 240–1, 246, 248, 249
Chilcot, Sir John, 112–13, 222–3, 244
Claffey, Una, 98, 229, 248, 250, 286

Clarke, Sally, 7, 10, 24, 52, 70, 109, 104–5, 123–4, 159–60, 231-2, 258, 310, 328
Cleary, Fr Michael, 117
Clinton, President Bill, 170, 238–40, 289, 299, 300–1
Clondalkin Paper Mills, 43–4
Cluskey, Frank, 3, 17–19, 24–6, 40
Collins, Lavina, 187
Collins, Stephen, 103, 105, 286
Comerford, Chris, 101, 104, 105
Conlon, Tom, 68–9
Constitution, 66–7, 69, 116, 245–6, 323. *see also* abortion; divorce
  Articles 2 and 3, 228–9, 280
  Presidential travel, 191–2
Contraceptive Bill, 1986, 41–2
Cooney, David, 174, 222, 243, 302–5
Corfu summit, 1994, 223, 227–9
Coughlan, Anthony, 275
Cowen, Brian, 148, 254
Cox, Pat, 134–5
Cranbourne, Viscount, 280
currency crisis, 1993, 158
Currie, Austin, 87–8, 92, 93
Cusack, Mary, 187

Dáil Eireann, 59–61, 90–2, 98–9, 195–6, 238–9
  financial scandals, 101–7
  government falls, 1992, 121–3, 135, 142, 143
  Haughey loses power, 65–7
  Reynolds resigns, 263–4
Dalton, Tim, 225, 244, 302–5
Danaher, Gerry, 149, 151
de Chastelaine, John, 300
De Rossa, Proinsias, 62–4, 103, 114, 143, 278, 279, 319
decommissioning, 244, 288–94
Deenihan, Jimmy, 37
Delors, Jacques, 177–8, 227
Democratic Left, 129–30, 321–2, 323

Democratic Left continued
  government negotiations, 1992,
  131–2, 134, 135, 143–4
  government negotiations, 1994,
  273–4
  Rainbow Coalition, 1994-97,
  278–319
Dempsey, Noel, 148, 230, 231,
  251, 258, 259, 261
Desmond, Barry, 3, 19–22, 27, 41,
  47, 51, 54, 70–1, 73–4, 82, 125–6,
  133, 137
  EP election, 1989, 59, 62–4
  and FF coalition, 140–2
  reshuffle, 34
  resigns from EP, 218
Desmond, Dermot, 101–2, 103–4
Desmond, Eileen, 40, 81
development aid, 152
disability, 152–3
divorce, 16, 33, 89, 266, 267, 295–8
Doherty, Sean, 107, 112
Donnelly, Jack, 137
Donoghue, David, 186, 204, 222,
  243
Dorr, Noel, 112–13, 186–7, 190,
  204, 282
Downey, Jim, 144
Downing, John, 173
Downing Street Declaration,
  111–12, 180–204, 206–8, 210,
  217, 228–9
Downtown Radio, 192, 193
Dublin Castle Summit, 200–3
Dublin Gas, 24–5
Duffy, Jim, 90
Duggan case, 259, 261, 271
Duignan, Sean, 7, 137, 138–9, 151,
  189, 232–3
Duke, Tom, 319–20
Dukes, Alan, 2, 12–13, 16, 20–1,
  27, 34, 58, 66-7, 96, 125
Dunne, Ben, 107, 110, 315
Durkan, Gerry, 108

Education, Department of, 152–6,
  162, 168, 320
Electoral Strategy, Commission
  on, 39
Enterprise and Employment,
  Department of, 155, 162
Environment, Department of, 7, 8
Equality and Law Reform,
  Department of, 153, 162, 267,
  295
Ervine, David, 200
European Commission, 29, 165,
  227, 228
European Court of Auditors, 218
European Parliament, 59, 62–4,
  70, 140–1, 218–22
European Union, 111, 158
exchange controls, 158
expatriate tax, 214–16, 230
extradition, 34

Fahey, Noel, 174, 175–6
Fahy, Joe, 70
Falklands War, 110
Farrell, Pat, 230, 231
Ferris, Cliona, 168–9
Ferris, Michael, 162, 167
Fianna Fáil, 38, 43, 70, 98–9, 120,
  125, 219, 280, 306
  Ahern leads, 268
  Beef Tribunal, 76, 118–19
  business scandals, 102, 122–3
  challenge to Haughey, 104,
  106–7
  coalition, 1993-94, 209–10,
  213–18, 229–36, 241–65
  Duggan case, 271–3
  election, 1989, 60–1, 65
  election, 1992, 126–31
  election, 1997, 317, 318–19
  government negotiations, 1992,
  131, 133, 135–40, 144–6, 148–63
  government negotiations, 1994,
  266–73
  Presidential election, 1990,
  81–95

Fianna Fáil continued
  Reynolds leads, 113–14
  Reynolds resigns, 263–4
Finance, Department of, 101, 155,
  166, 170–3, 209–10, 215–16
Finance Bill, 1994, 214–16
Fine Gael, 1–3, 96, 99, 148, 153,
  277–8
  coalition, 1982-87, 10–35, 37
  election, 1992, 124, 125, 128
  election, 1997, 317–18
  government negotiations, 1992,
  130, 131–5, 143
  government negotiations, 1994,
  273–4
  one-day conference, 1991, 98
  Presidential election, 1990, 81,
  86, 87–8, 92
  Rainbow Coalition, 1994-97,
  278–319
  Tallaght strategy, 58
Finlay, Frieda, 6, 9, 208–9, 250
Finlay, Sarah, 7
Fitzgerald, Brian, 199–200, 320
FitzGerald, Eithne, 3, 162, 165,
  306, 320
FitzGerald, Garret, 2–3, 5, 22–3,
  26–7, 29, 37, 67, 89, 133, 143
  and Robinson, 82–3
  Taoiseach, 1982-87, 10–11,
  15–17
Fitzsimons, Eoghan, 170–271,
  248, 261, 262, 268
flying, fear of, 282–3
Flynn, Bill, 237
Flynn, Padraig, 93, 133, 138, 225
  Structural Funds negotiations,
  175–8
Foley, Denis, 38
Foley, John, 160, 213, 215, 258,
  267, 282, 310, 328
  and Clinton, 240
  Kerry count, 36–8, 210
  passports issue, 223–7
  PLP meetings, 165–6
Food Industries, 72

food subsidies, 28
Foreign Affairs, Department of,
  164–5, 170, 183, 185, 227, 232,
  258, 282
  Anglo-Irish Division, 186–8
  Anglo-Irish division, 279–80
  Joint Framework Document,
  242–3
  neutrality, 152
Foreign Affairs Council, 174
fourchette, 178
Freedom of Information Act, 153
fund-raising, 306, 316

Gallagher, Dermot, 243
Gallagher, Jackie, 234
Gallagher, Patrick, 77–9
general elections
  1982, 1–2
  1987, 35, 36–41
  1989, 64–5
  1992, 109–10, 120–8
  1997, 316–21
Geoghegan, Simon, 209
Geoghegan-Quinn, Maire, 224,
  225, 241, 257, 268, 272
Geraghty, Des, 132
Giscard d'Estaing, Valery, 70
Gleeson, Dermot, 147, 273 278
Glennon, Chris, 106, 286
Good Friday Agreement, 283, 297
Goodman, Larry, 71–6, 98–9, 147.
  see also Beef Tribunal
Government Information
  Service, 10, 22, 28
government jet, 170, 227–8, 283
Grafton, David, 3, 148
Green Party, 322, 323
Greencore, 101, 103–4
Greene, Niall, 46
Greysteel, Co. Derry, 196
Guerin, Orla, 218–22
Guerin, Veronica, 105, 251–2, 314

Hacket, Edel, 323
Hall, Julie, 68, 69

Hamilton, Judge Liam, 239, 241,
  246, 248, 249
Hamilton Tribunal, 74. *see also*
  Beef Tribunal
Hardiman, Adrian, 108, 122
Harney, Mary, 103
Harrington, Walter, 97
Harris, Eoghan, 62, 85, 88, 94, 98,
  275
Harris, Pino, 100–1
Haughey, Charles, 1, 5, 10, 18–19,
  32, 96, 110–11, 114, 145, 156,
  209, 217, 263
  Beef Tribunal, 121
  financial scandals, 100–7, 315
  and Gallagher, 77–9
  and Goodman, 72–4
  Hillery phonecalls, 89–92
  Ombudsman issue, 69–71
  and peace process, 184
  resignation, 112, 113
Haughey, Sean, 217
Health, Department of, 51,
  312–14
Health Act, 1949, 21
Hepatitis C, 312–14
Higgins, Michael D, 40, 48, 57,
  114, 135, 162, 171, 209, 266, 306
High Court, Presidency of, 241,
  246–7, 254, 260
Hillery, Dr Patrick, 81, 89–90
Holkeri, Harry, 300
Holloway, Joe, 19
homosexuality, 210
Howe, Geoffrey, 32
Howlin, Brendan, 40, 54, 59–61,
  65–7, 93, 148, 162, 167, 209–10,
  266, 312
  on abortion, 116–17
  election, 1992, 109
  government negotiations, 1992,
  132, 134–5, 137, 141, 142
  haemophiliacs debate, 60
  Party reorganisation, 52
  Whelehan appointment, 249,
  257, 259, 261

Hudson, Chris, 199
Hume, John, 111–12, 184, 193–7,
  240
Humphreys, Richard, 267, 268,
  295
Hussey, Gemma, 12

Independent Newspapers, 13,
  27–8, 287
Independent Radio and
  Television Commission, 306–7
Inishvickillaune, 103
Institute of European Law, 82–3
Institute of Taxation, 214–16
Inter-Governmental Conferences,
  189–91, 192–3
International Body on
  Decommissioning, 289-301
interpretive centres, 209
IRA, 110–11, 208, 252, 288–9
  British contacts with, 186, 194,
  203
  ceasefire, 1994, 238, 240, 252,
  264, 290–3
  ceasefire ends, 1996, 301
  ceasefire possible, 110–11, 222,
  228, 236
  peace process, 180–204
Iraq export insurance, 118
Irish Congress of Trade Unions,
  105
Irish Distillers, 103
Irish Helicopters, 102
Irish Steel, 22–3, 24–5, 320
Irish Sugar Company, 72, 101,
  102, 105
Irish Transport and General
  Workers' Union, 46

Joint Declaration. *see* Downing
  Street Declaration
Joint Framework Document,
  242–6, 253, 266–7, 278–84
Joyce, Joe, 249
Justice, Department of, 225

Kavanagh, Liam, 128, 142, 162
Kavanagh, Ray, 40, 52, 54, 126,
    160–1, 219
Keating, Justin, 29
Kelly, Donal, 232, 286
Kemmy, Jim, 157–8
Kennedy, Fintan, 13
Kennedy, Geraldine, 33, 107, 168,
    271–2, 275, 286
Kenny, Stewart, 88
Kinkel, Klaus, 164–5, 173, 240
Kinnock, Glenys, 68–9
Kinnock, Neil, 68–9
Kinsella, Anne, 267, 295

Labour Left, 56
Labour Party, 99, 135–6, 253. *see
    also* Parliamentary Labour
    Party; Spring, Dick
    coalition, 1993-94, 161–3,
    209–10, 213–18, 229–36, 241,
    242–65
    constitution, 96–8
    Cork conference, 44–50
    criticisms of, 167–73, 172, 213,
    217–18, 227–8, 307–8
    criticisms of Spring, 28–9
    election, 1987, 35, 36–41
    election, 1992, 120–8
    election, 1997, 316–21
    EP elections, 1994, 218–22
    and FG, 23–4, 26
    financial pressures, 39–40
    in government, 1982-87, 4–35
    government negotiations, 1992,
    129–46, 148–63
    government negotiations, 1994,
    264–74
    Killarney conference, 96–8
    leadership election, 44–50
    Limerick conference, 287, 319
    in opposition, 1987-89, 54,
    58–61
    Presidential election,1997,
    320–4

Rainbow Coalition, 1994-97,
    278–319
    reorganisation, 51–8
    Robinson campaign, 80–95
    rumour campaigns, 42–3
    tensions within party, 306–7
    Tralee conference, 56, 57–8
    Waterford conference, 183
    Whelehan appointment, 248–65
"Labour's Alternative," 55
Lacey, Dermot, 124
Lake, Anthony, 301
Larchfield Securities, 78
Lawlor, Liam, 72
Lemass, Eileen, 71
Lenihan, Brian, 81–95, 99, 132,
    145
Lennon, Fr Brian, 205–8
local elections, 1991, 99
London bomb, 1993, 185
Lowry, Michael, 315
Lynch, Brendan, 52, 154
Lynch, Jack, 259

Maastricht Treaty, 193
McAleese, Mary, 322, 323
McAuliffe, Ita, 168, 328
McCabe, Jerry, 314
McCole, Brigid, 313
McConnells, 296
McConville, Seamus, 13
McCracken, Brian, 108
McCreevy, Charlie, 117–18, 259,
    261
McDonagh, Philip, 243
McDowell, Michael, 93, 226–7,
    288
McEntee, Paddy, 212–13
MacGiolla, Tomas, 114
McGuinness, Diarmuid, 149–50
McHale, Marie, 108–9, 123–4,
    323, 328
McKenna, Patricia, 322
McKenna judgement, 296, 297,
    298
McKernan, Padraic, 174, 178

McManus, Liz, 321–2
McMenamin, Peter, 85, 86
McQuaid, Dr J C, Archbishop of Dublin, 22
MacSharry, Ray, 51–2
Magee, Reverend Roy, 200
Magner, Pat, 3–5, 7, 29, 68, 114–15, 123, 159, 165, 212–13, 327–8
election, 1997, 315, 317
government negotiations, 1992, 132, 137, 141, 142, 143
government negotiations, 1994, 267
Party reorganisation, 52
Presidential election, 1997, 321, 323
Whelehan appointment, 258, 259
Major, John, 110, 193, 208
decommissioning issue, 288–9, 293, 299–305
Downing Street Declaration, 201–3
Joint Declaration, 111–12, 113
Joint Framework Document, 244, 281
peace process, 184, 185, 187-9, 193, 194, 196–7, 227–9
Malone, Bernie, 63, 218, 219–20
Manning, Maurice, 132
Mansergh, Martin, 15–17, 111, 136, 148, 151–2, 226, 236, 264, 268
peace process, 184, 185, 189, 204, 222–3, 242–6, 253
Mara, PJ, 65–6, 67, 81
Maryfield Secretariat, 181, 186, 225
Masri passports, 223–5, 230, 231, 264
Mayhew, Sir Patrick, 186, 190, 191–3, 280–3, 288–94, 301–5
media, 137, 157, 158–9, 227–8, 322, 327
Spring rumours, 220–1

Spring-Robinson "tiff," 285–8
training, 121
Merchant Banking Limited, 77–9
Militant Tendency, 52, 56–7, 57–8
Millan, Bruce, 174
Mills, Michael, 18, 69–71
Mitchell, George, 289, 300
Mitchell, Jim, 142
Molloy, Bobby, 65, 134–5
Molyneaux, James, 196, 201
Montgomery, Rory, 243
Moore, Joe, 18–19
Morgan, Donogh, 166, 210
Morrison, Bruce, 237
Moynan, Dave, 56–7, 124
Mulhern, Paul, 295
Mulroy, Angie, 54, 124, 323
Mulvihill, John, 320
Murphy, Mags, 323
Murray, Fr Raymond, 184
Murray, Pat, 47

Nally, Dermot, 25, 111, 112–13, 201
national debt, 58
National Development Corporation (NDC), 23
NCB, 102, 103, 104
negative campaigning, 130–1
nepotism allegations, 168–9, 171
neutrality, 152
New Agenda, 114
New Ireland Forum, 31, 149
Nixon, Richard, 261
"non-paper," 190
Noonan, Michael, 12, 313–14
Northern Ireland, 31–2, 110–11, 120, 140, 155, 161, 268, 320, 326. *see also* peace process
in 1992 government programme, 151
cabinet sub-committee, 277
Northern Ireland Office, 192–3, 222, 242, 303
Norton, William, 41 53

O Briain, Colm, 170–1
O Fiaich, Cardinal, 184
O hUiginn, Sean, 112–13, 186, 204, 236, 244
  peace process, 197, 222–3, 242, 253, 281, 302–5
O'Brien, Conor Cruise, 287
O'Brien, Deirdre, 51
O'Brien, Ronan, 319–20
O'Connell, Dr John, 40
O'Connell, Mick, 13–14
O'Donovan, Declan, 243
O'Dowd, Neil, 237
Office of Public Works, 209
O'Hare, Rita, 245
O'Higgins, Michael D, 130
oil terms, 26–7
O'Kennedy, Michael, 99
O'Leary, Michael, 1, 3, 44
O'Mahony, Flor, 40
O'Malley, Des, 59, 60, 65, 71, 75–6, 111, 130, 134–5, 140-1
  Beef Tribunal, 99, 108, 118–20, 122, 149–51
O'Malley, Finbarr, 108, 161, 225, 268, 327–8
Ombudsman appointment, 69–71
O'Meara, Kathleen, 297
O'Reilly, Emily, 83, 197–8, 199, 203, 229–31
O'Reilly, Tony, 26–7
O'Riordan, Sean, 10
O'Rourke, Mary, 100–1, 268
O'Sullivan, Gerry, 252
O'Sullivan, Lisa, 253
O'Sullivan, Toddy, 4, 253, 320
Owen, Nora, 133, 278

Paddy Powers, 88
Pairceir, Seamus, 101, 102
Parliamentary Labour Party, 223–4, 306–7
  coalition, 1993-94, 165–73, 263
  government negotiations, 1992, 144
  Programme Managers, 274–7

Parry, Tim, 180, 183
passports issue, 223–7, 230, 231, 264
Pattison, Seamus, 162
peace process, 217, 222–3, 227–9, 235-6, 275, 277–8, 300–5. *see also* Joint Framework Document
  ceasefire, 1994, 238, 240
  loyalist involvement, 198–201
  Six Principles, 196, 197–8
Peace Train, 199
Penrose, Willie, 124
Petersburg summit, 164–5
Phelan, Angela, 262
Phoenix Park, 210–13
phone-tapping, 12, 105–7, 112, 270
Pinochet, General, 285
Pitcher, Bartle, 13
PMPA collapse, 18–19
Prendergast, Frank, 13
Prendergast, Peter, 7, 10–12, 14
Presidency, 80–95, 320–4
Programme Managers, 156–7, 160–1, 165–6, 168, 210, 250–1, 274–7, 319
  early-warning system, 230–1
Progressive Democrats, 59-60, 65, 90, 98–9, 103, 125, 141, 145, 226–7
  and Beef Tribunal, 119–20
  election, 1992, 123, 130
  government negotiations, 1992, 131–2, 134–5, 144
  and Reynolds, 113–14
protocol guidelines, 287
Public Accounts Committee, 100–1
punt, devaluation of, 165, 166

Quinn, Conor, 296–7
Quinn, Ruairi, 46, 54, 82, 85, 120, 145, 148, 162, 297
  election, 1992, 127
  fund-raising lunch, 306

Index

Quinn, Ruairi continued
  government negotiations, 1992,
  132, 134–5, 137, 140–2
government negotiations, 1994,
  272–3
  Party reorganisation, 109–10
  Whelehan appointment, 249,
  254, 257, 263
Quinn McDonnell Pattison,
  296–7

Rabbitte, Pat, 131-3, 273–4
Reid, Father Alec, 111, 184, 185
Reidy, Sharon, 57
Revenue Commissioners, 40, 101,
  215
Revington, Joe, 3, 6, 10, 24
Reynolds, Albert, 71, 104, 118,
  188–9, 193, 272–3
  assessment of, 264–5
  Beef Tribunal, 108, 147–8,
  150–1, 232–6
  election, 1992, 121–3, 127
  Structural Funds, 164–5, 173–9
  government negotiations, 1992,
  131, 133, 135–40, 144–6, 149–63
  Labour coalition, 241, 242–65
  leads FF, 112, 113–14
  libel action, 308–12
  passports, 223–7
  peace process, 185, 194–7,
  201–3, 227–9, 236–8, 238, 240,
  244–6, 264
  resignation, 263–4, 268
  and Spring, 278, 319
  tax amendments, 214–16
  Whelehan appointment, 247–65
Reynolds, Kathleen 232
Rice, Rodney, 93, 133
Rimell, Katherine, 308–9
Roberts, Ruaidhri, 104, 105
Robinson, Mary, 53, 103, 127,
  133, 160, 227, 302–4, 321
  Belfast visit, 191–3
  Presidential campaign, 80–95
  South American visit, 284–7

and Spring, 82–3, 87, 94, 284–7
Robinson, Nick, 83–4, 86
Roche, Adi, 320–4
Rogers, Denise, 82, 328
Rogers, John, 3, 7, 8, 45, 48, 50,
  65, 94, 103, 165, 235, 258, 327–8
  Attorney General, 29–30
  Beef Tribunal, 150, 235
  economic policy, 52–3
  government negotiations, 1992,
  137, 140, 142
  passports issue, 223–7
  Robinson campaign, 82, 83
  Whelehan appointment, 248–9,
  267, 273–5
  'X' case, 117
Rosney, Bride, 80–1, 83–4, 85, 286
RTE, 77–9, 112, 125, 127, 138–9,
  213, 229, 233
  Orla Guerin, 218, 220–1
  Spring-Robinson "tiff," 286
Ruddock, Alan, 308–12
Russell, Matt, 252, 269

Saatchi and Saatchi, 126–7, 130–1
St Vincent de Paul Society, 55
Scally, William, 13, 26–7, 109,
  154, 165–6, 215, 276, 310, 319,
  327–8
  Beef Tribunal, 232, 235
  economic adviser, 3, 10, 24,
  52–3, 159
  government negotiations, 1992,
  137, 140–2, 148
  Guerin candidacy, 219
  Hepatitis C issue, 314
  passports issue, 223–7
  tax amnesty, 171–3
  Whelehan appointment, 254,
  258, 262, 263
Scheverdnadze, Edward, 164
school transport, 12
service charges, 12
Shankill Butchers, 199
Shankill Road bombing, 195–6
Shortall, Roisin, 274